NURSE

By the same author
The Daughters

NURSE

Peggy Anderson

ST. MARTIN'S PRESS
NEW YORK

Library of Congress Cataloging in Publication Data

Anderson, Peggy.
  Nurse.

  1. Benjamin, Mary.   2. Nurses—United States—
Biography.   I. Title.
RT37.B34A63   610.73′092′4 [B]   78-3994
ISBN 0-312-58021-5

CONTENTS

	Author's Note	*vii*
1	A Certain Day on Eight Cook	*1*
2	Reality Shock: The Acid Test of Nursing	*23*
3	Care: The Heart and the Hard Part	*39*
4	"Snowing": A Way Out	*51*
5	Thanksgiving Shift	*71*
6	Difficult Patients	*83*
7	Confrontations with Death and Dying	*99*
8	New Chances	*127*
9	The Problem of Sex	*139*
10	Weak Links, Tough Decisions: The Trials of Running a Staff	*159*
11	Kelly O'Brien Returns	*177*
12	Ron	*183*
13	Family Matters	*199*
14	Nurses and Doctors	*215*
15	Broken Ties to the Bedside	*243*
16	In Sickness and In Hell: Human Responses	*255*
17	Errors	*271*
18	Christmas Away: A Holiday to Remember	*289*
19	Last Resorts	*293*
20	The Old Year Passes	*297*
21	The New Year Begins	*305*

AUTHOR'S NOTE

The "I" in the text belongs to the young woman whose experiences comprise this book. She is head nurse on a general medical-surgical floor of a metropolitan hospital in a large American city. She is 27 years old. At her request, I have changed her name. The identity of the hospital itself and of all the other characters who figure in the narrative—doctors, nurses, and other hospital personnel; patients and patients' families; and the husband, family, and friends of "Mary Benjamin"—have likewise been changed, and certain situations disguised, to preserve the privacy of the people involved. One or two minor characters are composites. I have taken some liberties with chronology. But the stuff of the book is true. Every experience recorded here happened.

Throughout my work on this project, I was assisted in important ways by a number of people I cannot name. Their help made the book possible. I am deeply grateful to each of them. I am also grateful to people I can name: Leslie Pockell, my editor, and Jay Acton, my agent, for their unflagging enthusiasm and encouragement; Kay McMillan, my mother, an R.N., and Dr. Flora Gosch for their reading and appraisal of a particularly sensitive chapter; and Alan Halpern, Charles Peters, Bob Rice, Gene Roberts, and Babby Stone for their recommendations to the MacDowell Colony, where I began to write *Nurse*. The Colony is a remarkable place. Whatever appreciation I can convey to those who make it remarkable is inadequate to the gift of being there, but heartfelt. Finally, I owe special thanks to Donald Drake, Patricia McBroom, Michael Pakenham, and Olaf Saugen for saying just the right things at critical moments.

I can't begin to single out the other friends who have nurtured this project in some way by supporting me. My friends sustain me. It's that simple. To those friends, with love, I dedicate this book.

Peggy Anderson

NURSE

1

A CERTAIN DAY
ON EIGHT COOK

The fourth day of November. Kelly O'Brien was scheduled for surgery at 8:00 A.M. For the second time in less than two months, Dr. Kenneth Rose was going in to try to find out why Kelly was vomiting so much.

I woke up hearing rain. Since Ron had already left for school, I took my time in the shower. At 6:40, when I left the apartment, the rain was still coming down. Sky darker than usual, trees almost bare. Wet leaves covered the sidewalks. I walked the two blocks to work thinking about what had happened to Kelly O'Brien in the fourteen months since his cancer had been diagnosed and remembering a day three weeks earlier, the last really good day he had had on this admission.

He was the old Kelly that day, joking and kidding everybody. I went in to make his bed in the morning and heard laughter from all the way down the hall. It happened that we had two other retired policemen on the floor that week, Don Cline and Sol Schwarz. Both were in for prostate surgery. Cline was Kelly's roommate, as big a tease as Kelly was. For some reason men seem to find each other in the hospital and talk together more than women do. Somehow Kelly and Mr. Cline had found Mr. Schwarz. When I got in the room that morning, these three rough-and-tumble ex-cops were sitting around in their hospital gowns discussing the old days on the force.

1

"Uh-oh," I said. "The police mafia."

Kelly, propped up in bed, faked a bow. "At your service. Any patients give you a hard time, Mary, you just let us know."

I set the clean sheets on a chair.

"I'll keep that in mind," I said, "but usually the only patients I have trouble with are the ones in this room."

"Well," Kelly said, "I could have told you you'd have trouble with these two. So did the commissioner."

Schwarz gave it right back to Kelly. "Nothing compared to the trouble he had with you."

"Mr. O'Brien," I said, "could I please ask you to sit somewhere else so I can make your bed?"

Kelly moved. I stripped his sheets. Cline started in on me.

"Nurse," he said, "I have to pee awfully bad. I think I'll just take this girlie magazine into the john with me, and then maybe I'll be able to pee better."

I caught Kelly's eye. "Mr. O'Brien," I said, "you were such a nice man when you came in here the first time. But these two, they're just bad examples for you."

Kelly laughed. "You're not kidding."

Schwarz gave me a mock glare. "Why don't you ask us what kind of example *he* is."

I finished Kelly's bed and started to make Mr. Cline's. The patient leaned against the wall, watching me.

"You know," I said to Cline, tucking in the top sheet, "I think it's time for me to take out your Foley catheter."

Out of the corner of my eye, I saw Cline acting horrified.

"I don't want you to take my Foley out," Cline protested. "I want Miss Debbie. She's not married. I want to see her blush. You're a married lady. You're not going to blush."

"How do you know? I blush very easily. I can get embarrassed for you, if that's what you want. Now would you get on the bed so I can take your catheter out?"

"That's right, give him hell!" Kelly said. "Give him hell!"

After some coaxing, Cline finally let me remove his catheter. I told him I wanted him to drink lots of fluid.

"Right, make him drink!" Kelly kept egging me on. To Cline he said, "And she doesn't mean beer, either."

"No," Schwarz put in. "She means a gallon a day of straight bourbon whiskey."

"The best," Kelly said.

"You gentlemen are driving me nuts," I said. "I'll be back when things calm down." As I went out the door, I heard Kelly say, "Aw, come on, Mare. Don't wait for that."

I arrived at the hospital. It felt good to get out of the rain into the warm, light corridors of the Cook Building, good to see people and activity. At that hour there was more going on in the hospital than there was on the streets. I stopped in the cafeteria for a carry-out tea, then took the elevator to the eighth floor.

As I got off, I almost literally ran into Stephanie Jankowski, who was hurrying past the elevators. Stephanie had just worked the night shift. She was wearing a green surgical scrub suit and carrying a white bundle—her uniform, obviously, wadded up. She stopped short in front of me. I got a whiff of the bundle. It didn't smell too good.

"Guess who fell out of bed again!"

Stephanie was breathless and didn't wait for an answer.

"Looking for his cigarettes! Our mascot! When we checked him at 6:00 he was fine. Sleeping like a baby. Then all of a sudden we hear 'Aaaaaagggggghhhhhaaaaa' coming from his room.

"So we go running in, and there's John. He had climbed over the side rail, restraint and all. Diarrhea and urine all over the floor. He had slipped and fallen in it. So we picked him up, walking around everything, and got him back into bed, and I'm thinking, 'We got him into bed, and there's nothing on me.' Then I look down at the bottom of my pantsuit. Covered with feces!"

Stephanie was the best and the liveliest of the nine new graduates who had started on my staff four months earlier, in July. She seemed to have perpetually rosy cheeks. She was good technically, good with patients, and good at taking charge of the floor. If all nurses did their jobs the way Steph did hers, we wouldn't need head nurses anywhere.

"How is he?" I asked.

"He seems all right. He was talking to us while we were in there washing the floor. The resident on call came up and wrote an order for an orthopedic consult to see if he fractured anything, and X-ray was just up here."

"Did you call in the consult?"

"The night supervisor did."

"Go do something with that uniform," I said. "It really smells stinky."

"Chanel number 844B," Stephanie said, referring to John's room and bed number. She went off laughing. "Enjoy your day!"

I hung up my coat and checked the operating room schedule, which Ruth, the floor clerk, had tacked to the bulletin board in the nurses' station. In addition to Kelly O'Brien, only one Eight Cook patient was on the OR list that day. Roma Funicelli would be going down later in the morning for a left breast biopsy and possible radical mastectomy. Usually we have four or five ORs a day, and we've had as many as nine.

Since it was still a little before 7:00 A.M., I made rounds on the seven patients on the floor who were on intravenous—IV—fluids, checking to make sure that the fluids were dripping in at the proper rate and that the needles were in proper position. I got delayed. One of the patients needed pain medication. By the time I got into the nurses' lounge, report had already begun. Liz Roberts, who had been charge nurse on the night shift, sat with the patient-care Kardex files on her knees, giving a brief history of each patient and going over what had happened with each in the last eight hours.

". . . came in with gangrenous toes and toenails several inches long. The police picked him up in a boarding house. He refuses surgery, says he has to ask his brother. Social Services can't find a brother. His toenails were clipped in Podiatry yesterday. Slept through the night. Nothing new with him.

"842 bed A, Roma Funicelli, 68, admitted yesterday with a lump in her breast that she's had two years. She's sure she's going to have a mastectomy. They told me she was really scared on the evening shift, but she had a sleeper about 10:00 and slept okay. . . ."

I made a mental note to talk to Mrs. Funicelli before she went down.

The nurses' lounge is a small room behind the nurses' station. It has no windows, and it's narrow, with couches on either side and a few chairs at one end. No matter where you sit during report, you can't cross your legs without kicking somebody. In addition to Liz and me, there were seven other people in the lounge that morning—two more registered nurses, three licensed practical nurses, and two nursing assistants. Several were sipping coffee. As Liz gave her rundown, two or three people took notes.

"845 bed B, Virginia Medlock, cervical CA [cancer]. Virginia's getting really bad. I can't believe that I've still never heard one complaint out of her. She gets Dilaudid for pain Q 2 [every two hours], and we're trying zinc oxide on her buttocks to protect the skin from drainage.

"846 bed A, Charmaine Jenkins, 40, appendectomy on the second. We medicated her for pain once. Her wound looks okay.

"846 bed B, Marie Dwyer, 57, CA, excision of rectal mass. The wound is draining a pinkish-tinged stuff, and the surgical dressing is soaked. The doctors know about it. She's really a sweet lady. . . ."

Liz Roberts and Maureen Shay, who was sitting next to Liz, were people I counted on a lot. They were both in their second year on Eight Cook. They had started right after their graduation from nursing school, the same July I had come on as head nurse. They were both very good nurses, but in different ways. Liz was more geared to the emotional needs of patients. Although she came across as scatterbrained, she was an intelligent and caring person. Physically she was short, kind of chunky, with a pert nose and freckles.

Maureen was stronger on the physical care of patients. If we had a patient with a really messy abdominal wound, I'd try to assign the patient to Maureen, because she felt challenged by that kind of situation. Maureen was tall, thin, attractive, quiet, and much more political than Liz. She was always saying that nurses took a back seat. Liz and Maureen shared a house with two nurses from another hospital.

". . . 31, acute appendicitis, no sedation or pain medication. He's not complaining of severe pain. He's the one with the beard. This man really needs a shower!"

Liz looked up laughing as she closed the first of two Kardexes. She opened the other one.

"Okay, that's it for the 40s. On the 50s side, 851 bed A, Mr.

Born. This man had an impotency device put in. They inflated it yesterday. He's kind of hyper. I think he's scared. . . ."

"Not too scared to brag about the size of his penis."

The person interrupting Liz was Toni Gillette, a tall black nursing assistant in her thirties with bleached patches in her hair. Toni threw her eyes to heaven. "I finally told him yesterday that the size of a man has nothing to do with the size of his penis."

We all laughed. Toni was the best nursing assistant on the floor. She also had a mouth on her.

Liz took a sip of Maureen's coffee. "Bed B, Mr. Williams, 85, had a cystoscopy [test for bladder problems] on the first, has been voiding [urinating] in small amounts. We've had trouble with him and his matches. He started a couple of little fires in his wastebasket which his roommate and his wife put out. So please, monitor him when he smokes.

"852 bed A, Mr. Shelton. That's a nice smoking jacket he has there. He's supposed to go home Sunday. Temp normal. . . ."

This time I interrupted. "If he's supposed to go home Sunday, somebody should show him how to do his colostomy care."

Maureen took a puff on a cigarette. "Since I'm team leader in the 50s today, I guess that'll be me."

Liz went on. "852 bed B, Kelly O'Brien, 69, going down this morning for exploratory surgery. . . ."

Report lasted half an hour. As the meeting broke up and the day staff went off to start the A.M. care, Ann Sullivan came on the floor to check on John Harrison, the man who had fallen out of bed.

Ann is the day supervisor. She is indirectly responsible for patient care on Eight Cook and on two other floors over an eight-hour period. There are also evening and night supervisors. When Ann's on duty, her job is to see that problems get solved, to help out in emergencies or when the floor is busy or when I'm off, and to make sure that I do my job right. My job is to run the floor. I am directly responsible, even when I'm not on duty, for all the patient care on Eight Cook over a 24-hour period. I'm responsible for how the floor is organized, how it functions, and how the staff feels about working on it.

Ann and I have a good relationship. The first day supervisor I had on Eight Cook, Betty Fillmore, was constantly checking up on things and didn't allow me to feel that I was deciding what was happening on my floor. Occasionally there's a little friction between Ann and me about who's making what decision. But for the most part I feel we're working as a team. I assist her; she assists me.

She doesn't have heart failure if I don't tell her every time a patient falls, because she knows I'll follow through on it. Of course I don't try to keep something like that from her; it's just that once in a while things get so busy that I don't remember till later. Ann is 29, just two years older than I am, honey blonde, with her hair pulled back in a bun. She wears square, horn-rimmed glasses.

"I don't know what we're going to do about John," I told Ann. "He's such a devil. He knows he's not strong enough to stand by himself. You would not believe how fast he gets out of those jacket restraints. Last week we tried putting two Poseys on him, one forwards, one backwards. He was out of them in two minutes."

"Let's go take a look at him," Ann said.

John was lying in bed wide awake, a little old man of 78 with cancer of the bladder and Parkinsonism. Except for a divorced daughter who rarely visited him, John had no relatives. He had been on Eight Cook nearly four months. "A placement problem," the hospital social workers called him. One of them, Bev Bowles, was trying to get him into a home for people dying of cancer. John didn't need nursing care. He needed to be watched. He was always trying to get up, always trying to pull out the tube that irrigated his bladder.

We had given John the job of shaving himself. He hadn't shaved for days. His eyes were glassy, but he wasn't the least disoriented.

I touched his bristly cheek.

"John," I said. "What am I going to do with you? If you fall out of bed one more time, I'm going to lose my job."

The old eyes blinked. At some point John had had a mild stroke. He always took a long time to say anything. His voice was pretty weak. Still, he could usually get something out, and finally he said, "Don't worry, Mary. I'll take you in and take care of you."

John complained of a little pain in his chest. He might have fractured a rib when he fell. We wouldn't have the X-ray report for several hours. A rib fracture isn't serious. People walk around with broken ribs and don't even know. They just heal. Other than the chest pain, John seemed fine.

Back at the nurses' station, I signed the incident report that Liz Roberts had filled out on John Harrison. Incident reports are a record of unusual events—a fall, a medication error, a theft on the floor. The reports are kept as documentation in case legal questions arise. They go in a nurse's file only if there are enough of them to suggest a pattern.

Maureen came into the nurses' station to tell me that the OR had called for Kelly O'Brien. She had just premedicated him for surgery.

I was still at the desk when the escort arrived to take Kelly down. I paged Maureen in Kelly's room. In a few minutes, she wheeled Kelly out. He was lying strapped to a litter, groggy from his shot.

Dr. Rose had warned Mrs. O'Brien that the cancer could have spread. The residents had told me that Rose was afraid he was going to find cancer all over Kelly's stomach. But the first exploratory Rose had done in mid-September had shown no metastasis. One of the residents had told me that Rose had begun to wonder if the vomiting might be psychological.

I went around to the litter and took Mr. O'Brien's hand. "Kelly."

He had lost probably thirty pounds since I first met him. His stomach and chest had sort of chickened in. But he was still a good-looking man, with a strong jaw, bushy dark gray eyebrows, thick hair several shades lighter.

He turned his face toward me. His eyes were closed.

"Hi, Mare."

I could hardly hear him.

Not five minutes after the escort had taken Kelly to the OR, Mrs. O'Brien arrived. Pat, the O'Briens' married daughter, was with her. Thin, wiry women both of them, Mrs. O'Brien with short, almost silver hair. Kelly's wife was really sweet. I could tell from the way she acted with him as well as the way she was with the nurses. I had gotten somewhat close to her.

"How's Kelly?" Mrs. O'Brien asked.

"He seems okay. He just went down."

The two of them looked at me in amazement.

"I thought he wasn't supposed to go down till 8:00," Pat said.

"No, surgery starts at 8:00."

Mrs. O'Brien didn't say anything, but she seemed quite upset. From what I've seen, when somebody has cancer or is going through any major surgery, the family's first thought is, "He might not get off the operating table. If I don't say goodbye to him, I won't see him again." I'm sure that passed through Mrs. O'Brien's mind.

I put my hand on her arm. "We probably won't know anything till at least noon," I told her. "Why don't you go down and have some coffee?"

The O'Briens did go down for coffee, but in a little while they came back up to the floor and went into the solarium. They stayed there the rest of the morning, waiting for the news from the operating room.

In five years as a nurse, I have gotten close to maybe ten patients. Kelly O'Brien was one.

He was first admitted for evaluation right after I became head nurse on the floor. A well-built man who talked well, walked around a lot, and seemed very independent. A nice man. I don't know what kind of cop Kelly had been. Maybe he was the kind that banged heads together. But as a patient, in the way he related to his situation in the hospital, he seemed like a good person. A teddy bear. He liked to observe people. You could feel his eyes watching you.

There was a relaxed feeling between us from the beginning. I wasn't intimidated by him at all, and I don't think he was intimidated by me. Before he became so sick, we had kidded a lot. I was engaged at the time, and he would kid me about Ron.

"You treat a good man well, and he'll love you forever," he'd say.

I'd say, "What about him treating me well?"

"Well, that too. I've been married forty-three years, and I've treated my wife very well."

"It really seems as though you have. It looks as though you have a good marriage."

Kelly had surgery that first admission, and they found the

cancer. After he healed, he started on chemotherapy. That made him vomit and lose weight. But he was basically okay and went home.

A few months later he was back in. He was weaker, jaundiced, thin, and markedly depressed. He couldn't keep food down. He was dehydrated from the vomiting. We gave him fluids intravenously, and the doctors did some more tests and gave him some more chemotherapy. He began to feel better. I remember that he talked a lot about his family during that admission. About his son, Mike, also a policeman, about his daughter and her husband and their three children, about how good they all were, how good his children had been to his wife, and about how he loved his wife. He was discharged and had radiation as an outpatient. We didn't see him for a while.

The third time Kelly came in, he was vomiting, progressively more jaundiced, and suffering a lot of abdominal pain. That's when Rose did the first exploratory. He took Kelly down and opened him up expecting to find blockage from new cell growth.

There was no new cell growth.

Hoping to relieve the distension and discomfort, Dr. Rose put two tubes into Kelly's torso, a gastrostomy tube to drain his stomach and another drainage tube just below his gallbladder. After a few days in special care, Kelly came back to the floor. All the nurses were happy that Rose had found no more cancer, and we were glad to have Kelly back.

Pancreatic cancer doesn't have a very long prognosis, usually less than a year. It can be more, depending on when it is caught and on how the person responds to chemotherapy. We knew Kelly was eventually going to die from his disease. But he had already outlived the average prognosis. Since the operation had revealed no spread of cancer, we fully expected that Kelly was going to get better and go home.

He did get better. By the end of a month he was well enough to sit in the solarium talking, laughing, and carrying on with the other two members of the police mafia. He was still vomiting. He was eating regular food, but for some reason his stomach wasn't absorbing or digesting it properly. Five or six hours after he ate, when the food should have been starting to move into the small intestine, it was still in his stomach, and he would vomit it up, partially digested.

But he was getting stronger, and his spirits were good. Up until mid-October.

Then Kelly became very weak again. He was unable to do much for himself, other than get into the bathroom and sit there for a few minutes, wash up a little, walk back to bed, and walk around the hall for short periods. He was very depressed. He couldn't eat. He was still vomiting.

The doctors put Kelly on hyperalimentation. Hyperal is a high-caloric substance given to people who have had a long course of radiation or chemotherapy and who, because of nausea, can't keep food down. I don't know the precise chemical makeup of it, but it contains protein and carbohydrates for body-building. The particles are so big that if the fluid were put through a regular vein in the arm, it would cause sclerosis. So it is pumped into the heart through a subclavian catheter, a tube attached to a hollow needle which is inserted into a large vein under the collarbone.

Even with the hyperal, Kelly was vomiting constantly. He was always complaining of fullness. To relieve the fullness, he began to put his finger down his throat and make himself vomit.

That's when Rose scheduled the second exploratory.

After Kelly had gone down to the OR, I made sure that my staff had the A.M. care under control, and then I went to talk to Roma Funicelli about her possible mastectomy later that morning.

Mrs. Funicelli was a heavy woman, very plain, who was talking with her two sisters, a neighbor, and her brother-in-law. She was obviously frightened. As soon as I asked her how she was doing, she started saying, "You never want to know. You think God's going to take care of it. You don't want to know what's going to happen."

I sat down and talked with her for a few minutes. I don't know why, but to me this lady just didn't look as if she had cancer. I can't explain. I think you get a kind of sixth sense. I decided to take a chance.

"You know," I said, "I don't know whether I'm giving you false hope or not. But I'll never forget the lady who came in with a lump she had had for three years. By the time she finally went to the doctor, she was sure she was going to have her breast removed. The doctors told her she was probably right.

"When the escort brought this woman back on a stretcher from the OR, she was awake but still euphoric, I guess, from the medication. She felt around and realized her breast was still there. Suddenly she sat up and started slapping her hand on the counter of the nurses' station, and her body was sort of flopping around on the stretcher, and she was saying, 'It's all here! They didn't take it off! It's all here!' "

Mrs. Funicelli laughed a little. "Well," she said, "it's God's will." She seemed a little more relaxed.

I told her that she was going to wake up in the recovery room.

"The nurses down there will be taking your blood pressure and pulse every fifteen minutes," I said, "so don't think there's anything wrong. That's routine."

It seemed that I spent most of the morning taking off orders—transcribing the doctors' written orders from the charts to the Kardexes. Kardexes are folders containing a card for each patient in its own clear plastic envelope. The envelopes overlap along each side of the folder, as in a certain style of photograph album. We have one set of Kardexes for patient care, another for medications. The Kardexes are an easier reference than the charts, which have board covers and tend to get bulky.

At about 11:00 someone from X-ray called to say that John Harrison had fractured a rib when he fell.

I called the resident, who came up a little later. The resident didn't even put John on bed rest. He did write in the chart that we should keep a call bell next to John at all times.

When I saw that, I felt like calling the resident back to ask whether he didn't mean that we should tie a bell to John's wrist. What good would a call bell on the bedside table be to a patient who had fallen on the floor? If he wanted to, John could push a button next to his bed and light up a button on the monitor in the nurses' station at any moment of the day or night. The problem was getting him to do it.

Sam Polen came off the elevator. He was a third-year surgical resident, tall and skinny, with dark hair and glasses.

"You just ruined my day," I said to him. Polen and I tease each other a lot. When Ron and I became engaged, Polen and a couple of the other residents kept saying, "You fool! He's a medical student? You'll be divorced in six months." Now Polen was marrying a medical student. At Thanksgiving, in fact, just three weeks off. He had been in a bad mood lately. I had jokingly said to people, "Oh, it's just because he's getting married soon. He's nervous. Ignore him."

I said to Polen, "What's this about a med student who irons your shirts and picks you up every night? What's her address? I want to send her my women's lib book."

"What women's lib book?"

"The Female Eunuch."

"You wouldn't."

"Oh, yes I would."

"She doesn't believe in that stuff."

"She will after she marries you."

I was still taking off orders when Mrs. Payne interrupted me. Payne is a squat, square black woman in her forties, a very serious person, one of the best LPNs I've known.

"Mary," she said, "Mrs. Elson is refusing her pills again."

I knew that if Payne was having trouble with Mrs. Elson, I probably would too, but I said, "Okay. I'll go around and see her."

Mrs. Elson was a little old lady who had had some kind of abdominal surgery and was also senile. Everything was for the Lord. She said when I got in there, "The Lord Jesus or Dr. Lomax are the only ones that are going to get me to take my pills."

I said, "Mrs. Elson, the Lord Jesus came down to see me today. He told me that all the patients were supposed to take their pills, especially you."

Mrs. Elson didn't go for it. She said, "I want my nerve pill."

"This is your nerve pill."

"I'm not taking it."

I gave up. I wrote in Mrs. Elson's chart that she was still

refusing her medications and went back to the orders.

At noon I met Jackie Neill for lunch in the cafeteria. I usually don't go to lunch, only when Jackie's there. We talk about a lot of things. Otherwise I usually grab a Tab or a cup of tea. Jackie is the head nurse on Six Cook, the private pavilion. She's also my best friend at the hospital. Just knowing she's downstairs makes my days better. She's engaged to a resident at another hospital and probably looks like half the fantasies people have of nurses—brown eyes, long red hair, and not an ounce of fat on her.

"I'm glad you're on," Jackie said when I met her in the cafeteria line. "I really needed to get out of there. I must have every banana in the place on my floor today." Jackie started telling me about a wealthy bisexual patient on Six who had female visitors in the morning, male visitors in the afternoon. He also wanted to wear a scrub suit instead of a gown.

Eight Cook is one of five general medical–surgical floors at Central Hospital, a five-hundred bed hospital in the heart of the city. Central's patients range from people on public assistance to women from wealthy neighborhoods who come in to have their faces and rear ends lifted, their breasts augmented, or the bags under their eyes smoothed.

Eight Cook is laid out rectangularly. Stepping off the elevator, you face the nurses' station. It's a rather large area, with a counter in front and surrounding desks. There are several telephones, seven or eight chairs, two racks on wheels that contain all the charts, and an Addressograph machine used when we order lab studies, X-rays, or tests on patients. Order forms for all these procedures are in the desk drawers, along with other paper supplies.

Behind the nurses' station are the nurses' lounge and bathroom, utility rooms, a small kitchen we can use to prepare snacks for patients, hopper rooms where we empty bedpans, and a clean linen room. The dirty linen room is near the elevators. There are also bathrooms for visitors on the floor, and a big solarium, or sun room. When the hospital is crowded, we may have patient beds in the solarium or, for that matter, in the halls.

There's a hall on either side of the nurses' station. Both connect with the back hall. If you get off the elevator, turn in either direction, and keep walking, you'll end up at the elevators again. The patient rooms are on the outer rim of the rectangle. Each has a big window, so the rooms get lots of light. The Cook Building is fairly new. The floor is done in shades of orange and beige and always has a neat, fresh-painted look.

There are eighteen rooms on Eight Cook, with two beds to a room. We always have a few medical patients on the floor, but most of the beds are taken up by surgical patients.

People are always asking me the difference. A medical patient is one who is not being operated on during that admission. The person may have cardiac problems, for example, a urinary tract infection, or diabetes. Or it may be a person who's been vomiting a lot, who's obese, who has suffered weight loss. The patient may eventually end up in surgery, but he or she was not admitted for surgery. A surgical patient is anybody who comes in to be operated on or who has been operated on.

About half the patients on the floor at any one time have cancer. The rest have a variety of disorders. We may have five diabetics in for surgical procedures, including amputations. There may be four or five patients undergoing urological surgery. We may have a couple of people in for hernia operations, a couple in for removal of their gallbladders, maybe one person in with a gunshot or stab wound, perhaps another in for skin graft, a hysterectomy, an abortion of an ectopic pregnancy, or minor eye surgery. We get gynecological patients only if there are no beds on the "gynie" floor.

I'd say the average age of the patients on Eight Cook is fifty or sixty. Once recently we had about eight people in their twenties. All the nurses were threatening to throw a party. About half the patients at any one time are private patients. The rest are ward patients, people on public assistance or those who come into the hospital with no medical coverage. Most of the time I don't know which is which.

Most Eight Cook patients stay in the hospital less than two weeks. A few leave our floor and go to the special, cardiac, or intensive care units. Most go home. It's rare for us to have more than one or two patients dying at any one time. Patients whose conditions worsen, who get very sick, are usually transferred down to the intensive care unit, the ICU.

There are about twenty-five people on my staff, half of us RNs. Some of us graduated from two-year community college programs, others from three-year hospital-based diploma programs or four-year college programs, also called degree programs because graduates receive Bachelor of Science degrees.

The RN's main responsibility is to decide what kind of care is needed for each patient on the floor and to set up and provide that care. He or she delegates treatments ordered by the physician and evaluates the results. RNs probably understand the physiology of disease better than LPNs or nursing assistants, and we are taught that it is our place to make decisions. RNs at Central who have taken an IV therapy course can start intravenous infusions. We cannot diagnose, do surgical procedures, or order or prescribe treatments or medications.

Most LPN programs last one year. The line between an RN and an LPN is not always clear, because at Central, as at other hospitals, LPNs have always assumed a lot of authority when there aren't enough RNs to go around. Faced with a given situation, an RN and an experienced LPN are probably going to make the same judgment.

At Central there's really not much an RN can do that an LPN can't. LPNs can give tube feedings, suction patients, do sterile dressings and colostomy care, monitor IVs, and initiate cardiopulmonary resuscitation techniques, although in such an emergency an LPN is expected to call someone else to follow through. LPNs cannot hang blood, take verbal orders from a doctor over the telephone, or administer certain medications. Most of the LPNs on my staff are middle-aged black women with husbands and children. They're old enough to be my mother.

Most of the nursing assistants are also black, but somewhat younger. The requirement for being a nursing assistant at Central is a high school education. That isn't always needed if the applicant has had experience. The nursing assistants primarily give direct patient care. They help patients brush their teeth, take their baths, and eat. They run errands, give bedpans, clean up incontinent patients, help keep the unit clean, transport patients, and do a variety of other things under the supervision of an LPN or RN. They don't do sterile dressings, and they don't give any medications. Not even an aspirin.

In caring for the Eight Cook patients, the nurses work for the most part with the surgical residents. We see very little of the staff surgeons. At Central a staff surgeon is a doctor who has completed his or her medical training, has admission and operating privileges at the hospital, and practices general surgery, as opposed to, say, neurosurgery. Central has about a dozen staff surgeons. Kenneth Rose is one. The system differs from hospital to hospital, but at Central, the staff surgeons admit their own private patients and, under a rotation system, also direct the residents in caring for the ward patients.

Usually Central has twelve surgical residents in any one year. Residents are doctors who have completed medical school and are undergoing additional training to become surgeons. The residency period for general surgery is five years. Each year four med school graduates are chosen and hired as first-year residents. Of these, two usually do a year of general surgery and then go on to specialize in, say, neurosurgery or urology.

The two who are left become second-year residents, then third-year residents, then fourth-year residents, then chief residents, one for each of two groups of staff surgeons. Sometimes people will change hospitals midstream, but most programs are set up so that the residents can complete their five years at one hospital.

During these five years, each Central resident works for one, two, or six months at a time with one of the staff surgeons, then rotates to another. This gives the resident a variety of experiences, situations, viewpoints, and patients. When Sam Polen rotates to Dr. Rose, he is on Rose's service. That means he is taking care of Rose's patients under Rose's direction. At night or on weekends when the staff surgeons aren't around, the residents take turns being on call. If an emergency arises or something comes up they can't handle, they'll call the appropriate staff person at home. Otherwise they're in charge of the patients.

The nurse's job is to help the patients get well, or help them to die. This involves making beds, giving baths, taking temperatures and pulses, testing stools and vomitus for blood, testing urine for sugar and acetones, feeding patients who can't eat, giving Foley catheter care to patients who have been catheterized, giving wound care to surgery patients, giving out medications, cleaning up when patients vomit or are incontinent, scheduling tests, X-rays, and radiation treatments, giving enemas, prepping patients for surgery, checking IVs, recording every medication given, charting each patient's progress—a thousand technical chores, all done daily.

This is minimum nursing care. But nursing is not just technical. Anyone can do physical care. You can teach a robot to give a bed bath. To me a good nurse is someone who puts some caring behind the physical care.

Being a nurse is not like working on an assembly line. People are sick. You can't rush a post-op getting out of bed for the first time even when you're one nurse short that day. There are thirty-six different personalities. People are afraid. They're depressed. They may be angry. They may be alone. They may have no place to go. They may be dying. They have questions. They need reassurance. They may need to learn how to adjust their lives to changes in their bodies. They may need to cry. They may need to laugh.

They need support. Most often they get it from their families. But sometimes the families are unable to give it. Sometimes there is no family. Some patients get support from their doctors. But the doctors, like the families, come and go. Doctors may not be able to give what the patient needs.

Nurses may not, either. But we're the ones who spend the most time with the patients. Twenty-four hours a day. Seven days a week. Three hundred and sixty-five days a year. When a patient's light goes on, it's a nurse who goes into the room.

My husband says that from what he's seen as a med student, nurses play the same role on a regular floor that an electrocardiograph plays in the intensive care unit. They're the monitor. If the nurses fail, it's like a breakdown in a mechanical device.

I think, too, that nurses often help get better care for patients who are not the well-educated, 40-year-old suburban types who are aware of what's going on and will stick up for themselves. We stick up for the patients who can't or don't stick up for themselves.

I'm not saying that all nurses are wonderful. There are a lot of bitches in nursing, just as there are in other professions. But I think an awful lot is expected of nurses. People don't want robots. They want a calm person who stands there and supports them, and we've got to do all these other things as well. There are times when I feel like an octopus. I've got twenty things to do, and I say to myself, "My god. Where in the world am I going to find time to do all this?"

We've got to be a lot. People expect doctors and nurses, sometimes, to be more than we can be. I expect that myself, sometimes. I have to keep reminding myself that doctors and nurses are human beings. We have our needs too.

Dr. Rose got up to Eight Cook at about 1:00, just after Mrs. O'Brien and her daughter had gone down to get some lunch.

Rose is very tall, good-looking, with sideburns. I'd say he's in his early forties. I don't like him. The first time I ever met him, I was taking care of a patient who was on his way out. Dying. Rose walked in the room and said, "Well, how ya doin?"

The patient could barely manage to say, "Weeeeellll . . . lllooooo, Doooooc." He was really groggy.

Rose said to him, "What you need is some more big-busted things like her"—and he looked at me—"taking care of you."

I was so mad. It wasn't that it was so rude to me. I thought it was an insult to the patient. First-class crudeness.

I walked out of the room behind him, and I don't remember my exact words, but I said, "If you ever said anything like that to my father or to somebody I cared about, I'd be very upset. That's the last thing a patient ready to die needs to hear."

Rose just shrugged. It was a long time before I could look at him after that.

Rose has had good remissions with his cancer patients. For a lot of people, he represents hope. He also spends exactly ten seconds with each patient. Whether they're rich or poor, as Jackie Neill says. I've seen him spend more time that that with patients, but I've never seen him do a physical exam on a patient.

I don't know Rose as a person. He's strange. He hardly ever talks to me, usually just about says hello.

But for some reason Rose had been acting awfully nice to me

for a couple of weeks. When he got up on the floor that particular afternoon, he actually came over and told me about Kelly O'Brien's surgery.

The news, Rose said, was a lot better than he had expected. There was no sign that the cancer had spread. All he had found was radiation gastritis. He thought that that's what was causing the vomiting.

Radiation gastritis is supposedly common. I don't know how common it is, but it happens. Radiation treatments destroy cancer cells. The treatments also destroy some normal cells, those that multiply the most quickly. That's why some people lose their hair. The treatments can cause all kinds of side effects. They can also burn the skin and cause internal irritations, such as ulcers. People whose upper bodies are being irradiated sometimes end up with a radiation esophagitis, or inflammation. They have burning in their esophaguses, and they can't swallow.

People who administer the treatments shield every part of the patient's body that doesn't need to be irradiated. But in Kelly's case, they were irradiating his pancreas, which is so close to the stomach that I guess there was no way the stomach could have been shielded. Radiation gastritis isn't necessarily serious.

"People don't know a lot about it," Rose told me. "We do know that the effect of radiation is prolonged, and that it bottoms out. It takes a long time to heal the wounds, but if you give the patient enough support, the wounds do heal."

Rose had put a third tube into Kelly's body, a feeding tube through which we could soon put blenderized feedings directly into the small intestine, bypassing the stomach. As soon as Kelly got stronger, he could be taken off hyperalimentation. Once he was off hyperal, he could go home. Considering that he hadn't been the best surgical risk, he was doing pretty well.

Well enough, in fact, to be coming directly back to the floor, instead of going to special or intensive care for a few days.

I was really glad. "Whom shall I page when the family comes back?"

"You tell the family."

Rose's eyes were laughing. He was being sarcastic. Only the doctors tell patients what goes on in the OR.

I waited.

"Benson will be up soon," Rose said.

I breathed a sigh of relief. Jon Benson was a first-year resident on Rose's service. He was of medium height with sandy hair that was getting thin, and he wore gold-rimmed glasses. I didn't know Benson very well, but I had a lot of respect for him.

In fact, he was my favorite of the surgical residents I knew. Some of them were flip. Benson wasn't. Maybe that was because he was older than most of the others when he had started med school. Just how old he was I'm not sure. I knew he had two kids. Benson would come up and put his arm around me and say, "I get no respect on this floor." But he got it and gave it. I knew Benson would explain things to the O'Briens as well as things could be explained.

At a little after 2:00, Kelly O'Brien was brought back to Eight Cook on a stretcher. He was alert and looked better than I had expected him to. But he appeared to have been crying. His eyes were full of tears.

About five of us got him back into bed. While we were straightening him up, he said, "Knock me out, girls."

I said, "Knock you out?"

And he answered, "Yeah. Knock me out."

So I said, "As soon as we check your blood pressure and your temperature and your pulse, we'll give you a needle."

We did that, and he slept.

A little later, at change of shift, I was standing at the meds cart counting narcotics with a nurse coming on duty when Debbie, one of the new grads, came up to me. She looked really happy.

"Mary! Mrs. Funicelli has fibrocystitis! She didn't have a mastectomy!"

I walked home in a light rain feeling high. The news about Mrs. Funicelli was the best thing that had happened to me all day.

2

REALITY SHOCK: THE ACID
TEST OF NURSING

When I was 13, I wanted to become a nun. I wanted to give something to somebody and do something for people. Very idealistic. I was the first child of Catholic parents. My two brothers and sister and I all went to Catholic grade schools in a small town a short distance from the city where I now live.

Whether my parents wanted me to become a nun or not I don't remember. My mother did want us to be what she called service-oriented. She also wanted me out of bed on Saturday mornings, not sleeping half the day away, as some of my girlfriends did.

So when I was 14, she convinced one of the nuns at Mother of Mercy Hospital near our home to take me on as a volunteer. I volunteered for two Saturdays. Then the nuns offered to pay me. I worked there on and off until I finished nursing school.

For a couple of years all I did was take kids up and down to the X-ray Department and play with the kids. That was fun. They were basically well children who were just recovering from minor surgical procedures. The nurses were very motherly. I would do all the work they didn't want to do—clean the utility room, make the beds—and they loved that. I had no real responsibility. It was a very protected and good situation.

Then for a few years I worked in the Central Supply Room. There I cleaned syringes, sharpened needles, prepared bone marrow trays, powdered and sterilized gloves, and added up the charges to patients for what was ordered. I had a lot of responsibility in Central Supply. I worked there part-time until my second year of nursing school, when I became a nursing assistant.

Meanwhile, at the age of 15, I became an agnostic. I decided all religion was full of bunk. Fine for other people, but I was above all that. The next year I decided I didn't want to be a nun after all.

One reason was that I became interested in boys. At Mother of Mercy some of my girlfriends and I used to ride the back elevators with the guys who delivered the trays. They were also high school kids. I took one of them to my senior prom. I was having fun. I thought, "Who wants to be a nun and never get married?"

My mother wanted all of us to go on to school. My father thought this was a way-out idea. He is a laborer. Most of our relatives and friends were working-class people. My mother had the idea that the next generation should be better educated than her generation was. She encouraged me a lot. Eventually my sister and one of my brothers attended college, and my father got over thinking that the idea was way-out. But I was the first. It was a big thing.

I chose nursing by a process of elimination. For a while I considered teaching English. Most of my friends were going to teachers' college. But I wasn't that good in English. I couldn't afford a four-year program anyway. Although my father could have afforded to send us through, he believed that if somebody wanted something badly enough, the person would work for it. I just accepted that.

At Mother of Mercy I found that I enjoyed certain things that nurses did. I also liked the nuns. Although I never thought they were realistic about life, I was affected by what they taught me. My mother had raised me with the idea that you sacrificed, that you did things for other people. The nuns reinforced what I had been taught and thought was right. When I was 17, I announced my decision to become a nurse.

My family was pleased. They thought of nursing as a prestige job.

A friend of my mother's whose husband was a doctor recommended the nursing program at Metropolitan Hospital. I chose this program over that of a Catholic hospital where I was also accepted, mainly because Metropolitan was in the center of the city. I had only been downtown once in my life, to one of the big department stores one Christmastime.

I paid for my training with the money I earned working at Mother of Mercy. It was worth what I paid. Metro had a very sound program, I feel. While I'm sorry that I don't have that B.S. next to my name, because of what it means today, I feel I received good training.

I considered myself a very raw product when I started nursing school. But because of my Mother of Mercy experience, I think I had a better understanding of what a nurse was than many of my classmates did. Mother of Mercy helped formulate my ideas about what nursing should be. If I couldn't yet tell a good nurse from a bad nurse when I started at Metropolitan, at least I knew what nurses did.

Mother of Mercy showed me the realities of the floor. When I became a nurse, the realities of the floor did not come as a shock.

The realities of the floor cause many new nurses to become bitter or frustrated. Some of my friends hate nursing. Rebecca, my roommate in nursing school, hated nursing from the beginning. Joyce, with whom I shared an apartment when I first started working, hates nursing and can't wait to get out. I know of few people who have stayed in hospital nursing for a long period of time without becoming frustrated or bitter.

Many nurses don't stay for long periods. Staff turnover, especially in city hospitals, is very high. When I started as head nurse on Eight Cook in February 1975, my staff included six RNs who had graduated the previous June. Only two, Liz and Maureen, stayed on after their first year. This is common. Not all of them left nursing. But so many nurses do leave nursing that someone has written a textbook about it. The book is called *Reality Shock*.

The turnover problem partly explains why nurses at Mother of Mercy, as well as at other city hospitals, are so young. Nearly half my staff is made up of RNs who are 21 or 22 years old. Most of these have had less than a year's experience. I became a head nurse at 24. Ann Sullivan, my supervisor, is 29. Jackie Neill was made head nurse at 22.

Because of the turnover, a great deal of responsibility falls to people who sometimes aren't as mature as they should be. One of the new graduates on my floor recently transferred to obstetrics, where the patients aren't sick and the mood is happy. She left partly because of her inability to deal with doctors, a problem she saw as a weakness. If she had stayed longer, she would have realized that learning not to be afraid of doctors comes with maturity.

I think the problem begins with people's expectations. A lot of nurses start out with the dream Maureen Shay started out with. Maureen graduated from nursing school in 1974. She's one of the best RNs on my floor. "I went into nursing with the idea of being Florence Nightingale at the bedside," she often says. In her dream, Maureen put her hands on patients' brows, held patients' hands, comforted patients. On Eight Cook Maureen discovered that nursing wasn't at all what she had expected.

Maureen's dream might have been fine twenty or thirty years ago. But times have changed. Medicine is much more sophisticated than it used to be, and much more complicated. As a result of new medicines, new treatments, heavier surgery, and different types of monitors, we are able to keep people alive who in Florence Nightingale's day would have been dead fifteen minutes after they came in.

We're taking care of an entirely different population. Years ago people died in their forties and fifties. They didn't live long enough to get as sick as patients do now. Many of the people admitted to Eight Cook are eighty or ninety years old. They're diabetic. They're arthritic. There are changes going on in their brains, lungs, hearts, and even their skin. They have a lot of needs.

There was a time when registered nurses prepared food, emptied trash, and cleaned patients' rooms. They didn't even take blood pressures. Today's RNs know a lot about patients, and more about the machines used in patient care than many doctors do. In critical care units, or on general floors of hospitals having appropriate insurance coverage, today's RNs carry out procedures that used to be done only by doctors. They draw blood. They start intravenous feedings. They resuscitate patients whose hearts have stopped beating.

On Eight Cook the RNs are managers. We make decisions,

keep records, pass medications, and coordinate, teach, and lead staff. Our main responsibility is to see that patients receive the right kind of care. Often that care is given by somebody else. If a patient needs instruction in a two-gram sodium diet, I get a dietitian to come up. If I learn that a patient who has had a leg amputated is being discharged to go home alone to a second-floor apartment, I call in one of the hospital social workers. Most bedside care is done by licensed practical nurses and nursing assistants. At Mother of Mercy no RN ever touched a bedpan.

Maureen Shay thinks there's no such thing as a bedside nurse any more. That's true in the sense that no one person has the full care of a patient. The person the patient sees as a bedside nurse— the LPN or the nursing assistant—gives physical care but doesn't make any kind of plans. The person making the plans—the RN— spends much less time at the bedside than RNs used to spend.

That's a source of frustration for many RNs after they graduate, I think. They leave nursing school thinking they can do so much, and then they discover that they can't give the kind of care they want to give.

Another problem for many nurses is that nursing is undefined. What is a nurse? Nurses have been debating that question for years. A nurse used to be a physician's handmaiden. My husband's grandfather, an old-time pediatrician who died a few months after Ron and I were married in 1975, remembered a time when nurses stood up and saluted doctors. Central's director of nursing, a woman in her forties, remembers the days when nurses had to stand and give doctors their chairs when they came into the nurses' stations.

This attitude has not disappeared. But nurses are stepping out of that mold. Liz Roberts worked at a hospital in Houston before coming to Eight Cook. One day Liz was in the nurses' station working on charts. A doctor walked around her looking for a chart. The director of nursing happened to come on the floor. She took Liz aside. "When the doctors come around," the director said, "would you please get up out of the way and help them look for their charts?"

Ten years ago, Liz would have said, "Yes, ma'am." Instead, she told the director of nursing that she would be glad to help any doctor who had made a real effort to find the chart himself, just as she would help anyone else in that situation.

As Liz said when she told me the story, "You can't call yourself a professional and be a professional if you're just going to say, 'Yes, sir,' 'No, sir,' and not bring anything to the job yourself."

Many nurses want to bring their own intelligence to the job and are becoming aggressive about doing so. A lot of our time is still spent carrying out orders written by doctors. But more and more often nurses are questioning those orders. Questioning is considered good nursing judgment. So is making suggestions to doctors about things that might help patients. So is refusing to carry out an order that you disagree with, as long as you do it according to established procedures. I think a nurse must make decisions that affect what she's doing. If she's a robot, she's nothing.

Unfortunately, not everyone agrees on that point. Most nurses consider nursing a profession. Many doctors do not. In fact, some doctors don't even see nurses as having thinking brains. Many nurses I know are re-evaluating whether they're going to stay in nursing because they don't know whether they can cope with the constant battle to prove themselves professionals. If we don't view ourselves as handmaidens, but others don't view us as professionals, then what are we?

Since there's no general agreement about what a nurse is, there are no obvious limits to the job. A nurse's role tends to be whatever other people decide it should be. Nurses do whatever doctors and janitors won't do. If Escort doesn't want to do something, or Dietary doesn't want to do something, Nursing does it.

It seems crazy, but even a nurse's role in bedmaking has various interpretations, depending on the hospital. At Central people from the Housekeeping Department wash and make the beds, but only after the nurses have stripped the bedding. At Metropolitan nurses stripped the beds, Housekeeping washed the beds, then the nurses remade them. At Mother of Mercy the nurses had to strip, wash, and make the beds.

Nurses who don't become bitter about the ambiguities of their role may become bitter about the work itself. Nursing can be tedious. It's a pain in the ass to have to check blood pressures on thirty-six patients. Taking weights is boring. Adding up a patient's intake-and-output is boring; getting people to do these I&Os is a problem in all hospitals.

There is a lot of detail—forms to fill out, chores to be done, endless checking and rechecking. The detail involved in passing medications alone might come as a surprise to people who think of nurses as nothing more than pill pushers. To give the right dose of the right drug to the right patient at the right time, you have to be organized.

There's a lot of what some people call "dirty work" in nursing. Some nurses become really upset about bowel movements. They won't empty a bedpan or change a colostomy bag without putting on gloves. Cleaning up after incontinent patients can be messy, especially if the patient has had diarrhea.

It never bothered me to empty bedpans or clean up feces. After all, stool is just breakdown products. It's nothing but what goes into you. What does bother me is watching a patient vomit. It doesn't bother me every day. But sometimes there's an odor that really hits your nose, and if I'm getting my period, my stomach can turn queasy. I have held basins for patients and while they're vomiting, I'm turning my head and dry-heaving myself, with tears coming to my eyes, and I'm thinking, "Oh, my god, what if the patient sees me doing this?"

I guess every nurse is bothered by something. Maureen Shay gags if she looks at sputum before breakfast. Katie Cavanaugh, my first head nurse at Metro and the person who has influenced me most as a nurse, couldn't stand to suction somebody. She dry-heaved when she did that. If a patient needed suctioning, she would say, "Please! I'll do anything else, but that makes me sick at my stomach. Could you suction this patient?"

I don't mean that she wouldn't suction somebody in an emergency. I think anybody would do anything in an emergency. One of my friends did mouth-to-mouth resuscitation on a patient who had just thrown up and aspirated the vomit. All this green stuff was coming out of his mouth. She just wiped it off and started in. Several nurses to whom I told this story said, "Oh, my god, I would have let him die." But you don't think in a situation like that. Your instincts and training take over.

To me the most horrible job a nurse has to do is something that hurts a patient. A few times I've worked with people who were severely burned. The first time I ever smelled one of those patients, I remember thinking it was the worst smell I had ever experienced. The flesh of those patients was just like tar. We used to medicate them with narcotics before we took their dressings off with sterile water, but you could tell by their faces that they were still in terrible pain. That bothered me much more than any vomit or diarrhea I've had to confront.

Many nurses become bitter about the schedule they have to work. When a nurse leaves, and you ask her why, she's likely to say she can't stand rotating. General frustration may be the real reason, but rotating is the overt reason. Central's shifts are 7:00 A.M. to 3:00 P.M., 3:00 P.M. to 11:00 P.M., and 11:00 P.M. to 7:00 A.M. All head nurses work straight days. Supervisors are assigned permanently to either days, evenings, or nights. Some staff nurses choose to work permanent evenings or permanent nights for personal or family reasons. Everybody else changes shifts every two weeks, rotating from days to evenings to nights and back to days.

Straight days aren't ideal either. In winter I feel I'm living in darkness. It's dark when I get up and dark when I get home. That's depressing.

All of us work one weekend in two and one holiday in two. Half our days off are during the week, when husbands are at work and children are at school. I don't know how women who have children and a home to keep up do it. But a lot of my staff does. I've always been spoiled by being able to walk to work. They commute. Mrs. Payne lives an hour's drive away. When she's on days, she gets up at 5:00 A.M. I just can't imagine it.

Those of us who work in city hospitals are on city streets at dangerous times. I've heard of several nurses who have been raped or mugged on the way to or from work. Central now has security guards patrolling for several blocks around the hospital from 10:30 to midnight and again from 6:30 to 7:30 A.M., during change of shift.

Nursing is a restrictive profession. If a patient's heart stops, the doctor and the supervisor arrive, handle the situation, and leave. Nurses are confined to the floor. Any emergency can take a lot of emotion or a lot of time. That's true whether the patient lives or dies. When the emergency is over, it's the nurse who's left behind to straighten up, to try to get together what was interrupted. If we're upset, we can't leave.

Perhaps there is a patient who's combative or depressed or acting out. That one person can take a great deal of time and energy and put a lot of strain on the whole nursing staff. A doctor who comes in on consult is there for a few minutes. He may never see the patient again. The nurses are stuck there all the time. If we don't straighten out the problem, it will only get worse.

Sometimes I can't believe how little freedom a nurse has. My cousin works parttime for the government. People in her office frequently take an hour and a half for lunch. The day I take an hour and a half for lunch! We are allowed thirty minutes.

People in some jobs can work till midnight and go in late the next day. I don't have that option. If I'm feeling sick when I wake up in the morning, and I know the staffing is going to be short that day, I force myself to get in there. Any staff nurse will do the same.

In an office, there's some free time. People can goof off a little. They don't have to keep their minds on life-and-death matters all the time. A hospital doesn't allow people much freedom to goof off. In a hospital, events that would be considered ordinary elsewhere, like laughing in the hall when somebody tells you a joke, might be considered unprofessional by a patient's family. Yet nurses need to goof off occasionally as much as anyone else does.

Nurses have to answer to a lot of people. If the doctor wants something done, he tells the nurse. If the X-ray slip doesn't get over to the X-ray Department, the nurse gets the call. When family members want certain things done for Mom or Dad, they go to the nurse. Nurses are go-betweens. Everybody wants the nurse to do everything. Everything filters through his or her hands at one point or another.

Nurses are visible. We're the largest group in the hospital. We're more directly responsible for patients than anyone else is. We deal more closely with the business of the hospital than anybody else does. So Nursing gets blamed for a lot of things, I think. Sometimes it seems that everything that goes wrong is blamed on the nurse.

It's traumatizing to have people make demands all the time. You wonder, "What should I do first? Should I get the water for this patient first? Or do percussion on that patient? Or take off the order for Dr. So-and-so? Or get Mr. So-and-so ready for X-ray?" You know in your heart that the patient who's sickest needs you most, and ideally you'll go to that person first. But sometimes, unfortunately, it's who yells the most.

Most patients accept things. But patients used to be less sophisticated than they are today. Less educated. They didn't watch TV and go to the movies and see people dying of cancer. They didn't see Joe Gannon and Marcus Welby and the little nurses walking around in their white uniforms looking as if they had just stepped out of a commercial, instead of looking like most nurses look at the end of the day. My god, you watch the soap operas, and So-and-so has leukemia, and they're using the names of real drugs that are used to treat leukemia. If I say to a patient, "You're going to get Actinomycin," the patient may already know what it is.

I haven't noticed that patients expect more than they used to. Although we do hear comments from patients on what they expect in exchange for the $168 a day they're paying for a semi-private room, we always heard comments like that. Patients *are* asking more questions now about their own condition. They do want to know more about what's going to happen to them. They should know. But questions from everybody all day long can be annoying.

Nurses are up against a lot of stereotypes. Most of us are women. Liz Roberts, who can be sharp-tongued, figures it this way: "People have always thought women aren't too smart. Nursing is full of women. Therefore, nursing can't be much."

I think some people do look at nursing that way. Patients frequently ask questions like, "Oh, you're so cute; why are you still single?" or "When are you going to quit this and get married?" I'm sure women in other jobs are asked the same questions. But to some people, the idea that nurses consider nursing a profession and not just a way to mark time comes as a revelation.

Some people have the idea that nurses are an easy sexual mark. Maybe this idea started with the first nurses, who were prostitutes brought into hospitals to take care of poor people. I'm sure it was not considered appropriate even a few decades ago for a woman to see fifty million men's rear ends. One of Central's associate directors of nursing, a woman in her fifties, says that her family was against her becoming a nurse because nursing was not for "nice" girls.

People today are a lot less inhibited about bodies than they used to be. Still, some people apparently think that because a nurse works with the physical, she's more likely to give of the physical. Most people I know don't think this way. But before I met Ron, when I was dating medical students and would tell them or their friends that I was a nurse, it was fairly common for someone to say, "A nurse! Hmmmmmmmm!"

It's common to hear remarks on the street. A couple of times when I've walked home in my uniform late at night, men have said things like, "Nursey, nursey, I need an angel of mercy!" Or, "Nurse, nurse, it's getting worse!" Or, "Take care of me, take care of me!"

Some patients seem to think of a nurse as a glorified maid or stewardess. When they leave the hospital, they say, "The service here was very good." I honestly do not think people realize how that sounds. But nurses do not like to hear the word *service*.

Nursing is demanding physically. It's hard work to get a 350-pound patient up out of bed. It's hard work to be on your feet all day. Sometimes when I go to bed at night, my legs ache so badly they're in spasm.

Nursing is demanding emotionally. It hurts to watch a patient suffer or to watch someone you care about die.

You would think people would learn about the realities of the floor in nursing school. This is a very sensitive issue in nursing. There's a lot of feeling among nurses who work that nurses who teach often haven't had much practical experience. I don't know if this is true or not.

I do know that nurses who graduate from three-year, hospital-based diploma programs, as I did, have much less clinical training now than diploma graduates used to have. I graduated from Metropolitan in 1972. Four or five years before that, third-year students were running the floors on evenings and nights.

There were no RNs around. This was the case in a lot of hospitals, until the American Nurses' Association stepped in and cracked down on the hospitals for using the students as staff.

Today's three-year graduates have floor experience, but they don't know what it's like to be responsible for more than two or three patients at a time. The B.S., or four-year, college-based degree programs tend to teach the administrative part of nursing. People will argue that point. But that's my feeling. I've seen a lot of kids come out of the four-year program with little knowledge of what it means to take care of patients.

So no matter which program they follow, students don't discover the truth about nursing until after they've graduated. Only when they start to work on the floors do they find out that nursing is not the romantic picture they had in mind, but a demanding, difficult job.

If you become frustrated and bitter in hospital nursing, you're in a bind. It used to be that a nurse could get a job anywhere in the country. Lots of nurses chose places like Aspen, Colorado. While nursing there was the same as it was in Atlanta or Albany, the skiing was better. Now, however, the nursing shortage is just about over.

Nurses with B.S. degrees have some flexibility. Nurses who took the three-year diploma program, as I did, have very little. We're trained as nurses. Period.

Some people try administration and find they like that better than bedside nursing, but most hospitals now want or require head nurses and supervisors to have B.S. degrees. Most school nurse jobs now require B.S. degrees. A three-year grad who wants to change professions completely has to start from scratch. Some nurses, however bitter, find it easier to stay in nursing.

Sometimes they can reduce their frustrations by changing jobs within the hospital. That's why my former roommate Rebecca did. I have a lot of respect for Rebecca. She's a good person and an excellent nurse technically. But she hates anything to do with real bedside care. In nursing school she would come back from the floor screaming, "I'm not taking care of any more of those frigging patients and their bed baths! Why can't those patients stop shitting?"

Now Rebecca is working in a hospital recovery room. She

monitors. The closest she comes to doing bedside care is giving bedpans. She doesn't enjoy the bedpans. But her husband is in medical school, and they need her income. For now, she says, the job is fine, because it doesn't require her to get close to the patients. Rebecca lives for the day she can quit nursing and raise dogs.

I have wondered many times what keeps the nurse in a hospital who really wants to be there. What makes people really like their jobs? Because many nurses do. Many nurses work in hospitals by choice.

This is true of a number of the nurses on Eight Cook. I don't mean just RNs. I also mean LPNs and nursing assistants, some of whom I'd rather have taking care of me than some RNs I know. The doctors tell me I have a very good staff on my floor. I do. I'm very lucky. These women really care about patients.

That, I think, is the key.

It certainly is for me. You can't become like a family member to everyone. But I know that the people I never got to know, the people I held back from for some reason—these are the ones I've forgotten. The people I've cared about, felt something for, become close to, the people I've invested a certain amount of myself in— these are the people I've learned something from. They are the reason I stay in nursing.

I think the old idea of professionalism in nursing was that you didn't touch. You didn't become close. You didn't allow yourself to invest anything in this human being who was the patient. When my mother was in the hospital for minor surgery eight years ago, she grew fond of a nurse who was being rotated into different rooms. One day my mother said to her, "Gee, I really like you. Why can't you take care of me every day?"

The nurse answered, "Because we don't want to become attached to patients. If something happens to you, we'd be too upset."

This may partly explain how the idea got started that nurses are uninvolved or uncaring. I've heard so many people say that. "Nurses are harsh." "Nurses don't care if patients are in pain." I get very, very upset when I hear these things. You think to yourself,

"I'm trying to do everything I can. I think the majority of people I work with try to do everything they can. God, what happened?"

True, some nurses still avoid involvement because they're afraid of being hurt. Jackie Neill says she avoids dying patients for that reason. It's true that if you become involved, you will be hurt. I have been closer to certain patients than I am to my own father. I don't know how I will react when my father dies. I just know that when these people died, I felt as if something inside me had been hurt, even though I knew it was better for them to die.

But you get over the hurt. I think hurt makes you grow as a person. If you're not hurt a little bit, you don't grow at all.

To me the old idea of cold professionalism is wrong. If you're not going to care about patients, invest a certain amount of emotion in them, try to improve what you're doing for them, why be a nurse? There are many jobs that don't involve people which allow you to be a perfectionist. Why choose a job like nursing, where so many things can happen in a day to ruin a schedule? If you're not going to care about the people, then you'll get nothing out of the job. You might as well be working in a factory. You might as well find a job with better hours.

I see myself as taking a break from nursing before too long. Ron and I want to have children. To me it would be a sacrifice to work full time while my children are little. But I also think it's good for women to keep up their careers so they have something to turn to when their children are grown or if something happens to their husbands. So I see the break as temporary. I'll always go back to nursing.

On the days I work, my alarm goes off at 5:45 in the morning. I always turn it off wishing I didn't have to get up. I never feel gung-ho about work until I get there. I wish I did. Some people, I hear, just can't wait to get to their jobs in the morning. I wonder what those jobs are. I would just love to love to get up every morning and go to work.

Once I get there, I'm fine. I do have my frustrations. I'm not caring for patients as I thought I would be. My dream wasn't Maureen's vision of the nurse as comforter; I imagined myself more as a doer. Someone who gave out medications, gave a treatment, gave a bed bath, checked an IV. But I saw myself taking care of patients, not dealing with the bureaucracy. The days I have little contact with patients are my bad days. If I do nothing all day but tasks—passing meds, taking off orders—I don't come home feeling very satisfied.

But if I put a couple of people on the bedpan, wash some backs, stand and talk to a few people, I get a lot of pleasure out of the day. Some days I have done a lot of patient care, even nothing but patient care. I really love those days. I love to think about what goes on in people's minds. I love to watch their eyes and watch the way they react to things, to think about what they're thinking. I love to watch what happens to people. I've learned a lot from patients about human beings. That to me is the most interesting thing about nursing.

I love the contact with patients, but I also need it. I pride myself on the fact that I usually know what to do for patients. When I do physical care on them, they end up feeling better. That's where your thanks lie, and that's where I get my satisfaction.

3

CARE: THE HEART
AND THE HARD PART

Listening to report in the nurses' lounge the fourth morning after Kelly O'Brien's surgery, I noticed Sharon frown when she got to Kelly's name on the patient-care Kardex.

"Things with Kelly could be better," Sharon told us. "His temp was up to 100.6 at midnight. His stool is still positive for blood. Also, he's very depressed. He won't talk at all."

Sharon was one of the new grads, petite, dark-eyed, quiet, and somewhat lacking in self-confidence, I thought. But she approached her responsibilities seriously, and I appreciated her obvious concern for Kelly.

"Today's his birthday," Sharon continued, looking up from the Kardex and glancing around at the day staff. "November eighth. Jennie ordered him a cake from downstairs. Of course he won't be able to eat anything for a while. But maybe he'll feel better if she knows the nurses are thinking about him."

Sharon smiled at Jennie, who smiled back. Jennie was the only white LPN on Eight Cook. In her mid-twenties, she was a bit flighty, not as organized as I would have liked. Yet she cared about patients. She was also the socializer of the floor, often bringing in goodies, planning staff parties, visiting patients who had been transferred down to intensive care or even to the rehab hospital across the city. I knew that one morning soon I'd come in to work and find that Jennie had decorated the floor for Thanksgiving. One of the supervisors said that Jennie was like a character out of the *Nutcracker* who sprinkles fairy dust on everything.

Adding to Sharon's report, Jennie said, "Kelly is really down. Stephanie and I went in there this morning to wish him a happy birthday and told him we were going to give him a complete makeover to celebrate. He didn't say anything. He did turn his head when I patted him on the knee, but he didn't open his eyes."

I said, "Isn't he supposed to get his first tube feeding today?"

"That's just what I was about to say," Sharon replied. "He is."

"I'd like to give it to him. That will give me an excuse to talk to him a little." I wanted to see whether Kelly would respond to someone he had known for a while.

Given Sharon's report, I didn't go into Mr. O'Brien's room with high hopes. Seeing Mrs. O'Brien sitting in her usual chair at the foot of Kelly's bed and looking rather depressed didn't add to my optimism. She and I exchanged words. Kelly's eyes were closed.

I went to the side of the bed and touched his shoulder.

"Happy birthday, Kelly," I said.

To my surprise, he opened his eyes and looked at me. I tried teasing him a little.

"How old are you today?" I asked. "Twenty-one?"

Kelly said, deadpan. "That's right. Twenty-one." He grabbed my hand and put it next to his cheek.

Mrs. O'Brien and I looked at each other. Kelly's voice was weak, but I was really pleased with his reaction.

"How old really?" I said.

Kelly kept his eyes closed a moment, as if he were thinking. Then he said, "Sixty-nine."

"Oh, Kelly!" Mrs. O'Brien was laughing. "Sixty-nine!"

Kelly smiled faintly.

"Oh, that's right," he said softly. "Seventy. I'm seventy."

I got Kelly up and walked him out to the nurses' station. But he was having a lot of pain, so I got him back into bed and gave him a shave. Then I told him I was going to give him his first blenderized feeding through the tube Dr. Rose had inserted into his small intestine.

"It's Vivonex," I said. "That's a high-protein, high-calorie, low-residue diet, easily absorbed in the bowel. I'm going to mix it with grape. Is grape all right with you?"

"Am I going to taste it?"

"Probably not." Some people say they do notice a flavor, others swear they don't.

"Then use grape." Kelly laughed a little. I left the room feeling more hopeful about him than I had since Rose had told me the results of the surgery.

Mr. O'Brien was very weak post-operatively. We had expected him to be fairly weak. After several months of vomiting and losing blood, he was bound to be debilitated, and two major operations so close together would be hard on anybody. On the positive side, his post-op vital signs were stable. He was up walking with assistance. Though still very weak, he had begun to gain strength.

Even so, in the first few days after surgery, he showed less reserve than I had hoped he would. He was also very depressed. He seemed to want to sleep away his time. Of course he was still under sedation for pain. It was too early to tell if he was losing heart. But I wondered more than once in those first days post-op whether Dr. Rose was really as optimistic as he seemed about getting Mr. O'Brien well enough to go home.

Still, I argued with myself, the basic facts in the case were cause for optimism. Rose had found no spread of cancer. Radiation gastritis is usually controllable. Kelly had a good family. I mean unusually good. His wife was very warm and affectionate with him. So was his son. His daughter was in the room almost every day. All of them gave Kelly a lot of support. He knew he was surrounded by people who loved him.

In addition to having a good family, Kelly had a strong will. That's important. If somebody were to come into the hospital for a hernia operation and do nothing for himself, he would probably get well. The body would heal itself. But a patient like Kelly O'Brien has to put out some effort. As a nurse you can force people to a certain extent, and you can encourage them, and you can strive with them. But support means little unless the person wants it. From what I've seen, the will can determine whether a person gets worse or better.

I got my first hard lesson about will from Roland Pierce, the first patient I became close to after I graduated and started working as a staff nurse. Roland Pierce had had a stroke. He was a good-looking man in his late sixties who owned a typewriter store, and even with his condition, there was a certain dignity about him. I liked him a lot. I also got fairly close to his wife.

The stroke left Mr. Pierce with quite a bit of brain and motor damage. He had no control over his bowels or bladder. His hands were very weak. He had expressive aphasia. That is, he understood what people were saying to him, but he was unable to express his feelings.

Despite this damage, Roland Pierce was a candidate for rehabilitation. He was going to the rehab floor every day. Whether his heart would have withstood the rigors of full therapy I don't know. But a rehab candidate is somebody the doctors think is going to be viable. They don't try to rehabilitate people who have suffered irreversible strokes and aren't expected to live. Roland Pierce was expected to live.

He died. He virtually willed himself to die.

When a person has a stroke that affects the brain, the brain tissue swells, and a certain amount of damage seems apparent. Over a period of time, however, as the swelling starts to disappear, the person can get more return than is first evident. The doctors kept trying to impress this on Mr. Pierce. But he was so depressed right in the beginning that he wouldn't allow this information to sink in. He wouldn't accept it.

He refused to eat, no matter what we did. The doctors even put tubes down his nose so we could give him blenderized feedings directly into the stomach. Mr. Pierce yanked the tubes out. It was a constant battle, putting the tube down, restraining his hands. His weight went down to sixty pounds. He got bedsores all over. He was alert, but he refused to do anything. He would signal the nurses to leave him alone.

That was frustrating for all of us. It's very difficult to say to yourself, "I'm caring about this person and he doesn't care." As a nurse, you have two alternatives in that situation. You can say, "Well, shit, if he's not going to care, I'm not either." Or you can say to yourself, "He's depressed. He's upset. Maybe this is just something he's going through right now. Maybe it will pass. I've got to give him a chance."

The first month he was in the hospital, we were all working to give Roland Pierce a chance. We held numerous conferences on him. People spent a lot of time trying to get him to move, to care about himself, to go through the rehabilitation. We were very aggressive.

He just became angry. I remember saying to him, "It would be a lot easier for me to just ignore you and not to do anything. I want you to get better. You *can*." He would turn his face away.

What lay behind the man's decision to die I can't say for sure. He was obviously depressed about what had happened to his body. He was no dummy. He was intelligent and sensitive. I'm sure he realized that if he lived he would have to go into a nursing home. It also must have been hard for him to see his wife come in day after day, getting thinner, more tired, more drained. Maybe what he did was the best thing he could have done. It didn't seem so to me at the time.

In the end we all had to accept that Roland Pierce wanted to die. A nurse or doctor can only do so much. You can't make somebody want to live. But I still think he could have pulled through. I still feel that in some way the nurses and doctors failed him. I look back on Roland Pierce as a battle I lost.

Most of the lessons about will have much happier endings. While it's not rare for a patient to decide to die, the majority of people I've seen fight to get better. Many of them do get better. One of the more dramatic examples I know of involved Eleanor Vance, a patient we had on the floor fairly recently.

Mrs. Vance was diabetic. At the age of 70, she had a foot amputated and came to Eight Cook to be cared for while her stump healed. She was not, as someone on the floor said, your average little old lady. Eleanor Vance was a very well-bred person. Apparently she had once had money. She had also been a legal examiner for the government. She kept up with politics, loved to read, and had a command of language that amazed me. I thought she was very intelligent.

According to her care plan, Mrs. Vance was to be fitted with a prosthetic foot as soon as she felt well enough. As soon as she had learned to use the prosthesis, she would go home.

For a long time it looked as if Mrs. Vance's story would not end happily. Diabetics heal more slowly than other people, but this patient took an exceptionally long time to heal. She was on Eight Cook for 103 days. I felt she was not, deep down, a pusher psychologically. Maybe she tried as much as she thought she could. Maybe she couldn't accept what had happened to her. Her husband was dead, and she had no children, so maybe she just didn't care.

She became very depressed. Partly because she was depressed, she had trouble adjusting to the prosthesis. That made her even more depressed. Then she developed a bedsore on her remaining foot. The doctors told her she might lose that foot too. With nothing to look forward to but the likelihood of another amputation, even more time in the hospital, and an uncertain future, Eleanor Vance became so depressed that Sandy Nichols, Central's psychiatric nurse specialist, started spending twenty minutes with her every day.

Weeks passed. Mrs. Vance was finally discharged to live with a friend. Though she still had a blackened area on her foot, the bedsore was no worse. She was less than confident about using her prosthesis. She was still depressed. But there was nothing more to be done for her medically, and the doctors thought it would give her a psychological boost to get out of the hospital. I thought so too. She did look forward to going.

Three weeks later Eleanor Vance was readmitted to Three Cook to have her remaining foot amputated. Sandy Nichols told me that Mrs. Vance was so depressed that she wanted to die.

"She's too Catholic to try suicide," Sandy said, "but she may just stop eating."

Ten weeks after that conversation, Eleanor Vance left the hospital a different person. She was using a walker and a wheelchair, but she was wearing make-up and jewelry and looked, Sandy reported, like the businesswoman she once was. Mrs. Vance felt prepared—and Sandy believed she was prepared—to handle whatever might come up.

There was nothing miraculous in the transformation of Eleanor Vance. Basically what happened was that after the second surgery, the doctors started talking nursing home to her. She was horrified. She had a friend in a nursing home. The friend hated it. Mrs. Vance did not want to go into a nursing home herself.

But one of the doctors said to her one day, "You had trouble with one prosthesis. How can you manage with two?"

That comment apparently scared Eleanor Vance. She started talking with Sandy with the choices open to her. Sandy finally said, "If you want to take control of your own life, you can't just lie there and ask people to take care of you."

Exactly when that fact took hold in the patient's mind, Sandy didn't know. But at some point Eleanor Vance concluded that she had to learn to take care of herself. Once she made that decision, she stopped thinking of the prostheses as the enemy. She learned to get around. The more successful she became at getting around, the more her confidence increased. What brought her back to life was her will. She had had the necessary physical resources all along. She got better when she made up her mind to get better.

Since a person's state of mind can play such a vital role in healing, emotional support is a crucial part of nursing. Maureen Shay and other nurses even argue that nursing is concerned only with the psychosocial aspects of patient care and is not medicine at all. They have a point.

I don't mean that nurses look on every patient or family member as a psychological case. Most Eight Cook patients are short-term. They have surgery, they want to get better, they do get better, and they go home. They have family and friends. They don't need emotional support from the nurses. All they need is physical assistance. But many patients need some emotional support from us, and some need a lot.

Those who need the most are usually the patients who have been sick a long time, like Kelly O'Brien. They start thinking "What's the use?" and stop cooperating in their care. Kelly came out of the second exploratory wanting to get better. But the strongest will in the world can't cure cancer, and eventually Kelly would probably begin to lose the will to fight. In both phases he was going to need as much encouragement as the nurses could give him. Encouraging Kelly would be a big part of what was turning into a very big responsibility for the nurses.

In fact, though I didn't realize it at the time, Kelly O'Brien was on his way to becoming perhaps the heaviest nursing responsibility I had encountered in five years of nursing.

Once his surgery was over, Kelly needed little from the doctors directly. The doctors' role, I would say, was going in and saying hello to him, looking him over physically, and looking at the records to see what his intake and output were, what his blood studies showed, and how much fluid he was losing from diarrhea, vomiting, or drainage. Rose and the residents were legally responsible for Kelly. Of course they were directing his care. But what they actually did for him took little time out of their day. Minutes, really.

From the nursing staff, on the other hand, Kelly required a lot of time, more than any other patient on the floor most days. He could do very little for himself. We were shaving him, giving him mouth care, ambulating him, tube-feeding him, bathing him. Since surgery hadn't relieved his feeling of fullness, we hooked up his gastric tube to a pump and drained him whenever he complained of discomfort.

His wound care alone took nearly half an hour. His whole healing system had broken down, so his midline incision, which was huge, stayed open in spite of the sutures. The tissue was very fragile. We had to use sterile technique in treating the wound, and sterile technique takes time.

Then of course we were trying to provide emotional support, not just to Kelly but to his family as well. Kelly knew that he was eventually going to die of his disease. His family knew it. All of them had that to face. They had also been told that so far as Dr. Rose could tell, there was no technical reason Kelly could not go home and resume a reasonably comfortable life for a while. The family was hopeful. I think the nurses were hopeful. But Rose's optimism didn't stop Kelly from becoming depressed.

As soon as the original diagnosis was made, the nurses knew that what we had to do was try to keep Kelly physically and psychologically comfortable until the inevitable happened, however long that took, and whatever "comfortable" meant to Kelly and his family. The physical care we did on Kelly was time-consuming but not difficult. The emotional aspect took time, and it was often difficult.

That's a truth in nursing. The technical part of a nurse's job is not difficult. As long as you're interested, as long as you have a fairly decent nursing background and some sense and maturity, you can easily learn what a nurse has to do physically. The first time I ever irrigated a colostomy by myself, I was really afraid. I thought, "Oh, my god, I'm going to rupture something." I didn't. The irrigation went fine. At first even brushing a patient's teeth is awkward. But if you do it often enough, you learn to do it right.

Of course a nurse runs into technical difficulties that are difficult to solve. Bedsores are very difficult to clear up. No one knows for certain how to treat them. You just have to try different things.

Fistulas are difficult to treat. A fistula is a duct that opens between cavities in the body or opens onto the skin from an abscess inside the body. We had a patient, Mr. Loman, who developed an abdominal fistula after surgery in another hospital. When he was admitted to Eight Cook, his internal secretions were draining out onto his body, and his stomach looked like a piece of raw beefsteak that had been left out in the air. It was really ugly. But compared to the condition of some fistula patients I've seen, Loman's skin wasn't that bad. Some patients have gaping holes. Getting those holes to heal takes a lot of time and effort.

Still, while some technical problems are tricky, we rarely run into a technical problem on Eight Cook that we as nurses are incapable of handling, either by ourselves or with the right help. I used to be shaky going into a patient's room if I didn't know how to do something properly. Now if I don't know how to do something, I'll call somebody who does. Most tasks we do in the course of a day are familiar. We've done them so often that they've become routine.

Even codes become routine. A code is the emergency call that goes out over the intercom for the hospital's cardiopulmonary resuscitation team, or CRT. You call a code when a patient's heartbeat or breathing has stopped. If, for example, you can't get a pulse on a patient, or you walk into a room and see that the person isn't breathing, you pick up the phone in the room, dial 1010, wait for the buzz, and give the page operator the code initials: "CRT!"

Then you scream for another nurse to get in the room. The two of you start mouth-to-mouth resuscitation, somebody brings in the floor CRT cart containing all the medications and equipment that might be needed in an emergency, you get a board under the patient and start hitting his chest, and by that time the resuscitation team should be there to take over. You feel as if your heart's in your throat. You think, "If I don't perform, this patient is going to die." But so long as you have a basic understanding of what you're supposed to do, you just do it.

The real challenge of nursing is the psychological aspect. No two patients are alike. Each has an individual set of fears, convictions, quirks, problems. Learning what goes on in people's minds, so you know how to approach them, is hard. Being open to other people's values is hard.

A lot of factors work against nurses giving as much emotional support as some patients might need. Some nurses just can't handle the emotional needs of patients. Not knowing what to say or how to help, they leave the room. If this is a question of experience or maturity rather than personality, the nurse may get over it.

Nurses may stay out of the room for other reasons. We've had patients whose personalities were so offputting that nurses were reluctant to answer their lights. You read articles about nurses staying away from cancer patients. Some nurses do. But in my experience, when a nurse avoids a patient, it's more often because of the patient's personality than because of the disease.

Now and then you'll run into a supervisor who gets upset if nurses spend time giving emotional support. They don't view your time in a patient's room as patient care. I've never run into anybody like this at Central, but a supervisor at Metro once scolded me for spending so much time talking to patients, saying that if I'd spend less, I'd get out of work on time.

Time is a factor. A staff nurse spends about an hour a day with any one patient. Nurses rotate. Patient assignments change. Some patients come in on their last legs and die within three or four days. It's impossible to get to know their families well enough to give them the kind of support they need. Inside a hospital as well as outside, you have to establish a relationship with a person before you can provide emotional support. I will say certain things to people only if I feel I know them well enough, because I don't want to intrude, and I don't want to say things that people aren't ready to hear.

I suppose the most common obstacle to a nurse's giving emotional support is the number of demands on her time at any given moment. I found myself in that situation recently. One afternoon while I was sitting in the nurses' station taking off orders, Mrs. Johnson put her call light on. Mrs. Johnson was an older lady. She had had a leg amputated and had been having trouble passing her urine. She asked me for the bedpan, but she still couldn't urinate. As I took her off the bedpan, she started to cry.

"Oh, my god, I'm never going to get better," she moaned. "I'm going to die here."

My gut feeling was "Ohhhhhh." It was nearly 3:00. I was in the middle of taking off orders. I wanted to page a doctor, talk to the oncoming staff, do two other chores, and leave by 3:15, because I had to go to the bank, then get on a subway to meet Ron at school at 5:00.

I thought, "Should I say something to her, or should I ignore her and get out of the room? She has been having periods of confusion. I could pretend in my mind that she's confused."

For a few seconds, while I was trying to make a decision, my frustration level was at its peak.

Then I thought, "No, Mary, you can't do that. You can't leave. She's upset. She's crying. She's asking something. You've got to tell her."

I sat on the bed and talked with Mrs. Johnson until she seemed better and she said she was okay. Then I put a pillow behind her back and went out feeling fine, because I knew I had done what I should have done. I left seven minutes late that day. Seven minutes is nothing. It's just that seven often mounts up to twenty-seven. Some days you think you're never going to get out.

Such conflicts occur all the time. I have never walked out of the room when a patient asked to talk, but sometimes I have cut a conversation short. In a sense I failed those patients. Jackie Neill says that when this happens to her, she doubles the time she is supposed to spend with the patient the next day out of guilt, even if the patient doesn't need her.

My feeling is that most nurses want to give emotional support to patients and family. Some may be uncomfortable initiating certain kinds of support. I can't imagine any nurse turning down a request. If she can't fulfill the request herself, she may relay it, but she won't ignore it. I don't know of any nurses who don't consider emotional support important.

Yet as important as it is, giving emotional support, or trying to, is not always the most important thing a nurse can do for a patient.

When I had just graduated from nursing school, I didn't realize this. I thought if there was a choice between doing a task and giving emotional support, forget the task.

Now I see things differently. Extra attention is important. Tasks may be crucial. Patients can survive without that nice arm around them, but they might not survive if the floor isn't organized, if medications run out, if equipment isn't where it should be, if certain other things aren't done.

Sometimes it's more important to give the pain medication than to sit and hold the person's hand.

Kelly O'Brien's birthday cake came up from the kitchen at about 2:30. Jennie put a few candles on it and lit them. Then all the nurses on the floor who could get free for a few minutes went into Kelly's room singing "Happy Birthday." Dr. Benson happened to be on the floor, and he went in with us. I thought it was funny that all the nurses sang "Happy birthday, dear Kelly," but Benson sang, "Happy birthday, Mr. O'Brien." Mrs. O'Brien, who was also in the room, joined in the singing.

Kelly was sitting up in bed. Jennie put a tray down in front of him and put the cake on the tray. "Okay, now, take a deep breath and blow the candles out," Jennie said.

I didn't think Kelly would get that excited over a cake. But tears came to his eyes. After he blew the candles out, he just sat there and looked at all of us.

"Thank you," he kept saying. "Thank you."

We all stood around joking and eating. Everybody but Kelly had a piece of cake. When we had finished, just as we were starting to leave, Pat O'Brien came off the elevator with another cake. So of course we had to slice that one and pass it around too.

"The nurses are all making oinks of themselves," I said to Kelly.

He looked up at me.

"You girls," he said. His cheeks were wet with tears.

4

"SNOWING": A WAY OUT

Pain medications became an issue on Eight Cook just before Thanksgiving, not with Kelly O'Brien, who was somewhat better, but with Virginia Medlock, who was dying.

Virginia was a black ward patient of 53. When she was about fifty, she had been diagnosed as having cancer of the cervix. Cervical CA is a treatable cancer. A surgeon removes the cervix, or does a complete hysterectomy, and the prognosis is good. I don't know whether Virginia didn't understand that, or didn't accept that she needed the surgery, or just didn't want it.

But she refused treatment. When she finally entered the hospital, surgeons had to do a pelvic exenteration on her, which meant they took everything out of the lower abdominal cavity and diverted her urine and fecal waste into bags through artificial holes in the abdomen. The number of surgical procedures she had had since was unreal. Virginia was always skinny, but on her previous admission, she had gone down to about sixty pounds. When she came in this time, I knew she wasn't going to get out.

Virginia Medlock touched me more than almost any other patient I have taken care of. I really loved her. She was always puffing on cigarettes, and I would go back and sit with her while she smoked so she wouldn't ignite the alternating pressure mattress we had her on to keep her from getting bedsores, and we would talk about all kinds of things. I thought of her as worldly-wise. Sometimes one of the doctors would come in and sit on the

51

side of the bed. "Come here, sugar," she'd say. The doctor would lie down next to her. She'd put her arm around him and say, "Oh, that's cute!" and rub his head. She always had something nice to say to people. I think she had a special place in a lot of people's hearts.

As far as I know, Virginia was never married. Her twin sister and her mother visited her every day. Mrs. Medlock was a nice lady. Although she was in her seventies, she looked younger than Virginia. She was always properly dressed, with a little cap on, black shoes, and white stockings. She was a Baptist with deep religious feelings. You might consider her an old-fashioned black woman. Virginia's twin was an attractive, well-dressed woman. On Sundays people from the church would come with them. Sometimes all the women wore white. They had been helping with communion, Virginia told me.

Mrs. Medlock would come in, sit by Virginia, and just sort of look at her, shaking her head. I'd say, "Hi, Mrs. Medlock, how are you today?"

She'd say, "I'm fine, but I wish my gal would be okay."

I'd say, "She's really been through hell, hasn't she."

"She sure has."

Hell is the word. Virginia looked worse than concentration camp victims I've seen in pictures. Her body had been unbelievably destroyed by the cancer. Seeing her would have been extremely upsetting to anyone who didn't realize that many cancer patients don't die the way she did.

She had shrunk to 50 pounds, less than half her normal weight. She was nothing but bone. Her face was so thin that she looked like a cat. The veins stood out on her arms, her lips were dry and cracked and swollen, the skin around her mouth was all broken down, her chin was full of pimples. She had lost all her hair from chemotherapy. What had grown back wasn't like the hair of a human. It was like duck down.

Although she never complained, Virginia was in constant pain. Her buttocks were like one big bleeding bedsore. She was constantly oozing diarrhea from her vagina. No matter what we did, we could not keep that area clean. The doctors packed her, but the fluid oozed down past the pack. We were putting aluminum paste on her skin to protect it from the drainage, but the skin was so excoriated that every time we took the old aluminum paste off and put new paste on, she screamed with pain. It was a raw piece of body. One day it took me forty-five minutes to take the aluminum paste off. I was so upset by the end of it, with her screaming and saying, "I know you have to do it, I don't mean to scream out," that I felt like a torturer. I have never hurt a patient so much.

Nobody wanted to see Virginia die, but everyone wanted her suffering to end. Some of the doctors had known her a couple of years. Up to that point I think they had all tried to do everything they could to keep her alive. They felt really bad about what she was going through. Nurses would come out of the room and say, "I just wish it would be over for her."

The doctors were still ordering antibiotics, breathing treatments, medications, and intravenous feedings. But she was not to be coded. If her heart stopped, no one would be called to resuscitate her. In my opinion, it would have been a crime to code Virginia. There was nothing left of her.

Up until about ten days before Thanksgiving, Virginia was completely alert, although she was being medicated for pain almost every two hours. Then her kidneys shut down. She wasn't putting out any urine. Her blood studies went way off. She began passing blood clots from her vagina and oozing blood from her mouth. At the beginning of Thanksgiving week, the doctors increased her pain medication so she would not be awake to suffer.

I said to one of the residents, "It's not going to be any surprise to you when she goes."

"No," he said. "We're expecting it. We want it. She's had enough."

After the orders were changed, each nurse giving report reminded the staff that Virginia was to have Dilaudid every hour. Dilaudid is the strongest narcotic we have for relief of pain. A couple of days passed, and then Sharon and another one of the new kids, Jane, asked to talk to me privately.

"Mary," said Jane, "we're concerned about Virginia's Dilaudid order. If she's not awake to tell you she's in pain, how do you know she's having pain?"

I was not surprised by the question. Similar questions had

come up a couple of times before, with other patients. When a person is dying in excruciating pain, the doctors may order pain medication in a greater concentration than would be given just to control the pain. The doctors write these orders because they think the patient has been through enough. They want the person to sleep it out.

The doses involved would not kill a healthy person. If I received the same doses, I would probably sleep a lot, and perhaps my respiration would be lowered. It's not that the doses are so high.

But the drugs are given with such frequency that the patient remains too sedated to be aware of what's happening around him. Some nurses call this "snowing" a patient. At the end, the patient is completely under from pain medication, in what seems to be a kind of twilight. When someone is very ill, the body can't adequately process drugs given that frequently. The body doesn't get detoxified because the kidneys and liver aren't functioning properly. The patient builds up toxic levels of the drug and dies.

On doctors' orders, we had occasionally snowed patients on Eight Cook. Some nurses had objected. On doctors' orders, we were snowing Virginia. Jane and Sharon were objecting.

I had mixed feelings about their objections. Partly I was glad they were questioning, because that showed they were thinking. They weren't just doing their jobs by rote. Snowing can be very upsetting to new nurses. It's an issue almost every nurse grapples with sooner or later. I much preferred that Sharon and Jane questioned me rather than carrying out an order they considered wrong and saying nothing about it. I'm there to give guidance.

Yet I couldn't empathize with their feelings. My own grappling seemed far in the past. I had long since made up my mind about what to do in these situations. Besides, I couldn't imagine anyone looking at Virginia, seeing everything that had happened to her body, and thinking for one moment that she wasn't in pain.

But Sharon and Jane had their doubts.

"If she's not really awake," Sharon said, "and she can't tell us she's in pain, then we don't know she's in pain, and we're not giving the pain medication for the purpose for which it's intended, which is to relieve pain. We're giving it to snow her. To ease her out of this life."

"Yes," I said. "We're giving her the medication to help her die."

"If you were pulled into court," Jane asked, "What would you do?"

"I would tell them that she is in pain."

"You don't know she's in pain, because she's not awake. You're just giving her that medicine every hour. You're just going in and giving her an injection."

"When I call her name," I said, "she grimaces. To me that's pain. I go in and I say, 'Virge,' and she gives a croaky sound, like a moan, when I touch her. That to me is pain."

"Yes," Jane said, "but she's not asking for pain medication. The court could say to you, 'You know you're not supposed to do that. If a doctor orders pain medication for a patient who's not with it, and you give the pain medication, you're not using good nursing judgment.'"

I said, "I have done this before. No family has ever made an issue of it."

"But there might be one family that will call it into court and say that you didn't use your training as you should have. What would you say?"

"I would say that she's in pain."

"But I don't know that Virginia is," Sharon said, "and I don't feel comfortable giving the pain medication." Jane obviously felt the same way.

I said, "That's fine. I'm glad you've told me your feelings. This has happened once before. What we decided to do was that the nurses who felt comfortable giving the pain medication would give it, and the nurses who didn't would not."

I emphasized to Jane and Sharon that I didn't want them doing anything they didn't want to do.

"I don't want you feeling uncomfortable or feeling that you're doing anything you could be put in a legal bind over," I said. "It's okay with me if you don't want to give Virginia's Dilaudid. But don't just withhold it for eight hours. Call the supervisor or call me over. I don't feel uncomfortable giving it, so when I'm here, I'll give it. If I'm not here, and nobody else on the floor wants to give it, notify the resident on call, and he'll come up and give it himself. I'll call the doctor and tell him that this is what we're doing."

Jane and Sharon seemed satisfied with that.

I called the doctor and explained the situation to him.

"Some of the nurses are beginning to feel uncomfortable about Virginia's Dilaudid," I told him. "I don't feel uncomfortable doing this, because I've done it many times before. While I'm here, if no one else wants to give it, I'll give it.

"But I don't want these kids feeling uncomfortable or worrying about getting into a legal problem if anything is ever brought up, and this is what they're afraid of. So I've told them that on evenings and nights, if nobody on the floor will give the medication, then they're to page the doctor on call."

He said, "Fine. That's all I want done."

And that's what was done.

I did feel guilty about Virginia Medlock. Most people don't die as slowly as she was dying, don't deteriorate as much as she had deteriorated. She was a very difficult nursing responsibility. Though I fought it in myself, I couldn't help feeling glad that she was going. Not just glad for her sake. Glad for the nurses' sake. When Virginia died, we would be free of this seemingly neverending physical care and of the heavy emotional burden. I have felt that gladness with a few other patients. Feeling glad always makes me feel guilty.

But my guilt about Virginia had nothing to do with the snowing. I felt fine about that. To me giving her the Dilaudid in the dosages prescribed by the doctors was the most humane thing to do. She was suffering horribly. I would never want to suffer like that. I don't feel that we're killing somebody. We're not giving a medication that's going to end the person's life. Virginia's life was already ended. We were giving her something that kept her comfortable.

The first person I ever did that with was Joy Li, a 35-year-old Chinese woman. At least that was the first time I consciously understood what I was doing. Joy was a patient at Metro when I worked there. She really had a horrible death. Like Virginia, she had cervical cancer and had postponed treatment. When she began having vaginal discharge and bleeding, she and her husband and children were living in Taiwan. She had been too embarrassed to see a doctor. By the time they moved to the United States and she was finally diagnosed, it was too late to do very much for her.

Joy had two long admissions at Metro, during which I got to know her very well. Apparently her family had been quite wealthy. She had been a radio announcer and a model in Taiwan and had also designed women's clothes. She showed me pictures of herself as a model. She had been gorgeous. She still had the olive complexion, but she had gotten very pale and thin.

We talked a lot. Her husband owned a Chinese restaurant in town and their children were young, so sometimes her family couldn't get in to the hospital. On weekends when I was off, if I knew Joy was going to be lonely, I'd go in and just sit by her bed and talk to her. I really came to love her.

Maybe we got so close because she depended on me. I felt very motherly toward her. I don't know whether there's a motherly instinct or not. But with someone as debilitated as Joy was, you feel very protective. You forget that the person is older than you. My god, I was two of her, almost. She weighed about 70 pounds. Lying there shrunken up in bed, she was like a child.

Her dependence on me was more psychological than physical. Until she got very sick, Joy would not let the nurses do any of her physical care. She had a thing about her body. She didn't want us seeing it or touching it. She had a maid, a squat, dumpy-looking woman about five years younger than Joy who didn't understand much English. The two spoke to each other in Chinese. The woman slept in the room and did everything for Joy. We only supervised her care.

Joy Li wasted away to nothingness. The cancer metastasized throughout her chest, arms, legs, and into her bones. Toward the end, everything on her body looked horrible. Her skin was so dry it looked like an old lady's skin. Her lips were cracked. She had ulcers all over her mouth. She had sores all over her body. Her arms were black and blue from IVs infiltrating, slipping out of the vein and into the surrounding tissue. Her vagina was draining feces.

Lying there, Joy would compare what she had been to what she had become. "Look at my body," she would say. "I don't want to live like this." Getting her to walk down the hall was nearly impossible because she didn't want anybody to see her. Also, even though we held her up, one person on each side, her feet hurt so much she could hardly walk. She sort of tiptoed.

I've never seen anybody die the way Joy Li died. She was having a lot of bone pain and was in pain all the time. When she was feeling it most, you could see her eyelashes fluttering. She had a tendency to bite her top lip. Tears would roll out her eyes and down her cheeks.

More than most people do, she verbalized her pain. She was no stoic. I don't think it's necessarily good to be a stoic. Each person has to do things in his or her own way. When Joy was having pain, she let you know. She moaned. Cried. Not loud. Very low. But you could hear it when you'd pass the room. I felt very sad for her and cried with her more than once.

She was afraid. Petrified. It's horrible to say, but she did not face her death well at all. She completely fell apart. She did not want to talk about dying. When I'd bring the subject up, she'd turn me off. She made no plans. She just wanted to get it over with. She wanted to block everything out and die. I would go in at night to check on her, and she would be awake, but as soon as I came in the room, if she didn't want to talk, she shut her eyes. She kept her eyes closed most of the time.

Toward the end the doctors gave Joy her pain medication intravenously so she would not wake up. She was getting morphine every two hours. They decided to give it to her intravenously because there was nowhere left on her body to give an intramuscular injection. Every time they'd put a needle in her, blood would spurt out, and we couldn't control the bleeding.

Joy already had an IV line in her arm. At the base of the line was a resealable brown bubble. Ordinarily when you give fluids intravenously, you ignore the bubble. You just hang a new bottle and plug the tube leading from it into the line. The patient doesn't have to get stuck each time. The fluid just drips in. To give the morphine, however, a doctor would use a syringe, sticking a needle into the bubble and injecting the fluid into the vein through the line.

This method of giving medications is called "IV push." The Metro nurses were not allowed to do it. We weren't covered.

We're not allowed to do it at Central either. Nurses in the critical care units can, but on the floor we're not allowed to give anything IV push except anticoagulants, commonly referred to as blood thinners.

The reason has to do with the rate of absorption. If a medication is given orally, it has to go through the intestines and then be absorbed before it goes into the bloodstream. A drug given intramuscularly is absorbed by the tissue, and then blood flows into that area and picks up the drug and carries it into the main stream. In either case, if a mistake is made, the effects can be counteracted fairly rapidly by another medication.

But a drug injected intravenously goes directly into the bloodstream. That's the fastest method of administration. In its IV form, a drug is readily used by the body. It's absorbed rapidly, and it acts rapidly. If a mistake is made, the effects can't be counteracted as quickly as with intramuscular or oral administration. So in most hospitals, only the doctors can give medications IV push. If a mistake is made, it's the doctor's fault, not Nursing's fault. This is legal protection for the hospital.

The IV push rule became a problem for us with Joy Li. Because she had received radiation treatments, she was being followed in the hospital by the Radiation Therapy Department. She was on that service. At Metro, no radiation therapy residents were on call in the hospital at night. This meant that after the department staff went home, no one in the hospital was responsible for those patients. If we ran into a problem, other than an emergency, we were supposed to call the senior resident, who would take care of the problem from home.

The senior resident gave Joy Li her morphine during the day. But we couldn't get him to come back to the hospital every two hours all night. Getting another resident in the hospital to cover and give Joy Li IV morphine half a dozen times between 5:00 P.M. and 7:00 A.M. would have been like asking God. From the residents' point of view, why should they be awakened at 2:00 in the morning to take care of patients who aren't even on their service when they're going to be awakened at 2:15 to take care of somebody who is?

That meant that unless we were willing to call a resident on the phone every two hours, and finagle him into coming up, Joy Li would not get her pain medication all night.

There was only one alternative.

I took it, and one or two other nurses took it. We began giving Joy her IV push injections ourselves. We had the okay of the attending physician. Katie, the head nurse, pretended she didn't know what was going on.

I remember well the first time I broke the rule. It was at about 2:00 in the morning. Joy was crying in pain. I had tried giving her an intramuscular injection earlier in the evening, but she had bled so badly from it that I was scared to give her a needle again. I couldn't stand to see her in such pain. So I gave her the morphine intravenously. It was not technically difficult. I had been watching the doctors do it for days.

But I felt shaky. I knew I was doing something I wasn't supposed to do. I knew I wasn't covered legally. Also, I was scared that I was going to hurt Joy, afraid that that moment would be her time to die, and that I was going to be the one giving her the push medication as it happened.

At the time, I thought, "If anyone takes this to court, I'll never admit it." If I had been backed into a corner, I honestly don't know what I would have done. But in my conscience, I knew I was doing the right thing. I knew I was giving Joy Li something to relieve pain. I knew nothing was going to happen. The woman had cancer all over. She was in agony. She was lying there screaming and begging for her pain medication. I thought it would be better for her to sleep toward her death.

As far as I remember, no one on the staff raised an objection to what we were doing. The five or six RNs on the floor had all worked for more than a year. While that's not a long time, it's long enough to see what illness can do to patients and to families. We had all known Joy when she was a real person. She had lost that part of herself. There was nothing anyone could do to get it back.

After a while Joy Li just slipped out of this life.

Recently I read yet another article on Karen Quinlan, the New Jersey woman who was comatose for months and whose parents finally received court permission to order the doctors to disconnect her from the machines that were keeping her body going. I think the case was blown far out of proportion. As this article pointed out, decisions are made every day to let patients go when lifesaving measures are no longer deemed appropriate. The usual decision, at least in my experience, is to do nothing heroic, to give only comfort measures.

Sometimes, as the article said, these decisions are made in closed-door sessions between the doctor and the family. From what I've seen, joint decisions are uncommon. The staff doctor decides. He doesn't leave it up to the family. Not long ago we had a patient on Eight Cook who was going bad. I asked the doctors, "Is she to be coded?" They said, "No, no, no." There was no family discussion there. She had CA with metastasis all over.

In my opinion, doctors should make the decision. I don't think many families are prepared to cut everything off. Asking family members to consider doing so puts them in a difficult position. The doctor who does ask really has to know the family. I've known a few families whom the doctor has asked. In each case the family came to me the next day and said, "Nurse, what do you think we should do?"

I tried to get them to open up and say what they thought. My feeling was that they wanted somebody to tell them what the right choice was. Nowadays you read about people or see people on TV who say they want to make their own decision. In my experience, people want someone else to make it.

I do think the public is aware that when a patient is obviously getting no better, or is getting worse, the family or the patient can ask specific questions. Of course these should be dealt with truthfully.

It depends on the doctors, but in many cases I've seen the doctors do not say to the family, "We're going to start giving pain medications to keep the person comfortable as he dies." I don't even think they tell the family that nothing heroic is going to be done. They usually just say, "We're going to do everything we can to keep your family member as comfortable as possible. There's nothing more we can do." I think most families understand the implications of giving a patient pain medication every two hours. I think most families prefer that course to having a family member be in pain.

In a few instances I've heard doctors say to patients, "We're going to keep you comfortable." At the beginning when I give the injection, I usually say, "Here's your pain medication. It's going to make you more comfortable." Or I say, "The doctor ordered this pain medication so you won't be uncomfortable." I guess people in the end stages of cancer know what's implied by that. After they've been getting it a while, I say, "Here's something for your rear!"

I don't think I'm putting anything over on patients. Most of them are aware at the beginning that they're getting pain medication every two hours. The few exceptions are patients who have ceased being alert before the doctor writes the order. The others usually know before I tell them. Often patients will say, "My doctor said he ordered something so I'm never going to be in pain again." Or, "My doctor told me I could have it every two hours." When they wake up, they remind you again. "My doctor said you're supposed to give it to me."

As they receive higher dosages of the pain medication, of course, they're sleeping more. In a lot of cases they're aware you're giving them the pain medication, but that's about it. They're really foggy. Of course if they're completely under and only moaning in pain, then obviously they don't have the option of not being snowed. My feeling is that they made the choice when they were alert. After that I assume that they have made that choice or that the doctor has. And I have.

Some people don't want to be in any pain and don't want to have to think about the people they're leaving behind. They want to slip quietly out of the world. You could really be doped up if you want to be. I don't think anybody who has a cancer disease has to be in pain. The doctors increase the dosage and frequency of medications like Thorazine, a major tranquilizer which potentiates Dilaudid, and you're snowed, and you slide out of this world not even knowing what's happening.

Jackie Neill says most of the patients she has seen die on her floor, the private pavilion, have been overloaded with medication—at their own request—to the point of being quote gorked. That's a disrespectful term, and I don't use it often, but I don't know any other term that signifies the same thing. "Unresponsive" comes close. It means the person has absolutely no response to painful or verbal stimuli. The condition could result from medication, from brain surgery, from an automobile accident, or from anything else that puts the patient in a vegetative state.

Jackie says her patients dictate to the doctors. She had a patient recently who announced when she came in, "I'm here to die." She told the doctor she wanted to be put out of her misery. The doctor wrote in his notes, "Of course we can't do this, but we will make her as comfortable as possible."

That's what I want when the time comes. As I have already told Ron, if I have a disease that's going to waste me away, and I'm going to be in a lot of pain, I want him to make sure that the doctors don't do anything that's going to keep me alive unnecessarily, and that I'm put on medication to keep me pain-free. I don't care if that means an intravenous continuously into my body.

Some people don't want to go that way. They are in pain, but they don't want their minds destroyed. They'll say, "I don't want that pain medication. I want to be aware of what's going on around me till I'm finished." Of course the doctors and nurses abide by that wish.

Sometimes patients who have been getting pain medication every two hours wake up enough to talk to their families a little bit. They may not want their next dose of pain medication. We had a patient who died not long ago, a little Italian man who was getting Dilaudid every two hours. When he knew his family was coming in, he would say, "Don't give that to me now. Wait till after they've gone." So he was alert enough to choose. Not at the very end, but when the pain medication was started.

Customary dosage for a dying patient in pain is two to four milligrams of Dilaudid around the clock until the person is out of it. Or the doctor may order 15 milligrams of morphine around the clock, with Thorazine. Sometimes the order is written "PRN" for *pro re nata*, a Latin term meaning "as needed."

But if you're giving these medications every two hours around the clock no matter what, technically you're giving them for the purpose of knocking somebody off. Some nurses, and doctors too, refer to such orders as giving a patient "the Thorazine–Dilaudid trip."

A nurse has every right to question an order like that. I don't know what the legal ramifications are, but some nurses are saying,

"I'm not signing my name as having given that pain medication. If that chart were pulled into court saying that we killed that patient, if a family member said, 'You snowed my mother, you gave her that morphine every two hours, you let her die, you helped her over the edge,' it's possible that the court could say to the nurses, 'If that patient was unresponsive, why were you giving the pain medication? That's for pain.' " Some nurses, like Jane and Sharon, refuse to give the pain medication on the grounds that the patient is quote a gork.

About twelve to fifteen patients a year die on Eight Cook. A few of those don't have pain. The rest have mild to severe pain. Most of the patients I have seen die have reacted to pain. My feeling in those cases is that we're giving the pain medication to keep the patients comfortable, and it just eases them into what's going to happen.

When Jane and Sharon have spent more time around dying patients, they may come to feel as I do about this. My own conviction took several years to form. It began with a realization that for a patient who is in agony or has deteriorated horribly in mind and body, life is not necessarily better than death. That realization was also gradual. In nursing school death didn't really involve me. My ideas about it were unformed until I started working with dying patients after nursing school. Then I began to see how ugly dying can be.

In nursing school I never heard of the Thorazine–Dilaudid trip. Until Joy Li, I don't think I had any idea that patients were sometimes eased out. Even then I don't think I knew at first what was really going on with Joy. When I realized what the IV push morphine was for, it seemed right to me that Joy was being helped toward an end of her suffering.

I'm sure I was influenced a lot by the fact that Katie also believed we were doing the right thing. To me Katie was *the* nurse. I idolized her. I thought she was fantastic. I still do. She made me feel more comfortable with myself about many things, she was not intimidated by authority, and she was one hundred percent for the patient. She cared about patients' rights. She cared about patients as people. She had a deep respect for living and for leading a quality life. This came out in the way she talked about her parents and about old people in the hospital. She believed that when the human body and the human spirit have done as much as they can, they deserve some peace.

At the time I started thinking along those lines because of Katie, I was also beginning to read a lot about death and dying because of what I was seeing on the floor. I must still have been trying to make up my mind about helping patients to die or I wouldn't have read as much about it as I did. I think I wanted to know that others felt the way I was beginning to feel. The more I read, the more I believed in Katie's approach. Each person I saw die firmed the belief in my mind. By the time I left Metro, I had no doubt about the value of helping patients die in the cases in which I had seen that done.

Work experience alone may not make Jane and Sharon take a different position from the one they took with Virginia Medlock. The issue is an ethical one. Where a nurse stands on it depends at least as much on how she feels about life as on her work experience.

When I was new at Central, we had a patient on the floor for about a month who was like Virginia. He was in a lot of pain. Almost comatose. He wanted to die. He kept saying, "Let me die. Let me die." One day he had a seizure. He was without oxygen for a short period of time, and his brain stopped functioning. They took him down to the intensive care unit for a while. They gave him all kinds of medications, hoping he would get better. He didn't get better.

When he came back up to Eight Cook, he was hardly with it at all. Some time earlier, the man had told both his family and the doctors that he didn't want heroic measures. Talking this over among themselves, the family and the doctors agreed to abide by the request and just keep the patient comfortable. In fact, the sons were adamant. The nurses were giving the man Thorazine and Dilaudid every two hours.

The day supervisor of Eight Cook at the time was Betty Fillmore, the person who was always checking up on me. Apparently one or two of the new grads then on the staff mentioned to Betty that they were concerned about the dosage. Betty found me on the floor one day and said, "How do you know this man wants to die? He's not asking for pain medication. The family is. Maybe they want his money. Are we legally justified in what we're doing?"

Betty was excited and coming on pretty strong. I replied in kind. By this time I felt so strongly about the issue that I couldn't let a supervisor back me down on it. Later I was proud of the way I had talked to Betty, because I still tended to be intimidated by authority, and I had never stood up to her before. I told her that according to Dr. Rose, the patient did not want to be kept alive to die a prolonged death. I went further. I told her exactly how I felt and how I had come to feel that way.

Betty is a fair person. She heard me out. Then she said, "Well, you feel as you do for moral reasons and because of what you've seen. I don't feel the way you do. I'd never do what you're doing. I'd never give medication like that. But I haven't worked with as many cancer patients as you have. These new kids haven't either, and I don't think they feel the way you do."

That was the case in which we decided that the every-two-hour pain medications would be given only by the nurses who felt comfortable giving them.

I was nonetheless annoyed with Betty Fillmore. She certainly had a right to question me. I didn't mind that, but I did think she was interfering. More than that, I wondered how she could feel the way she did when she had been in nursing longer than I had.

Yet even as I wondered, I was aware that the answer to my question had little to do with Betty's experiences as a nurse. What she did not say, but I knew, was that she was Catholic and that her father was dying of cancer.

When I related this incident to Jackie Neill, she told me that her own feelings about giving pain medications under such circumstances are ambivalent. A favorite patient of hers who was dying had orders for Dilaudid and Thorazine every two or three hours. When the woman began gurgling and Cheyne-Stoking—breathing in an irregular pattern, which indicates neurologic dysfunction and is a sure sign that the person is near death—Jackie would give the pain medication thinking, "I just can't stand to see this woman like this. Am I giving the injection for her pain, or am I giving it for my pain?"

I think any nurse who has a question like that ought to continue to ask it of herself. I think Sharon and Jane were right to refuse to give Virginia's Dilaudid. I think Betty Fillmore was right to take the position she took, just as I feel I'm right in taking the opposite position. Personal feelings and experiences should enter into the way a nurse does her job. They're part of her.

I wouldn't want people to be afraid that if they have cancer, someone is going to decide that they're not going to live any longer. I wouldn't want patients' families to feel that nurses and doctors are walking around deciding who's to live and who isn't. That is far from the truth. I'm not talking about patients who have just gotten sick and somebody has decided that they should have pain medication. I'm talking about terminal patients who have no hope of getting better or who may get better only for a few days, who are in excruciating pain and who need a lot of medication in any case to keep them pain-free.

Some patients die without pain. They don't receive pain medication. A person dying of cardiac failure will get diuretics and other meds to keep him comfortable, but no pain medication. Patients with renal failure who aren't candidates for dialysis die from a build-up of toxic products in their blood, and they may become groggy and sleep their way out, but we don't give pain medication to ease them out.

When I talk about snowing, I'm talking about people who are without hope of going back to any kind of a life. I'm talking about people who have so deteriorated in mind and body that there's nothing left of them to bring back.

I'm talking about people who are hopeless.

The question of Virginia Medlock's Dilaudid arose on the morning before Thanksgiving. A few other problems came up during the day, so at 4:30 I was still sitting at the desk taking off orders. I thought I was alone in the nurses' station.

"How come you're sitting here pushing charts around?"

I jumped.

Dr. Benson laughed at my surprise. "You should be home making your husband stuff the turkey," he said.

"You know I can't stand to be in the same room with my husband."

Benson threw his eyes to heaven.

"Anyway," I said, "I'm here tomorrow. We're having dinner late with Ron's parents. What about you?"

"I'm here tomorrow too. My in-laws are in from New York, and my wife and mother-in-law will do the honors."

Benson pulled some charts from the rack. "How's Kelly?"

"He's good today. Better than I've seen him in weeks, in fact. Of course his stools are still bloody, but his lungs are clear and his temp is fine. He hasn't vomited all day. Mrs. O'Brien is in there clipping his toenails. He was out walking in the halls earlier. He's in really good spirits."

"Rose wants to get him out of here," Benson said. "Even just for a day. See if that will give him a boost. He's been here how long now?"

"Something like three months."

"Do you think we could get a visiting nurse to do his care?"

"No problem. I'll just have to let Beth Augustine know a few days in advance." Beth is in charge of Central's visiting nurse program.

"We could teach Mrs. O'Brien to do some things too," I suggested to Benson.

Sending Kelly home seemed like a good idea to me. From what I could tell, he was neither a lot worse nor a lot better as a result of surgery. At one point, after a bowel movement that was nothing but blood, he had nearly bled out. He became so sick that he almost needed a nurse to himself. Benson had told Mrs. O'Brien then that things looked bad. He told me he thought Kelly and Virginia were going to beat each other out to St. Peter. If Kelly hadn't stopped bleeding, he would have been gone.

He was still bleeding. But it was microscopic blood, not gross blood. From what I could tell by looking at him, he had progressed. He was up walking around every day. His morale was pretty good some days. Whether his inside picture had changed I didn't know. He did still have his down periods. Going home would make no difference in his prognosis. But maybe if he spent time with his family away from the hospital, he'd begin to relax and feel more peaceful. At least he'd get some relief from the aggravation of being stuck for blood every day and being awakened every night to have his temperature taken.

As Benson left on rounds, a button lit up on the nurses' station monitor. I answered the light. Mr. Weinstein, a patient who was in for urology surgery, needed to get to the bathroom. I helped him in and told him to put the light on again when he was finished. When I got back to the nurses' station, John Harrison was sitting in front of the elevators in a wheelchair, waiting for an escort to take him to physical therapy.

"Checking out of this fine hotel?" I asked John. He was Poseyed into the wheelchair, tied in with jacket restraints. Despite his cracked rib, he looked halfway chipper. He blinked. A slow grin appeared on his face.

"Nooooo," he finally answered. He was absorbed in the Thanksgiving decorations Jennie had put up around the nurses' station—colorful cutouts of turkeys and cornstalks, big brown letters saying HAPPY THANKSGIVING. The decorations had been up for more than a week. John looked around at them in a puzzled way, as if he had never seen them before.

A few minutes after John had gone downstairs, I saw that Mr. Weinstein's light had gone back on. I went in. He was still in the bathroom. I knocked. "Can I help you?"

He mumbled. I opened the door a crack.

He said, loud and clear, "I'm gonna die if I don't have a bowel movement."

From the next room, I could hear two women visitors stifling laughter.

"Okay," I said to Mr. Weinstein. "You had milk of magnesia at 11:00. . . ."

He said, "Oh, god, I can't stand it any longer!"

People and their bowels. I guess when you're constipated, it is uncomfortable, but you might think some people were dying. They'll say, "Oh, I haven't had a bowel movement for a day and a half." When I suggest that they start drinking more fruit juices and eating lettuce, they'll say, "Oh, I take milk of magnesia at home every day." Or "I take Dulcolax every day." Or "I give myself an enema every other day."

That's when my eyes sort of cross. I try to explain that such treatments are not good for their bowels. But if they've been doing it for ten years, they've already ruined the sphincter control they might have had.

Then there are the little old ladies who have us boiling their prune juice at 7:00 in the morning. Cold prune juice won't do. Oh, no. It has to be hot prune juice.

I tried to reassure Mr. Weinstein. "Sometimes it takes eight or nine hours for the milk of magnesia to work."

"I'll die if I wait that long."

There was nothing else I could do but get Mr. Weinstein back into bed, which I did. As I walked out of the room, I sort of threw my eyes to heaven, thinking, "Oh, my god, get me out of here!" One of the visitors from the next room was just leaving. She saw the look on my face.

"I could never be a nurse," she said. "God bless you."

I wanted to say, "Honey, if that were the worst thing, it would be easy."

5

THANKSGIVING SHIFT

I wasn't exactly looking forward to working on Thanksgiving.
But I didn't really mind either. For one thing, I had four days off at
Christmas to look forward to.

For another, the floor census is usually down on a holiday.
Doctors try to avoid admitting patients. They discharge everyone
who is well enough to go home. True, the patients who stay are
pretty sick, and they're usually depressed, because it's no fun to be
in the hospital when everyone else is out celebrating. Holidays are
a very anxious time for patients. But we would only have twenty-
seven or twenty-eight people on the floor. No ORs were
scheduled. With decent staffing, we shouldn't have any real problems.

It was even possible that I would get to do some patient care.
When I got off the elevator that morning, I fully expected that
Thanksgiving would be a good day on Eight Cook.

Thanksgiving was chaos.

To begin with, one of our RNs was pulled to work on the
special care unit. As if that weren't enough, we had six patients
who were disoriented. Half of them were falling out of bed. One
man who fell had to have two stitches in his head. We had to Posey
all six, and even restraints did not solve the biggest problem, a
54-year-old black male patient who called himself Marshall Francis
Gripps, King of Europe.

Mr. Gripps had come up from special care a week earlier. He

71

had entered the hospital with a bladder obstruction. The doctors wanted to do urology surgery on him. He wouldn't let them. He was behaving so strangely that a psychiatrist who examined him diagnosed him as a fruitcake, writing in the chart that Marshall was paranoid and had delusions of grandeur. He also had syphilis.

No one could find out if Marshall had a family. The only information he gave was the address of his boarding house. One of the social workers found out that he had come up from the South a year or two earlier. Apparently someone who found Marshall wandering the streets had taken him to the boarding home, which his medical assistance check paid for. God only knows what kind of place it was.

Since Marshall was so crazy, and since no family could be found, none of the doctors wanted to take the legal risk of doing surgery. All they could do was to rest the urinary tract by letting his urine drain out through a Foley catheter and a suprapubic tube inserted into the bladder through the abdomen. The residents also wanted to put him on medication that would calm him down.

As soon as he came to Eight Cook, Marshall pulled out both the suprapubic tube and the catheter. He refused all medications, ate only what he wanted to eat, took baths rarely, and wouldn't let the nurses touch him unless he felt like it. Worse, he disturbed the other patients on the floor. He did broadcasts. He would pick up his phone, dial once, put the phone down, and start talking in a loud voice.

"Ready for a broadcast? Now broadcasting! I am the king! Marshall Francis Gripps! King of Europe! My brothers are governors of all the states! Don't you mess with the King of Europe! The nurses in this place are rotten! They get people in off the streets to take care of the patients in this hospital! They are terrible to the patients! But I am the King! Marshall Francis Gripps! King of Europe!"

He broadcast all the time. At four in the morning he'd lie in bed doing his broadcasts. When he first arrived on the floor, he controlled his voice somewhat, but once he grew accustomed to his surroundings, he became loud. Hearing him yell and carry on, the other patients got upset. I certainly couldn't blame them. If you walked in off the street and heard Marshall yelling and stomping around the room, you might think he could go into a patient's room and hurt somebody.

Actually, I wasn't positive he wouldn't. Although Marshall the King could be amusing, he was also abusive. When he was in a good mood, he told the nurses that he had left us each a million dollars in a Swiss bank. But when he was mad at us, which was most of the time, he threatened us, calling us bitches and telling us to get the fuck out. Because he was such a skinny thing, I wasn't afraid of him. Some nurses were, and I probably should have been. I'm sure he could have hurt any of us if he had tried.

His behavior with the doctors was entirely different. Marshall never gave the doctors a bit of trouble. The one exception was a woman, Dr. Breston, the psychiatrist who was trying to work with him. If he saw her coming toward his room, he'd scream, "Woman! Get away from me! Dr. Breston! You get out of here!" She'd get out. "Patient recognizes me but won't let me in the room," she'd write in his chart. The male doctors couldn't believe that he acted as nastily and noisily as we said he did. With them he was meek little Marshall.

Having the King of Europe on the floor would have been easier if we could have gotten him to take tranquilizers. But not a pill would he take. He rarely let us near him for a shot. One day somebody got the idea of grabbing the ginger ale off his tray before the people from Dietary took the tray into the room. We opened the bottle, dropped in a Stelazine tablet, and put the bottle back on the tray. For a couple of days Marshall drank the ginger ale. Then he started refusing it.

So not only did we have trouble keeping him quiet, we also had to spend a lot of time trying to con him into letting us do his care. He wouldn't let us wash him or even change the bed. He was really dirty.

Marshall chose Thanksgiving Day to be particularly obstreperous. I went into the room in the morning to try to give him an antibiotic and some Thorazine, which he was supposed to get once each shift. He wasn't letting us give him anything unless we told him it was pain medication.

He saw that I was holding two syringes. Eyeing me suspiciously, he asked, "What have you got two needles for, girl?"

"I said, This one is to make you feel better, and this one is to get rid of your pain." That was a bunch of bull that I hoped would inspire Marshall to cooperate.

He became very angry.

"Shut up, girl! Shut up! Don't you tell me, you people at the desk out there, having control of somebody's body! I'm going to fire all of you!"

I replied calmly, "Don't you talk to me in that yelling voice. I'm a human being too."

"Girl, you get out of here! You leave me alone, girl! You white woman! Not two needles! One needle, girl! You treat me like some nigger from Mississippi! Treat me like you came off the streets! I'm going to kick you in the stomach!"

He could have kicked me. The jacket restraint left his feet completely free. Afraid that he was going to really give it to me, and not wanting to risk exciting him any more than he was, I didn't even try to get him to turn over. Instead, I went out to look for Dr. Benson, who had been at the nurses' station a moment before. He was still there.

"Yoo-hoo, Dr. Benson!" I told him I was having trouble and asked him to come in the room with me. The minute Marshall saw Benson, he turned over. I gave him both needles. Benson looked at me as if to say, "What's the problem?" and walked out. I could have killed them both.

Unfortunately, my work with Marshall wasn't finished. I had noticed while giving the shots that Marshall had dribbled diarrhea all over the back of his gown. The gown looked disgusting and smelled worse. I asked Marshall to give it to me. Instead, he gave me another suspicious look.

"What am I going to wear?"

"I'll get you another one."

"No."

"Marshall, why do you want *that* gown? Because you have shit all over it, I think that's why. Can't I wash it for you?"

"Why do you want to wash it?"

"Marshall, it smells."

He smiled at me. Out of the blue, he said, "How about you being my private nurse?"

I had to smile too. "Marshall, I'm in charge of the whole floor. I can't be anybody's private nurse."

"And who gave you that job? The King of Europe gave you that job, didn't he?"

"Yes, Marshall. But you wanted me to do this job right. So why don't you let me have your robe."

"You're really going to wash it?"

"Yes."

"How long will it take to dry?"

"Two or three hours."

"You won't be here when it dries."

"Marshall, I'm going to be here till 3:30 or 4:00. It's only 9:30 now."

He finally gave me his gown. After I had washed it out, I hung it in his bathroom so he'd know I meant for him to have it back. By the time I got out of the room, I was thinking, "My god, I'm going to end up just as nuts as he is."

Since we were an RN short that day, I had to give meds for the floor. I started with Mr. Carter, a diabetic with an infected toe. Mr. Carter had been confused for several days. He hadn't been eating or taking his pills. The night before Thanksgiving, he had tried to climb out of bed, so the night nurses had put a Posey on him. I gave him his pills, gave him his juice, and watched while he swallowed the pills. But he only appeared to swallow them. Suddenly he spit everything out.

I began to feel pressured. "Oh, god," I thought, "it's 10:00, and I have all these pills to give out, and here's this man spitting his juice at me."

I tried to give Mr. Carter the pills again. Again he spat them out. I tried to reason with him.

"How come you're not going to take your pills?"

"Because I don't want to."

"You came into the hospital to get better. If you're not going to take your pills, you might as well go home."

"I don't want my pills."

"You know," I said, "I'm getting a little angry." That was no ploy. I was getting angry.

"That's all right."

There was nothing more I could do. If the man refused to take the pills, I couldn't force him.

Two rooms down I ran into more problems. In one of the beds was a big lady with undifferentiated carcinoma, congestive heart failure, occasional shortness of breath, and senility. I gave the woman her pills. She swallowed half of them and choked. Her lips turned blue, her face turned red, and I'm thinking, "Oh-oh," trying to raise her chin so her head would go back and saying to her, "Look up! Look up!"

Finally the pills went down, and the woman started breathing again. I went over to the patient in the next bed, Mrs. Shapiro, who was completely senile. Within ten seconds this lady had spit out all her pills at me.

I could feel the tension building. I'd given pills to five patients. One had choked, two had spit, and I still had eighteen people to go. I never take Valium, but I was ready for one at that moment.

Fortunately I had no problems with the rest of the pills and even had some pleasant conversations with the other patients.

I went back to the desk to catch up on orders. Before ten minutes had passed, someone told me that Mrs. Martinez was having severe chills.

Mrs. Martinez had pancreatic CA. She had come in for surgery. After surgery she began retaining a lot of fluid, and at about 5:00 Thanksgiving morning, she had started running high temperatures. Her doctor ordered cultures and a chest X-ray. We wouldn't have the culture results for forty-eight hours. The X-ray was fairly normal. We started giving Mrs. Martinez aspirin, hoping to bring her temperature down.

When I went back to see her, she was shaking so badly that I could hear her teeth chattering. I could scarcely feel a pulse. In addition to being sick, the lady was obviously frightened. There was not much I could do to reassure her. Mrs. Martinez spoke only Spanish. I don't speak a word of Spanish.

Jane knew a few words, like "pain" and "water," but Jane had Thanksgiving off. Of course other people on the hospital staff speak Spanish. But you can't get them up on the floor every time you want to converse with a patient. Poor Mrs. Martinez. She had been depressed all day. She knew she was sick. Yet she couldn't even communicate that she was afraid. I had to guess what was wrong by looking at her face.

I sat down with her. Though I knew she couldn't understand me, I explained that the temperature was causing the chills. When the aspirin started working, I told her, the temp would go down and the chills would stop. I hoped she could tell by the tone of my voice that the situation wasn't desperate. But I felt frustrated to know I really wasn't getting through.

It was lunchtime when I left Mrs. Martinez. Jackie Neill was also working that day, and we had been planning to have Thanksgiving lunch together in the cafeteria. No way. Mrs. Davis was too disoriented to eat by herself. Everyone else was too busy to feed her. I called Jackie and asked her to bring me a Tab on the way back from the cafeteria.

Mrs. Davis was nutty. So was her roommate, Mrs. Elson, the lady who only wanted to take her pills for the Lord Jesus or Dr. Lomax. She was really crazy. As I walked toward the room, I could hear Mrs. Elson singing a blue streak. "Blessed Lord. Sweet Jesus! Blessed Lord. Sweet Jesus!"

The two women had been roommates in Special Care, a stepdown unit from Intensive Care. Mrs. Davis had come up to Eight Cook a few days earlier. The doctors had done a total hip disarticulation on her, removing her leg by separating it from the body at the hip socket. As Jennie was getting her settled into bed that first day, Mrs. Davis suddenly sat up and said, out of the clear blue, "Am I confused or is that Mrs. Elson singing?" She hadn't even seen Mrs. Elson. Jennie nearly died.

Mrs. Davis was still suffering from ICU psychosis. That's a common occurrence. She had been in the ICU and SCU for a couple of weeks, I think, and it's very easy to get disoriented down there. You don't know what time it is. Everybody's always poking at you, pulling at you, doing things to you. Older people especially get disoriented. Mrs. Davis could tell you she was in the hospital, but she didn't know what day it was, what year it was, or who was president.

"Okay, Mrs. Davis," I said, putting a pillow behind her back so she could sit up. "I'm here to give you your Thanksgiving dinner."

I sat down on the edge of the bed and pulled the tray table over beside me.

Mrs. Davis said, "You think you're going to get me to eat, don't you, girl."

I decided to ignore that. I just didn't have time to deal patiently with delays. I started to feed Mrs. Davis. All of a sudden she began to slap at her body, whacking at her body with her hands, giving orders. "Get those bugs off! Get those bugs off me!"

"Mrs. Davis, there aren't any. . . ."

"Girl, don't you tell me there ain't no bugs! Bugs crawling up my arm!"

"Mrs. Davis. Please?" I was becoming upset.

She ate. But she smacked away at the pretend bugs the whole time I was trying to feed her.

At about 2:00 I got a call informing me that a patient named Emerald Lynch would be coming up soon from special care. When I heard why the patient was in the hospital, I groaned.

I didn't know Emerald Lynch, but I had certainly heard of her. She was an obese black diabetic woman on public assistance who drank, smoked, ignored her diet, and generally did all the things she wasn't supposed to do, given the poor state of her health. She had had surgery so many times that half the nurses at Central knew her. They all talked about her because she never complained and rarely got depressed. People really liked her. Apparently she was fresh-mouthed and feisty, a real character.

On the phone, Admissions told me that Lynch had had one leg amputated eight weeks earlier and two days earlier had come into the Emergency Room complaining that she had no feeling in her other leg. The doctors were furious. Lynch knew the signs of gangrene from the first amputation. Yet she had sat at home for several days while the sensations in her leg went from pain to pins and needles to cold. By the time she came in, her second leg was gone. The doctors amputated it immediately.

The escort brought the woman up on a litter at about 2:30.

Mrs. Lynch's belongings were piled around her. Lynch herself, though still subdued from surgery, was friendly.

"Hiya, girls, how are ya?" she said when I introduced myself and the nurses who would take her back to her room. While they were getting her into bed, one of the nurses told me later, Mrs. Lynch had very matter-of-factly lifted her gown to show the scars from her previous surgeries, joking about her railroad tracks. Lynch would probably be on Eight Cook for weeks. I wondered how she would handle what had just happened to her.

Every hour all day long I had to interrupt whatever I was doing to go in and give Virginia Medlock her Dilaudid. Virginia looked ready to go. Deep in my heart I was hoping she would. I could not imagine anybody suffering more than she had, and I couldn't believe she had withstood all the hell she had been through. After attending holiday church services, her mother and sister came in. They stayed only a few minutes. When I saw them leave the room, I went up to them.

"You know," I said, "things are really bad for Virginia. I don't think she has much more time."

This wasn't news to the Medlocks. I just wanted them to know I was conscious of their being there and facing what they were facing.

"Yes, dear, I know," Mrs. Medlock said. "I was with her Tuesday and Wednesday, and I know this is the end. God is going to take care of her now."

"Yes."

Not until after the evening shift had come on did I get a chance to go in and see Kelly. Mrs. Payne, the LPN taking care of him that day, had told me several times that he was depressed and anxious. His whole family, including the three grandchildren, had been in at different times to visit him, but only Mrs. O'Brien was still there when I went in. She was knitting. We chatted a little about our Thanksgiving dinner plans. When he heard us talking, Kelly opened his eyes.

"How's my sweetheart?" I said.

"I'm never going to make it out of here."

That comment was the first inkling I'd had that Kelly was

seriously discouraged about his condition and not just going through post-op depression. I sat down next to him on the bed and took his hand.

"Kelly," I said, "did Dr. Benson tell you they want to send you home?"

He nodded.

"Wouldn't you like to go? Even for a day?"

Tears came to his eyes. "I'd like to go home even for a few minutes."

"Well, let's work for a day. At least."

Mrs. O'Brien said, "That would be wonderful."

Kelly said to her, "You'll have too much to do if I come home. You'll have to work on me all day long, and you won't have a chance to do anything else."

Mrs. O'Brien answered him gently.

"Well, I don't do anything else now," she said. "I come to the hospital, spend the day in the hospital, and go home. When I get home, I'm too tired to do anything. So what difference is there if you're at home? I'd probably get more done if you were."

I took a tissue and blotted the tears on Kelly's cheeks.

"I'll call Beth Augustine," I said. "She'll arrange for a visiting nurse to come in and help with your care. We'll teach your wife to give you your pain injections. How's that?"

"That's good."

All in all the day was very depressing. The only really nice thing about it was the two patients in Room 845, a pharmacist and his six-year-old son. They had been shot in a robbery at the pharmacy the night before. Neither was badly hurt. The father had been hit in the arm, the little boy in the thigh. Ordinarily we don't have children on the floor, but because the father was also admitted and the boy wasn't that sick, it was decided that after that traumatizing experience, they'd be better off together.

The little boy was so sweet I could have mothered him to death. Everybody fell in love with him. It seemed as if the family was very close. The mother was in all day. Many family members came in. They brought the boy lots of stuff and really seemed to care about him. There was a lot of touching and holding. I think it made everybody feel good to see them.

Another nice thing was that some family members had ordered special Thanksgiving guest trays, and they came in and ate dinner with the patients. Other people brought in turkey and stuffing or pumpkin pie they had made at home. You could tell it was a holiday.

But nothing was made of the day by anybody who was working. The nurses were too busy. By the end of the day, we were all on each other's nerves. Everybody was just glad to get out. It didn't feel like a holiday at all.

In fact, I left at 4:30 feeling that the holiday had been ruined. It wouldn't have been so bad if it had been a quiet day. But the patients were all so loony, in plain English, that I arrived home tired and frustrated.

Ron wasn't there. His aunt had been sick, so he had studied part of the day, then gone out to see her. I was to meet him at his parents' house. Because of my schedule, his mother was serving the turkey later than usual. We wouldn't have much time with his family, and I wouldn't see my own family till Saturday night.

I took a bath and got myself ready and went. We had a nice time. But I couldn't have cared less whether it was Thanksgiving or Flag Day.

6

DIFFICULT PATIENTS

The first thing I heard as I got off the elevator on Eight Cook the morning after Thanksgiving was Marshall the King doing a particularly loud broadcast.

"The other one got runned out of California because he didn't believe in Negroes having equal rights!" he announced. "That was Mrs. Louise Day Hicks!"

He started on another tack. "Objection! Objection! Is that objection overruled or objection sustained?"

I looked at Stephanie, who was standing in the nurses' station. She shook her head, saying, "He's really frisky this morning. Jennie went in a few minutes ago and found him burning holes in the sheets with his cigarettes. When she tried to take the cigarettes away from him, he told her he was going to kill her."

"Okay," I said, "that's it! I'm having him shipped over to the psych floor."

If I had had my way, Marshall would have gone to the psych floor before Thanksgiving. But the residents didn't want that. They wanted him out of the hospital. Since he had refused surgery, he wasn't of much interest to them, and they didn't want to go through the red tape involved in having a patient committed.

"Let's get him into a nursing home," Lee George said when I first mentioned sending Marshall to the psych floor.

George was my least favorite resident, a bigmouth, defensive, demanding, and rarely interested in listening to anyone else's opinions. I tried to tell him that only a state nursing home would take an abusive patient who refused to do anything for himself. The state homes had long waiting lists.

George wasn't convinced. With Virginia so sick and all the other problems on the floor, I didn't have time to pursue the problem of Marshall the King until the morning after Thanksgiving.

My first step was to call the psychiatrist. Dr. Breston agreed with me that Marshall should be sent to the psych floor, but she couldn't commit him, because Breston is not on the Central staff. By law, Marshall would have to be asked to commit himself voluntarily. Neither Breston nor I thought Marshall would agree to a voluntary admission. Therefore, someone in the hospital who had seen Marshall would have to agree to petition the court for an involuntary admission.

"George will have to do it," Breston said.

I called George. Knowing how he felt about anything involving work, I anticipated a lot of arguing. I decided to give it to him straight as firmly as I could without being nasty.

"About Marshall," I said. "I'm not allowing him to stay on this floor any longer. First of all, we cannot put another patient in that room. Second of all, he's disturbing everybody else on the floor with his yelling. These patients are sick. They don't need that kind of carrying on. This isn't the place for him. We're getting him transferred off."

"No, you're not," George said.

I took a deep breath. "Yes, I am."

George gave in. He came up to ask Marshall to admit himself voluntarily. When you do that, you have to read people their rights and let them know where they're going. George did nothing of the sort.

"Well, Marshall," he said, "we're going to send you to another floor."

"Fine," said Marshall.

"But you have to sign some papers saying that you don't mind going over to that floor."

"Okay," Marshall said. "Fine." I can still see him doing his meek little Marshall number.

When we left the room, I said to George, "That's not a voluntary admission. You didn't tell him anything. That won't stand up in court."

"What do you mean? He's too crazy. He's not going to know."

"The heck he isn't. He's no dummy. He knows enough to be nice to the nurses when he wants cigarettes. He knows what's going on."

"Tough," George said. "We're using a voluntary admission."

Oh, god. I knew a voluntary admission would never work, and George was obviously not going to change his mind. Unless I could find someone willing to get an involuntary admission, we were going to have to keep Marshall.

I spent the next two hours on the phone getting a runaround. The residents on the psych floor knew Marshall was a dump job and didn't want to take him. I called Breston for help, but she was leaving her office and said she'd have to call me back. Finally I got to one of the two chief residents. She gave me some hope.

"The psych residents are just being turkeys," she said. "It's all political. You call this person."

I didn't even know whom I was calling, but I got a doctor who sounded very sympathetic. He promised to send a resident right over.

"Don't worry, dear," the doctor said. "If worst comes to worst, I'll come over and admit the patient myself."

Later I found out that I had been talking to the head of the whole psych department for the hospital.

A resident came over and got the involuntary admission.

At about 7:00 that evening, Marshall Francis Gripps, King of Europe, was shipped to the psych floor. I wasn't there when he left, but when I heard the next morning what had happened, I had to laugh. I had told the head nurse on the psych floor that Marshall might give the escorts a hard time. So she sent two big orderlies with jacket and wrist restraints. The orderlies pulled the wheelchair into the room and said, "Okay, Marshall. We're going over."

"Okay," said Marshall. Without a word of protest, he got into the chair, said goodbye to all the nurses, and off he went.

By law, every patient who is admitted to a psych floor involuntarily must receive a court hearing within 72 hours. The judge released Marshall. As we heard the story later, the judge said that while the King was definitely nuts, he wasn't harmful to anybody. I thought the judge was wrong. Who knew what Marshall would do if somebody provoked him?

"Marshall's out on the streets," I said to Toni Gillette after I had heard the news.

"Well," Toni said, "I'll tell you one thing. If I ever get on a bus and hear someone yell 'This is Marshall Francis Gripps, King of England, France, and Europe,' I'm getting off at the next stop."

Marshall was psychotic. We rarely have patients like him on the floor. Occasionally we get people I call nuts who aren't necessarily certifiable. But when I think of all the patients I've taken care of in five years of nursing, the proportion of people who are a little weird seems very small.

I haven't seen many who are nasty or uncooperative either. The world is supposed to be full of rotten people, but I don't know where all these people are. I rarely see them as patients in the hospital.

It *is* common to have a patient on the floor who's a management problem, as Marshall was. These patients can really test your commitment to nursing. They may be dangerous, manipulative, important—VIPs—or a combination of these. All require special handling. All take extra amounts of time, patience, resourcefulness, and good will.

One of the most difficult patients I have ever had to deal with was Duke Causey, a young black kid of about 21 who had been burned as a result of smoking in bed. Causey was admitted some months after the accident for further grafting and came up to the Eight Cook from the special care unit. He was on the floor about a week.

We had no problem with him for the first few days. He did smoke pot in his room, but as far as I know, there is nothing in the hospital rules that specifically prohibits smoking pot. At Metro, the director of nursing advised us just to ignore anyone who did. So I just ignored Causey's pot smoking.

Nor were Causey's visitors a problem at first. Three big kids came in every evening. They were a little noisy sometimes, and they liked to play rock music stations. I thought the kids or the radio might bother Causey's roommate, a white, middle-aged lawyer. I asked the man if he wanted to change rooms, but he said he was fine. I think he enjoyed watching the interaction.

A few days passed, and then we began to suspect that Causey was abusing his pain medications. He was constantly asking for a painkiller. We didn't know if he was really in pain or just accustomed to drugs. He did not look like a person in pain.

Then one night we caught one of Causey's friends sneaking around the back of the nurses' station. Later one of the nurses discovered that money was missing from her purse.

We called the security guards. They came up and made out incident reports. You can't accuse anyone, but I did alert the guards to keep an eye on Causey's friends. When the doctors heard what had happened, they told Causey that if his friends didn't shape up, he would be discharged from the hospital.

The patient apparently thought the warning applied only to his friends. In the middle of one night the security guards found Causey himself up on Ten Cook, and then he started turning up at odd times in the nurses' station or in patients' rooms. Watching Causey and his friends took time we should have been spending in other ways. The three-to-eleven nurses, who were on when the friends came in, were becoming afraid.

Matters reached a head the day that Causey asked a young nursing assistant, Cheryl, to get him some narcotics from the narcotics cabinet.

"He asked me to get any drugs that were lying around," Cheryl told me. She was upset, and I would see why. "He knows me," she said. "He's from my neighborhood, and he's bad action."

I got really mad. If Causey was after drugs, we'd all have to be careful to make sure he didn't get any, which meant we'd have to be even more watchful of him than we had been, taking even more time away from patient care. Also, it made me angry that Causey would try to take advantage of a staff member. Causey's friends were visiting him that afternoon, and as soon as they left, I stomped in and let him have it.

"Look," I said. "You can do what you want on the outside. But don't think you're pulling the wool over our eyes. We know you're smoking pot and. . . ."

"I'm not smoking pot," Causey interrupted. "My friends are

smoking pot. I don't have any control over what my friends do."

"Well," I said, "if you have no control over what your friends do, we're going to forbid your friends from coming in. We have a lot of sick patients on this floor. We don't have time for this nonsense."

Without planning to, I did something I had never done before—and haven't since. I confined Causey to his room and the back hall.

"You're not to be out near the nurses' station," I said. "The same goes for your friends. If I see any of you out there, or if I hear of any of you threatening my staff, I'll call the guard."

Causey threw down a pack of cigarettes he had been fiddling with. "You're not going to push me around."

"I'm not pushing you around. But I don't want you out near the nurses' station where the drugs are."

Causey snapped, "I'm leaving!"

"Fine."

Usually if a patient who is confused or upset wants to sign out of the hospital, I try to sit down with the person and talk out the problem. Or the doctor may try to convince the person to stay. But with somebody like Causey, I just call the doctor and say, "He's leaving," and the doctor comes over and has the patient sign a form releasing the hospital and the doctors from the responsibility of further care. The doctors wanted Causey out. The one I called was delighted that he was leaving on his own.

Only after Causey left did I begin to think that it might not have been such a good idea for me to confront him. I'm rarely afraid of people and wasn't afraid of Causey when I went in there. First of all, his roommate, a big guy, was lying in the next bed. There was a doctor in the nurses' station. I get to know most of the patients, and I really think if I had screamed for help, somebody who was ambulatory would have come running.

But afterward a couple of the nurses said to me, "I don't believe you went back there and did that." Gillette seemed seriously afraid for me. "You better watch out when you walk home," she warned me. "He's going to get his friends and come after you."

I got upset. Gillette raised a possibility I hadn't even thought of. For a day or two I looked around the streets when I left work.

But Causey didn't show up, with or without his friends, and I haven't seen any of them since.

From the point of view of the amount of time the nurses spent acting as guards during his admission, Causey was the most disruptive patient I've known. He was also the first patient I ever yelled at. It doesn't happen often that I have to come on like a police sergeant with a patient. I think in retrospect that that was the right approach with Causey. I must say, though, that confining him to his room was one of the quote highlights of my career.

Duke Causey was a difficult patient from an administrative point of view. A patient I found difficult for personal reasons was Shirley Brown, an attractive black woman in her thirties with lupus, a potentially fatal disease involving the bones and connective tissue. Shirley spent three months at Metro when I was a staff nurse there. She was the first Jehovah's Witness I had ever known, and she talked a lot about her religion. I thought she was interesting. Even though I sometimes thought she was trying to convert me, I became fairly attached to her.

But she was a strange person. How much that had to do with her illness I don't know. Personality changes are common with lupus, and Shirley was also on cortisone, which can affect mood. She would go through crying spells, then be euphoric.

Whatever the reason, she was so demanding and manipulative that after a while, none of the interns or residents wanted to take care of her. Deep down, I felt she manipulated me too. She took advantage of the good relationship between us. She knew if she wanted extra things, I would try to get them for her.

What she mostly tried to get from all of us was pain medication. She was always complaining of pain. As with Causey, I could never tell whether she was really having pain or not. She would sit and talk with her visitors and look perfectly comfortable. As soon as they left, she would ask for her pain medication. Finally the doctors ordered us to try Shirley on a placebo injection. Instead of Demerol, we injected her with plain water for a week and a half. The shots relieved her pain.

Then she found out. A student nurse walked into the room holding a white medications card on which the word *placebo* was written. The patient saw it.

Shirley was not dumb. She screamed for me at the top of her lungs. I heard her from down the hall and ran into the room. When I got there, she said angrily, "What's this? Why does it say 'placebo'? You people have been making a fool out of me. How long have I been getting this?"

I didn't know what to say. I could have killed the student, and I wanted to hide myself. I don't like lying to patients, and we *were* lying to Shirley.

I tried to explain to her that emotions play a large part in a person's reaction to what's happening in his or her body. She would have no part of it. She chewed me out as if I had betrayed her.

We never became comfortable with each other again. She was still nice to me, but the trust wasn't there on her part. Because I didn't feel trusted, I couldn't relax. Toward the end of her stay, we did talk a little about what had happened, but the barrier remained. When Shirley finally went home, I was happy to see her go. Taking care of her had become a burden for me. Besides, I was hurt. Shirley was the only patient I've ever grown close to who turned against me.

Fortunately, I rarely have to run the risk that a VIP will turn against me. Most VIPs who check into Central go to Jackie Neill's floor, the private pavilion. VIPs aren't necessarily difficult patients, but taking care of a VIP can be difficult if you feel pressured to give special treatment. Jackie runs into this problem fairly often. I hear about it over lunch.

One situation that sticks in my mind involved a woman who had donated two million dollars to another hospital. The morning the patient was admitted, Jackie was told three separate times—by Administration, by the attending physician's office, and by a resident—that the woman was thinking of making a donation to Central.

The woman turned out to be neurotic. She began her hospital stay by wrapping the toilet seat in her room in toilet paper. She was so concerned about cleanliness that she refused to have anything touch her body that wasn't sterile. Of course this meant extra work and extra planning for the nurses on Jackie's staff.

Feeling they were being asked to go to extremes for the woman, they were upset and indignant. Jackie was in conflict. She felt pressured from two directions. As she said when she told me the story, "You have to walk a tightrope to please the patient and the staff at the same time."

Occasionally we get patients on Eight who are considered VIPs because of a connection to the hospital. The closest I've come to a problem with one of these patients was the time Mrs. Sampson, whose daughter is the head nurse in Central's cardiac care unit, insisted on moving into another room. I had to refuse. We had no other beds available. But the daughter kept asking my supervisor about a room change, and I felt under more pressure to comply than I would have if Mrs. Sampson had not been a VIP.

Among the least difficult patients, in my experience, are those you might expect to be the most difficult—people who have been involved in crime or violence. The one prisoner I've had as a patient was no problem at all. When I first started at Central as acting head nurse, we got a 19-year-old kid on the floor who had committed a robbery and then been shot in the abdomen during a police chase. He was in about ten days. Two armed policemen stood guard over him the whole time.

Some nurses were afraid that if anybody came in to finish the kid off, there might be a shootout. The other patients and the visitors were upset by the presence of the police. But the boy himself gave us no trouble. He was just a scared kid. I felt sorry for him.

The police were the problem. They were really in the way. If I drew the curtain around the bed to give the patient a bath, one of the cops would come and sit inside the curtain, so I'd have to maneuver around him. Both cops were supposed to stay in the boy's room. Instead, one would sit in the room and watch the kid, and the other would sit in the hall and watch the nurses. They were young guys. When one of us turned or moved, they watched. We were uncomfortable. They loved it.

Little in nursing is more difficult than taking care of a hostile patient. By the same token, getting a hostile patient to respond to care is one of the most satisfying aspects of nursing. I'm thinking of Al Fortin.

My problem with Mr. Fortin began before I even knew about

his hostility. He was a 350-pound diabetic in his mid-fifties who took such poor care of himself that a sore on his foot became gangrenous. Part of his foot had to be amputated. The infection spread. The doctors took off his leg below the knee. Finally they amputated his whole leg. He was in special care for a while after that, and then he came to Eight Cook.

When I first looked at him, I was disgusted by the size of his body. "Oh, god," I thought, "how could you let yourself get like that?" I found the man physically repulsive. He made me think of a eunuch. Diabetes can cause impotency, and Mr. Fortin had been impotent for twenty years. With his genitals having lost some of their tone and his abdomen so flabby that it just about engulfed his scrotum, you could hardly see his penis at all.

He turned out to be one of the most difficult personalities I've ever encountered in a patient. He was verbally abusive, always making sexual remarks or derogatory remarks against black people. He was constantly rubbing his arm or his leg against the nurse doing his care. He refused to do anything for himself.

Even more frustrating from the nurses' point of view, he was abusive to anyone who tried to get him to do something. Getting up was part of his therapy. I'd push him to get up, and he'd say, "Mary, you are so hard. You are so nasty. You can be so obnoxious." One day he said, "Get out of my room. You don't do any good for me. I hate you. Leave."

At the time, I was very hurt by his remark. It's rare for a patient to say he hates you. Most patients, realizing the nurses are doing things for their own good, try to cooperate. I felt I was trying to do everything I could for this man.

A few days later when I was again in the room trying to get him up, he said, "Mary, look at me. Do you really want me to get up out of bed looking like this? Just look at me. I'm nothing. I'm a mess."

He didn't sound hostile. He sounded pathetic. I suddenly realized that Mr. Fortin probably hated himself a lot more than he hated me.

Seeing a change in his attitude, I decided to hold a staff conference to discuss how we might change our approach to Mr. Fortin. I asked Sandy Nichols, the psychiatric nurse specialist, to sit in. She and I met in the nurses' lounge one afternoon with everyone who was on the nursing staff that day. We talked out the problem. The more we talked, the more we understood Mr. Fortin's behavior and the clearer we became on how to proceed with his care.

Al Fortin had been a construction foreman for many years. He was used to bossing men. Now he was flat in bed, overweight, minus a leg, unable to manipulate his surroundings, and instead of bossing, he was being bossed—by a bunch of women. Maybe none of us went in and said, "You're a pain in the ass, and you're going to do this." But we all went in thinking, "We know what's good for you, and you're going to get up."

In a sense, we reminded ourselves as we talked about Mr. Fortin, every hospital patient is subject to that kind of approach. A hospital takes away a lot of rights from patients. A patient has his temperature taken when the nurse wants to take it, gets his meals when the hospital wants to serve them, is awakened several times during the night because that's what the doctor has ordered, goes to X-ray or physical therapy when it's convenient for the hospital. A patient doesn't make any of those decisions.

Some patients don't mind. But as Sandy Nichols pointed out at the meeting on Al Fortin, it must have been hard for a construction foreman to be in the hands of a group of women offering him no choices.

Several older LPNs made some suggestions that I thought were very good. We'll give Mr. Fortin choices, they said. We don't want to accept his not showing us respect, yet we do want to allow him a certain dignity, a certain freedom.

So why not go in, they suggested, and say, "Mr. Fortin, the doctors want you to get out of bed today. Would you like to do it now?" If he says no, we will ask him when he does want to get up. He would have the freedom to decide. The choices would be small, but at least Mr. Fortin wouldn't feel he had lost all say in what was happening to him.

That meeting marked the beginning of a different relationship between the nurses and the patient. It took a while. But a leveling was gradually reached between us. As Mr. Fortin began to see that people respected his wishes, he became less hostile. He began to do things for himself, and he began to improve.

I'm not claiming that the nurses turned him around single-handedly. But we did contribute to his decision to get better. He went from Eight Cook to a rehabilitation hospital where he learned to walk on a prosthetic leg. Some time later we heard that he had returned to work. Most of us never grew to really like Al Fortin as a person; we just felt sorry for him. But there wasn't a nurse on the floor who didn't feel good about what had happened to him as a patient.

Patients as difficult as Marshall the King, Al Fortin, and Duke Causey are fairly rare. While they're on the floor, they take up a disproportionate amount of the nurses' time and energy. In the course of a year, though, they don't take up nearly as much time and energy as the most common variety of difficult patients, the complainers.

Many patients never complain. But there are lots of patients in the hospital with chronic diseases—lung disease, heart disease, arthritis—and if you're in the room for half an hour, they're complaining for half an hour. Some people complain so much that you never know what their condition really is.

I could go through a whole dissertation. "I didn't get my towel this morning. Nobody has made my bed yet. My oatmeal was cold. My coffee was cold. The doctor only spent ten minutes with me, and I wanted to ask him another question. Why don't you put the blanket at the bottom of the bed; I don't like the blanket up here. Why don't you move my phone over there; I don't like the phone where it is. The nurse didn't put the call light on. The nurse last night didn't give me my sleeping pill.

"I don't like my roommate. My roommate and I don't get along. My roommate puts the TV on till 2:00, and I don't want to watch TV that late at night. My legs are swollen. My arm aches. My back hurts. The IV hurts. My tray isn't right. I'm having chest pain. I'm having stomach pain. I can't sleep at night. I can't move my bowels. I can't pee."

Of course some complaints are justified. Nurses make mistakes, just as other people do. I'm sure I forget to do something or fail to do something the way it should be done at least once a day.

But our nerves get frazzled. I'll walk by the conference room and hear nurses saying to each other, "This is really getting to me." Rarely does a patient ever say, "I feel comfortable," or "That nurse was really nice last night." Complaints are one of the main reasons nurses leave nursing.

In training we were taught that when patients complain a lot, it's because there's something wrong with them emotionally. From what I've seen, that's true. The real sickies are not the complainers, or else their complaints are valid. But some people who are not very sick get upset when the wrong lunch tray comes up. They'll say, "I ordered coffee and I got tea," and they're nearly sobbing. Their reaction is way out of proportion to the incident. Obviously something else is bothering them.

We were taught that the best way to handle a complainer is to sit with the patient, discuss what's needed, and plan care around those needs. Nurses should also stop by patients' rooms occasionally without waiting to be summoned by the light. It's hard to do these things when the floor is busy, but if you can do them, they usually work.

With some complainers, however, nothing seems to work. In those cases, I think you have to tell the patients to turn it off. I don't think you can ignore it just because the person is sick. I mean it's fine to verbalize feelings of frustration, anxiety, and depression and get them off your chest. But certain people are born *kvetchers*. Unless you do something to get them out of the habit, they're going to keep right on *kvetching*.

You can do it nicely. I'll say, "Look, I know it's really rotten to be in the hospital. I wouldn't want to be in the hospital, either, and be as sick as you are right now. But there has to be something decent that's happening to you."

A few times I have been nasty and said to patients, "Do you realize what you sound like? I've been in here for fifteen minutes, and you haven't said one nice word. For god's sake, can't you say something nice?"

Some nurses are uncomfortable talking that way to patients. But if you don't say something, you can get really upset. Who wants to listen to five hours of complaints? Furthermore, nonstop complaining isn't good for the complainers. It drives family away. The nurses sometimes turn off. Nobody can stand to be in the room.

Patients can learn to control their complaining once they are aware of it. Occasionally when I've talked with a patient who complained constantly, the person has started crying and said, "I didn't know I was doing that." I believe it. I don't think people realize how they sound sometimes. If they did, they might stop sounding that way.

Maybe I'm wrong. I don't know if I have God's blessing, the doctors' blessing, and the nurses' blessing to talk to patients about their complaining, but it's something I feel I have to do.

I don't think it hurts to tell patients if you find other aspects of their behavior difficult to deal with. When patients have said or done something that hurt me, I have usually told them so. I told Mr. Fortin he hurt me by saying he hated me. Deep inside myself, I think, "These people are saying these things because they've gone through hell." But I also think they're being unfair. If I don't speak up, it's as if I'm accepting the fact that I'm a bitch or I'm hateful or whatever it is they're saying I am.

That's not reality. Outside the hospital, nobody would take the comment "I hate you" and go back for more.

So I have tried to find out why a patient has said something abusive, and then I've told the person how I felt. And I've honestly come away with a better understanding of that person than I would have had if I had ignored the comment.

Understanding is what helps me deal with a person whose difficult behavior I can't change. When patients get on my nerves, it's good to stop and think that this could be me or somebody I care about. A patient complains about not getting a box of tissues. That may seem unimportant. Yet if the person is lying there with his nose running and he can't get up, that box of tissues becomes monumental.

Being a patient is very confining. I think nurses sometimes tend to forget—I know I do—how it feels to lie in bed and not even be able to get a box of tissues for yourself.

Two patients we had on Eight Cook while Marshall the King was there were difficult for me in a way I had never experienced before. They made me feel I might not be the nurse I wanted to be.

These two were men in their fifties. Mr. Lamb and Mr. Dechter. Believe it or not, they were in the same room. I forgot why they were in the hospital. They were really strange. They sat in bed with most of their clothes off. When one of us would go in, there they'd be with their gowns up, their legs crossed, and their penises exposed. Both of them walked around with their rear ends hanging out. One day I asked them to keep themselves covered.

"Bodies are beautiful," they said. "Don't get embarrassed."

"That may be the way you react," I said, "but you're in a hospital now."

"Oh, don't worry about it, honey."

"I said, "Then just keep your door closed."

But they didn't. They thought I was being funny.

That was one problem with Lamb and Dechter. The other was that everything they said or heard had a sexual connotation. Everything. When Stephanie was in there one day with a medical student, Dechter was saying, "I can't stand being in here any more. I'm used to being physically active. I feel like I could do a few push-ups."

The student said, "Are you used to doing a lot of push-ups?"

"Yeah," Dechter said, "I do them best when I'm on top of my wife."

Stephanie said the med student's tongue almost fell out of his mouth. I find such comments vulgar. If that's where a person is at, fine. But I do not think it's fair for a patient to put the people taking care of him in the position of having to listen to that kind of talk. Everybody on the floor was reluctant to go in the room.

My response to Lamb and Dechter was to ignore them. I answered their light. I would talk to them long enough to find out what they wanted. But I stopped watching their faces. I avoided eye contact. I could not stand to look at either one of them. Especially Dechter. He almost sickened me.

Before, I might have said to myself, "Why do they act like that?" I would have tried to get involved somehow. At the very least I would have behaved sympathetically toward them. Instead, I said to myself, "I've known people like that before, and I don't want to get involved."

I saw that as a change in me. It was a change that bothered me a lot. I felt I wasn't allowing myself to get as involved with patients as I had when I first got out of nursing school.

I had had that feeling a few times before. Once or twice in talking to patients, I had found myself thinking that the way I was answering their questions seemed pat. When I started out as a nurse, I had often found myself floundering while I was talking to patients. I was quite aware of people's reactions to what I was saying. As I became more experienced, I became less aware. Now sometimes I'd say something and wait for a response, but the interaction was different. The wonderment wasn't there.

With Lamb and Dechter, I found myself holding back. Whereas before I might have gotten involved with everybody, now I was being selective, removing myself, not getting involved with people whose personalities offended me.

Maybe that's maturity. But nurses should be involved with patients. That's just the way I feel.

Of course involvement is harder for a head nurse than for a staff nurse, and there's only a certain amount of time in any nurse's day. If we wanted to, we could sit and talk to every patient on the floor. Most of them would want to talk to us. We'd get home at nine or ten o'clock. I used to allow myself to sit and talk more. Now I find myself drawing back, thinking to myself, "I can't."

But that kind of thinking makes me impatient with myself. A head nurse can do everything she has to do, get out on time, and still sit down and talk to a couple of patients in more than a cursory way.

The experience with Lamb and Dechter made me afraid I was losing my ability or desire to get close to patients. Of course I felt involved with Kelly O'Brien and Virginia Medlock and a few others. But I had known Kelly and Virginia a long time. I had not become close to any new patients in nearly two years, and besides that, here I was, reacting to two new patients in a way that could only be described as clinical.

I found myself wondering that last week in November, five years into my career, whether I was going to turn into one of those cold, clinical nurses you hear people talking about.

7

CONFRONTATIONS WITH DEATH AND DYING

On the Saturday after Thanksgiving at 3:45 in the afternoon, Mrs. Payne came up to me in the nurses' station and said quietly, "Virginia just died."

For a moment, Payne and I looked at each other without a word. She had grown close to Virginia and her family, closer, in fact, than I had seen her get to any other patient. I knew Mrs. Payne had been deeply distressed by Virginia's suffering. In that moment of silence between us, I felt something very heavy being lifted off us both.

"Oh, I'm so glad."

Payne nodded. "I am too."

We went back into Virginia's room. Mrs. Payne had pulled the curtain around Virginia's bed. I went behind it and just looked at Virginia. I tried to get a pulse. A formality. A nurse is not supposed to pronounce a patient dead until a doctor says so, but there isn't a person on my staff, no matter what her training, who needs an opinion any more expert than her own to know when life has ended.

"Okay, Mrs. Payne. I'll get somebody to help you."

I went around to Virginia's roommate, who had been admitted just two hours earlier. Taking her into the hall, I told her what had happened. The woman nodded.

"She was really sick, wasn't she?"

"Yes. She had cancer all through her body, and she has really been through hell. This is the best thing that has happened to her—to die and get a little peace."

I told the woman I thought she might be more comfortable if she stayed out of the room while the nurses were taking care of Virginia's body. I also wanted the family to have the freedom to say or do whatever they wanted when they came in to see Virginia. The roommate agreed to sit in the solarium.

"Were you reading anything?" I asked her.

"The *Daily News*. It's on the bed."

I got the newspaper and took the woman into the solarium, then called the chief resident to give him the news. Just as I hung up, Virginia's sister and a friend walked off the elevator.

I went to them. "Virginia just died."

The sister looked at me. "I thought so," she said. "I had a feeling today was the day."

"Is your mother at home?"

"Yes, she's there by herself."

"Then let me call the resident back so he doesn't call her," I said.

"Oh, yes, do that, because I want to tell my mother myself. I want to be with her when I tell her."

The sister and friend went into the room. They stayed for about ten minutes. Virginia's sister didn't cry. The friend did cry, I think, because she hadn't seen Virginia and wasn't prepared for how she looked, whereas the mother and sister had watched her change.

After the sister and the friend left, the nurses on the floor washed Virginia's body with soap and water. They made it as presentable as possible. Then they wrapped the body in a thick paper morgue sheet and covered the morgue sheet with a clean bed sheet. I called the supervisor, who in turn called Escort for a morgue cart.

In a little while an orderly came up with the cart. It's like a stretcher. You put the body on it, then put another stretcher over the top, like a lid, and cover the whole thing with a sheet, so it isn't obvious that a body is being wheeled.

While some of the nurses got Virginia's body onto the cart, I closed the doors of all the rooms between Virginia's room and the elevator. I also asked the visitors I saw to clear the halls for a few minutes. I've always been taught that you do that. But people know when somebody dies. I guess somebody hears the nurses talking, or somebody sees a family member crying, and the word is passed along. They all know.

When a female dies, a female nurse must accompany the body to the morgue. There's a rumor that at one hospital in the city, one of the orderlies who took patients to the morgue had sex with the bodies of women. I have never heard of that happening at this hospital. But that's what's behind the practice of having a nurse escort.

Katie, my first head nurse, used to stress that it's very important for the nurse who has been involved with the patient to have the chance to follow through after the patient dies. That should never be taken away from the nurse, Katie said. The head nurse or supervisor should never run in and say, "Okay, the patient's dead, I'll handle this, you go do the rest of the baths."

So when Virginia's body was wheeled out of the room and down the hall and onto the elevator on its way to the morgue, Mrs. Payne walked alongside.

As a child growing up Catholic, I believed in a hereafter. But I always disliked the concept of heaven and hell. It used to upset me. Now I think you go into the grave and that's it. I think there's an absence of anything more. There's nothing. My feeling is that you make the best of your time here.

For a time I held that view as an atheist. Now I hold it as a Jew. I converted when Ron and I were married. Two things in particular drew me to Judaism. One was the importance given to family, the idea that the family is at the center of life. The other attraction was the idea that there is no hereafter. You make your life in this world. Your good deeds are rewards in themselves. If you do a good deed or you help somebody in this world, then you will be remembered in the hearts of your children or your neighbors as a good person. If you're a bad person, you are not remembered at all.

I still haven't decided what my feelings about God are. I don't know whether I believe that there is a supreme being. My interpretation is somewhat different. I think of God as peace.

For that reason, and because of what I've seen, I don't look upon death as depressing. Maybe when it's my death, or the death of somebody I love, it'll be another story. But I'm not in awe of death for myself. I don't think death is the most horrible thing in life. From what I have observed, unrelieved pain is harder on a person than death. Watching someone you love go downhill, till the person's whole body has changed and the mind is no longer functioning, is horrible. Lying there knowing no one cares is harder than dying. I think it must be more horrible than dying to go through life never knowing that anybody loved you or never feeling you did anything worthwhile.

So when patients have gone through hell, I'm happy when they die. They're out of their pain. They're at peace. I never feel sorry for the person who's dead. His problems are over. It's the family that has the death to face. The people who survive have to live with the person's memory and try to build some kind of life without someone they loved. From what I've seen, death is worse for the survivors than for the person who dies.

People talk about a dead body as though it's ugly. I don't think it is. I agree with one of my mother's friends who lost her elderly father. The two had had a very close relationship. But when the woman looked at her father's body, she wasn't upset. She said, "That's not my father lying there. My father was his mind."

I hope that's how I'll react when the time comes. A few patients I've seen die were really alert toward the end. But usually the person's mind is gone. There's just a body. Toward the end, most terminal patients are not the functioning persons they had been. Once the mind is gone, the body is nothing.

Some nurses will cry after a patient dies. It really upsets them. I guess I have become a little hardened. I'll cry when I see the person suffer. When I stand at the bedside and see the family going through agony, starting to feel the death or preparing themselves for it, that will bring tears to my eyes. When the patient's family starts to cry, it really upsets me. I have felt bad—for myself—when patients I felt close to died. But after someone dies, I try to divorce myself from that person. I say to myself, "It's good that he's dead. He has had enough."

I don't know how I would feel if I lost somebody I loved, such as Ron or my mother. I've never experienced that. The only person I have lost who was close to me in the sense of family closeness was Ron's grandfather. He was an old-time physician, really patriarchal, probably the one person who made me decide to become Jewish. I really had a lot of respect for him. I thought of him as a good person who wanted to do the right thing. There was a great deal of love between him and Ron. He was happy that Ron was a medical student. He accepted me as part of the family.

Still, I didn't know the man as a person. When he died, shortly after we were married, I did not feel as if part of me had died. If my mother died, I would feel that way. So I don't know if I'm intellectualizing about death and not dealing with it at a gut level. I guess I won't know until I do lose someone I care deeply about.

But so far, at least, death doesn't scare me. I'm very comfortable with people when they're ready to die. I'm not uncomfortable about their dying. I always think death is interesting. I don't know whether that's grotesque or not. But when a person dies, I want to watch him die. I want to be in the room. How people are when they're ready to die has always interested me.

How their families behave has also always interested me. When I see a spouse sitting next to the bed of someone dying, I always wonder what's going on in the person's mind. Especially if I've seen the two of them touch or kiss or hold each other earlier in the hospital admission, I think about what it must feel like to be reduced to looking at somebody you love just lying there, the body clammy and cold. My god, the person in the bed is the person that spouse has lain beside for years.

I think the family members who watch somebody die are thinking of themselves. They know the patient isn't going to be in pain any more. They are. Maybe they lose a mother or a husband they've lived with for years. They have a normal routine. Getting up in the morning. Making a cup of coffee. Whatever. For all those years that other person has been there, sharing that routine. Then suddenly the person is not there. My mother and I don't live together any more. I don't get up and say good morning to her. But I still talk with her on the phone for two hours once a week or visit her every other week. If she were gone, this part of my life would be gone.

So I'm sure the families of dying patients will miss all kinds of things. They sit by the bedside wondering, "What am I going to do now?"

I've wondered if watching a patient's reaction to dying, and the family's reaction, is my way of removing myself from what's happening. I've often thought that my curiosity might be intellectual. Sometimes I have wondered if that's not being cold. I was always afraid that if I told people I liked watching someone die, they would think I was a morbid, horrible person.

But I don't think I'm cold, because when I've known someone, I'm really upset if that person suffers. I'm upset for the family, because they're going through so much. I think watching is my way of dealing with what's happening. I don't know if I'm patting myself on the back, but I think it's better for dying patients to have someone like me in the room, holding their hands, being near them, than to have somebody who is not comfortable with dying.

Eventually I would like to work full time with dying patients. That's the thing I'm really comfortable with, and that's the kind of nursing I like. I want to work with oncology patients on an oncology floor, where a majority of patients would know they were going to die sooner than most people without a cancer diagnosis and at least have a chance to prepare themselves. I think I could give a lot in that situation. Maybe I'll never get to the point where I feel I can do it. But that's what I think I want. And I'd want to be a staff nurse, not a head nurse, so I could work closely with the patients.

Jackie Neil has trouble understanding this plan. "I couldn't stand working with dying patients all the time," she said when I first told her about it. "Just this past week we had two people die on Six. It's so depressing. Won't it depress you?"

"Some days it probably will," I told her. "But people won't be dying all at once. Maybe two or three would die a week on an oncology floor. And don't forget, working with amputees depresses some people."

Jackie is uncomfortable with the idea of death and dying. Given something that happened when her grandmother died, I can understand her feeling. When Jackie was a freshman in nursing school, her grandmother was laid out in an open casket. At the wake Jackie's mother leaned over and kissed the grandmother goodbye. Jackie couldn't do the same.

"I'll never forget that I couldn't bring myself to kiss my grandmother," Jackie has told me. "I touched her hand, and the thing that shocked me was the coldness of the hand. I still remember that. The coldness of the body."

Jackie is Catholic. She believes in God. She believes in life after death. She has read about patients who have technically died, then returned to life to tell about their experiences with death, which they describe as beautiful. To some extent, Jackie says, death fascinates her.

It also scares her. About a week before Virginia died, a Six Cook patient who was a favorite of Jackie's died. The woman had been sick a long time. At the end Jackie avoided the patient, even though it upset her to do so.

"Before she was terminal," Jackie told me, "I'd go in and we'd talk. I'd make a special effort to say goodbye before going off duty. But as she got sicker and sicker, I would just leave. I would go in that room only if absolutely, positively necessary. At times during the last week, I wouldn't go in by myself. I'd have to have somebody with me. Something inside me just gets sick to see this lifeless, lifeless body."

Many nurses and doctors are uncomfortable with death and dying. Part of the reason may be personal experiences, but at least part of the reason is professional. People in the health field are taught they are to take care of people so they get better. If patients die, they're failures. Or they think they are.

Not long ago Jackie attended a conference at which a panel of physicians discussed how they felt when their patients died of bladder CA. One physician said, "Face it. Our job is to save lives. When a patient doesn't do what we want—doesn't live—we're madder than hell. We're angry at ourselves, at the patients, and at the patients' families. We may express it as frustration, but deep down it just comes to anger."

At a party once, I got to talking about this with a psychiatrist Ron knows at medical school. His feeling was that a lot of doctors shirk their responsibilities when it comes to death and dying. They think they're infallible. They're never going to die themselves. They have no concept of what it feels like to be dying. Nobody ever taught them anything about it in medical school. This psychiatrist is trying to start a program to teach medical students to deal with death and dying. He wants to teach them that it is their responsibility. I've heard of other medical schools and some nursing schools that are starting similar programs.

Doctors and nurses aren't the only professionals who may be uncomfortable with death and dying. I discovered that when I was taking care of Tony Seletti, one of my favorite patients at Metro. Tony was about sixty and dying of leukemia. Being very Catholic he often asked to see the priest. One day just before he died, Tony was sitting up in bed looking horrible—sweaty, pale, blank—when a priest stuck his head into the room, said "Hang loose, Tony," and disappeared.

I left the room fuming. "How can a priest say that?" I asked Katie. "He has administered last rites to this man. Now he's telling him to hang loose."

The priest had actually administered the sacrament of the sick. The church no longer calls it extreme unction. The sacrament is not to be taken as a sign of dying. But because of my background, I still considered it last rites. And I got mad.

Katie said, "I would have told him how I felt."

I thought that was a good idea. So the next time I saw the priest, I took him aside and said, "You know, Father, when you came into the room the other day and told Tony Seletti to hang loose, it really upset me. That man is ready to die."

The priest said, "I didn't notice he was that sick."

I said something like, "Well, I think you should know something about the patients you're coming in to see."

I have a lot of respect for anyone who becomes a priest or a minister. There are bad priests and bad rabbis or whatever, but there are many good ones. I think they go through a great deal, and unless they're rotten people, I think they deserve respect. But at the time, I thought that this priest should have known more than he apparently knew about dealing with a dying patient.

Then I started reading books about dying. One was written by a Catholic priest. He wrote about how little training priests had received in matters of marriage, sex, and death. He remembered going into the home of an old lady whose husband had just died and having no idea what to say to her. He was so ill prepared that he was afraid. Then he explained how he came to grips with death and dying. I thought the book was beautiful. It certainly put a new light on the incident with Mr. Seletti.

Since that happened, of course, death has become the new sex. According to my mother, who works in a college library, death and dying is the subject most students want to read about these days. Everybody's reading about it. Everybody's talking about it on talk shows.

I'm glad. It has been hidden away too long. Once Katie said to me, "As a nurse, you're supposed to be the strong person for a dying patient's family, instead of another human being. But if people can't handle dying or death or morbidity within themselves, how can they portray themselves as having that strength?" I think the more people talk about death and dying, the easier it will become for all of us to think about death and dying, and for nurses and doctors to help patients to die.

How I became comfortable with death I'm not sure. I wasn't always. But I can't pinpoint any one moment or situation that changed me. I suppose it was a combination of my experiences.

The first person I ever knew who died was my grandfather. I was seven or eight at the time. I remember my mother telling me he had died from drinking too much. We used to go over to see Grandpop on Sundays, but since I was not close to him, I wasn't that shocked when he died.

I remember that my mother told us children that we didn't have to go to the funeral. She kept saying, "Funerals are worse than viewings, because at the viewing the casket is open and the person is still there, whereas at the burial, the person is covered." But I went to the viewing, and so did Jeff, the oldest of my brothers.

What upset me was how white my grandfather looked. I couldn't believe it. But I also remember people coming up to Jeff and me and patting us on our heads as if to say, "Poor little things."

As if we had been close to our grandfather. I think the whole experience entranced me more than anything else.

But the story my mother told about her grandmother's death really affected me. My mother was nine. She and a cousin Marge, who was sixteen, were living with their grandmother. One night they were awakened by the grandmother at 2:00 in the morning. "Come and help me get ready," the grandmother said. "I'm dying."

My mother and her cousin went downstairs. Their grandmother said, "Give me the wash rag. Let me wash my face." My mother, frightened, kept saying to herself, "You're not dying. You're not dying." But the grandmother washed herself, changed all her clothes, sent Marge out for a priest, lay down on her bed and died. When my mother tells this story, she ends by saying, "So I've been with a person who died very peacefully." I thought the story was beautiful. I still get very emotional when I hear it.

Although I don't recall the incident, my mother remembers my telling her that one day when I was working at Mother of Mercy, a sister told me to go to a certain room and pull a box out of the wall. I did. There was a body in the box. The room was the morgue. Maybe that incident left no impression on me because I didn't know the person. If you hear that twenty people died in a car accident, you think to yourself, "Well, that's too bad." If you haven't invested any emotions in people, their deaths don't strike home.

In nursing school, we never dealt with the subject of dying in the classroom. We dealt with it somewhat on the floors. Students would work with patients on a floor, and if a patient was dying, we would discuss that patient in our weekly conferences. But we were immature in both our understanding of what dying meant and in our handling of it. We often made flip remarks, saying such things as, "Well, five went this week!" I guess our flippancy was a defense mechanism.

Something happened during nursing school that stands out vividly in my mind because of the difference between how I reacted then and how I would react now. Four or five of my friends were working the night shift on a floor when an old man died. They all went in to do post-mortem care together. They got to joking around and manipulated the man's finger into an obscene gesture.

Then, because rigor mortis had started to set in, they had trouble getting the finger out of that position.

I can imagine if any layperson heard that, or even if most nurses heard it, they would think, "Oh, god, what kind of nurses are they? How could they do that to another human being? That's horrible." That's just how I felt at the time. I was shocked.

"How would you like somebody doing that to your father?" I remember saying when my friends told me what they had done. "I don't think it's funny at all."

Now when I look back, I don't consider the incident so disrespectful. My friends were upset about the man dying. He was the first person they had ever taken care of who died. They were so afraid that they could hardly look at the body. They did what they did for comic relief. Now if I heard of such an incident, my thoughts would be, "It's just a body. What difference does it make? They were really upset about the man's death. Maybe they had to deal with it in that way."

It was in nursing school that I first became aware of my own curiosity about death. When people died, I wanted to know what they were feeling. My friends wanted to be out of the room. I was afraid to admit that I was curious.

During our second year of nursing school, everybody was assigned a nine-week rotation on one floor. Along with one other student, I was assigned to the eleventh pavilion, which was oncology. It was a very good experience. The head nurse there was excellent. She seemed involved. She didn't just sit at the desk; she went into the rooms and did things. I liked her, and I liked the way the floor was run. It was very organized.

Although I don't remember developing a special interest in cancer patients that year, I did apply to work on the oncology floor after I graduated. Since others had applied earlier, I ended up on a medical pavilion. There the patients themselves began to teach me about death.

I was still very uncomfortable with the whole idea. Once, not long after graduation, I went in to bathe a man who was dying, and I remember going at the procedure very efficiently and quietly and maybe even sternly, because the man said, "Just because I'm dying doesn't mean you can't smile."

That really struck home. I thought, "You're right." Then one day another patient who was dying asked me to talk to him.

"I can't," I said. "I'm too afraid."

The man said, "You're not going to hurt me by what you say. Say anything. Just sit with me."

That struck home, too. I was always afraid that I'd laugh or giggle or say something inappropriate. I think that's what a lot of nurses fear. They keep thinking, "I'm going to say the wrong thing."

This man made me see that the wrong thing would be to walk out of the room. So you say the wrong thing to dying patients. What are you going to say that's so wrong? They're already facing the worst thing in their lives. Plenty of times I've said stupid things, or things I later thought seemed totally inappropriate, because my train of thought was elsewhere. Though I worried about how insensitive it must have sounded, the patient probably forgot about it in two minutes.

I received my next lesson in death and dying from one of the first patients I became close to after I graduated from school. Dorothy Smith was a refined woman in her late fifties, neat as a pin, with white hair that had a purplish-blue glow to it. She was dying of a type of blood cancer.

I was afraid of her. She was so sick that I wasn't sure if I knew enough, either technically or psychologically, to take care of her. Sometimes now I recognize that feeling in the new grads. They don't talk about it—who wants to admit we're afraid to take care of a patient?—but I'll see a puzzled look on their faces, especially on weekends, when we're understaffed and don't have the backup we have during the week. Fortunately for me, Katie was a nut for work, so when I was starting out on her floor, I had her to back me up most of the time.

Gradually I overcame my fear of caring for Dorothy Smith. I got to know her. I think she had been an English teacher. She did a lot of reading. At night we used to sit and talk about books. Though I don't remember now just what was said, she was the first person I remember truly talking with about dying.

She was afraid to die. But she had a lot of inner strength. What struck me was that even when she was close to death, she still talked about books and still thought about other people. Her doctor was a big wheel on the staff. One day when he was on the floor, she called me over and introduced us.

"This is the best nurse around," she said to him. "She takes really good care of me."

Today if a patient said that in front of me, I might ask myself whether the patient was manipulating me. I took Mrs. Smith's comment at face value. What she said made me feel very good. It also surprised me. That a person could be dying and still think of other people made me begin to see that it was possible to face death without panicking.

Katie affected my approach to death and dying as well as my thoughts about it. Her approach was an example for me in the case of Joy Li and in one other situation at Metro that stands out in my mind. The oncologist there was a doctor everyone called Black Ollie. He never told patients their diagnosis, never told the residents what was happening to the patients, made rounds at strange times, and often wrote sarcastic notes on patients' charts.

Katie believed patients should know their diagnosis. I began to feel strongly about that myself the first time I took care of one of Black Ollie's patients who was dying. The woman kept asking me questions. I had to keep lying to her. That made me mad, because I was being put in the middle. I also thought the patient should be getting honest answers. At Katie's urging, I told Black Ollie how I felt. He listened but laughed off what I said.

That wasn't the end of the lesson. When Tony Seletti came in on his last admission, though both he and his wife knew that Tony had leukemia, neither knew how close he was to the end. Black Ollie wouldn't tell them. Katie decided to let them know.

I helped her. So did a few of the other nurses. No one actually told the Selettis. What we did with Tony was to give him information about his white count every time he asked. Like most leukemics, he asked frequently. If the white count goes high enough, the person can have more chemotherapy, which could mean a longer prognosis. Nurses at Metro weren't supposed to tell a patient his white count. Only doctors could do that. But we told Tony. He was quite aware of what it meant when his white count stayed low.

Then, as Katie put it, we undertook to prepare Mrs. Seletti for

Tony's death. You don't have to actually use the words *dying* or *death* to prepare somebody. We just showed our own feelings. I felt a lot for Tony. I used to cry when I went into the room. If you're putting your arm around a person, as I did with Mrs. Seletti, and that person sees tears in your eyes, she is not going to think that her husband is getting well. In addition to letting her know the situation, we were as supportive to her as we could possibly be.

As I think back to Tony, I realize that all the patients I got closest to in my three years as a staff nurse at Metro had cancer. All died. Maybe we got close because they spent so much time in the hospital. Each of them taught me something important about death and dying, but no one taught me more than Ted Roger.

Oh, that was a man. He was about thirty when I knew him, dying of leukemia, a salesman who sold helicopter parts and told traveling salesman jokes up until a few hours before he died. His jokes were all sexual. They were also very funny. While some of them used to embarrass me slightly, I just accepted them as part of him. Ted was nuts. He had three long admissions over the course of a year, and everybody grew to love him.

I think some of the nurses identified with the Rogers. We were young. They were young. Ted's wife was a few years younger than he was. They were very tender with each other; there was a great deal of physical warmth between them. Here they were, a young couple with two little children, attractive-looking people who were going somewhere in the world, good people with everything to give, yet something so horrible, so devastating, was happening to them. At the time, though Ron was attending school in Michigan, our relationship was growing serious. I'd go home after work thinking, "How could I ever face it if somebody I loved was going through what Ted is going through?"

I felt a definite physical attraction to him. More than I have felt to any other patient. A lot of the nurses were attracted to him physically. I don't mean everybody was madly in love with him. When you see somebody lying in bed with ashen skin, a 102° temperature, sweat dripping off his body, somebody who has lost twenty pounds, lost his hair from chemotherapy, was anemic, is throwing up, you don't think, "Oh, I'd like to go to bed with him."

But I remember thinking often, "My god, he's such a good-looking man."

Because of the kids, there were times when Ted's wife couldn't get in to visit. He would be really lonely. I'd stay late and go back into his room and sit and talk and watch TV with him. A few times I sat there while he slept. Because of the temps and the sweating, he would wear just his pajama bottoms. Light from buildings across the street would come in through the windows and flash across the bed. I remember sitting there thinking, "What a waste of a body. He is so attractive."

A lot of his attractiveness was because of his mind. Ted was a very deep person. He didn't just talk about himself. He would sit and listen to what other people had to say. He wasn't always jovial. Sometimes he would break down. But I really admired him for being able to deal as much as he did with what was happening.

Apparently he was well liked, because all the people in his office donated blood platelets and frequently came to see him and bring him things. One whole wall of his room was covered with cards that his wife had pasted up. He'd say, "I'm so lucky to have so many friends. My life may have been horrible in some respects, but I'll never forget the wonderful people I've met. Men at work I hardly know, coming in and giving platelets."

Or when he felt well enough, he would go out on a pass and get a hamburger and milkshake with his wife. He was on harsh chemotherapy regimes which made him very nauseated. When he would come back from a pass, he'd be plugged into the chemotherapy again and throw up everything he had eaten. "Doesn't taste so good coming up," he'd say, "but it was worth every bit of it because it tasted so good going down!"

Knowing Ted showed me that a nurse could get close to a patient and learn a lot. There was a strong emotional bond between us, stronger than I had had with any other patient. I can say that I really loved him. He had a horrible death. I was very, very upset when he died. I cried for a long time and felt a real sense of loss. But what I remember most now is caring about him. I learned that a sense of loss does not last forever.

I also learned from Ted that it's possible to approach death in a practical way. When he learned his prognosis, he and his wife talked about how to proceed. She was a year's credit short of a teaching degree. He told her to go back to school and complete the degree so she could support the children. She did. In fact, she started teaching even before he died.

I remember thinking it was unbelievable that a couple could be so close and know each other so well that they could plan for death. It was a real sharing of adults. In my experience, that is rare. From what I've seen and read, families in similar situations are rarely that open with each other.

Ted was very realistic. He accepted the fact that he was going to die, he made his plans, and he made the best of the time he had. His major aim before he died was to turn the family's attic into a room for their son. Apparently the children had been sharing a bedroom. Ted told everybody about his plans for the attic, told us all about the colors he was using—red and blue—and kept us posted on the progress. He worked on the attic between admissions to the hospital. By the time he died, the room was finished.

I became interested in death a few years after Elisabeth Kubler-Ross's book *On Death and Dying* was published. Since few of my friends were interested in the subject, and I didn't have anybody to talk to, I started reading books. Kubler-Ross was the pioneer. Her book was the one everybody was talking about. It was the first book on the subject I ever read.

I reacted to it very negatively. What the author said about the five stages people go through as they gradually come to accept death seemed dogmatic to me. Although I hadn't had that much experience with dying patients, the experience I had had didn't bear out what Kubler-Ross was saying. I thought, "Does everybody really go through those five stages? Why can't I accept that? Maybe I'm blocking something."

Then I read some more, and I started talking to people. I soon realized that there's disagreement about the existence of five stages. In later articles Kubler-Ross herself wrote that everyone doesn't necessarily go through all five. Some people get to one and never go any further. Some people never accept dying. Some stay angry. Reading these things, I began to see that I wasn't crazy. Later articles I have read of Kubler-Ross's have been very nice. Comforting and really beautiful.

Since coming to Central, I have talked a lot about all this to one of the hospital social workers. In talking with her, I realized that I had taken what Kubler-Ross said as gospel, when that wasn't how she had meant it to be taken. What Kubler-Ross had done, I realized, was to start people talking about something they hadn't talked about before.

Recently I read a beautiful book that Kubler-Ross edited, *Death: The Final Stage of Growth.* The title describes perfectly how I have come to feel about death and dying.

In my five years as a nurse, I have seen dozens of people die. Most have died fairly peacefully. It's a very quiet thing. I'll never forget how Tony Seletti died. I was sitting on the bed feeding him cherry Jell-O. We were talking. I put a spoonful of Jell-O up to his mouth. He took it with his tongue, put his head back, and died. He didn't swallow. He didn't choke. He just died.

I have never seen anybody else die quite that peacefully. But with many people, it seems as though one minute they're here and the next minute they're not. Often, I think, the death is peaceful because the person is at peace. This is true of older people especially. They know their time is coming. They're prepared. They've talked to whomever they want to talk to. They know their family's taken care of. They're not afraid to die.

Terminal patients can prepare themselves for what's going to happen only if they know what the situation is. I think patients—all patients—should know what their situation is. I don't mean one should say to a terminally ill patient, "There's no hope." I wouldn't want anybody to do that to me. Rather, I think it's wrong to try to fool patients.

Most patients end up knowing anyway. From what I've seen, few people come close to death without knowing it. People are smart. When they see that their bodies have shrunk to half their normal size, when they see tubes all around, they know. They watch television. They read newspapers. They hear "chemotherapy," or "radiation treatments," and the first thing they think of is cancer. It's hard to hide things from people.

They start asking questions. "What's wrong with me? I'm weak. I'm losing weight."

"It's the radiation treatments."

"Why am I getting radiation treatments?"

"To clear up the problem in your stomach."

I think when a person asks these kinds of questions, he's guessing the truth. He knows his diagnosis. He's just asking to convince himself. It's like a child saying, "Mommy, am I beautiful? Daddy, am I beautiful? Aunt Mildred, am I beautiful?"

All the doctors I work with now believe in telling patients their diagnoses. Some family members do not. People have said to me, "Nobody's to tell my husband that he has cancer." If I see an opportunity, I'll try to change their minds. I'll say to a wife or a daughter, "You know, when you lie about something like that, if the person finds out, he's not going to believe anything else you've told him. He's going to think, 'Well, she lied about that; maybe she's lying about other things.' "

I don't say it, but I think to myself, "Like when you say 'I love you.' "

Of course some patients don't want to talk about the truth. Virginia Medlock did not want to talk about dying. Joy Li didn't want to. At the time, I was hurt that Joy wouldn't open her feelings to me about something so important when she had talked to me about so many other things. I really cared about her. I thought she cared about me. Why didn't she want to talk to me? From the reading I had done up to that point, I thought Joy would have a more peaceful death if she did talk to me. I felt I was a failure.

Now I know that you can't force a person. All you can do is let a person know you're there and willing to talk. Joy just wasn't ready. It wasn't her time.

When a patient makes the decision Joy Li made—not to talk about death at all—I feel others should respect it. Too often, though, I think the truth is avoided not because the patient is afraid to discuss it but because other people are. I once heard a cancer specialist say that this is why family members visit a cancer patient in groups. They're protecting themselves.

If you are afraid to talk about something, you're never going to help the person you love. In my experience, if you put your arm around a patient who is dying, or just sit there and listen, sometimes that person's feelings come pouring out. This can happen even when the patient seems completely unreceptive.

Ray Powell was a classic example. He was a fireman dying of lymphoma. When he came to Eight Cook from special care, he was hostile. He complained constantly. He wouldn't talk seriously about anything. His wife told me that her husband had worked very hard to provide the family—the Powells had five children—with the material comforts his parents had never known. I found that information helpful. One day when I was taking care of Mr. Powell, and he was almost surly with me, I thought to myself, "This man has had enough."

I said to him, "It must be terribly hard for you to have worked so hard and gotten your life to where you wanted it and now to be so sick."

He burst into tears.

We talked for a long time. After that day it was easier for all of us to support Ray Powell, and I think his last weeks were easier for him.

Talking honestly about the situation is one way a nurse can help when a person is dying. It can also be important for a nurse to suggest that children or grandchildren visit the patient. I learned that from Katie. Generally, families leave children out of a death. I don't always suggest that children come in. I don't think it's my place to say to somebody I don't know, "You should tell your children and bring them in." But when I have gotten close to a family member, as I did to Ray Powell's wife, or if I see that somebody is trying to figure out what to do—Joy Li's husband asked me one day what he should do about their two children—I will say something.

I think it's better for kids to see a family member die than not to see. I've read many articles which say that if you don't see the person dying or dead, you don't accept the death. All the literature I've read says that children should be given as realistic an idea as possible of what's happening. If you tell children "Daddy went to sleep," they'll be afraid to go to sleep themselves. If you say, "God took your mother away," then children might think God is horrible.

If a father or grandfather has a lingering disease, like cancer or a severe cardiac problem, the children should see the patient right along. Otherwise they see Daddy one day, and he's well, and then he goes to the hospital and he's sick but he's going to get better, and then he's dying. The child comes in and sees someone who weighs 25 pounds less than Daddy and looks terrible. Or Daddy just doesn't come home. Either way, it can be a shock for children.

My feeling is that children should come into the hospital often enough so that the changes they see don't stand out in their minds. I'm almost sure in my heart that that's what I'd do with my own children. I would want to show them that this is part of life.

When I see the relative of a really sick patient come in, I always let him or her know how the patient has been that day. If the patient turns bad, I alert the family. Sometimes in this situation a family member will ask me how long the patient has. I'll say something like, "I really don't know. I've seen people who looked like your mother and they've lived on for two or three days. Looking at her, my feeling is that she is ready to die sooner than that."

You really don't know. Dr. Rose will say to a patient's family, "I'll give him seventy-two hours." But even he doesn't know. We were once snowing a patient of Rose's, and Rose came up one day and said, "He'll be dead by tomorrow." The man was alive for a week. Rose accused us of not giving the pain medications.

I always try to emphasize to the family that their presence in the patient's room counts for something. Often there's a lot of guilt involved in family relationships. When a person is dying, the guilt sometimes comes out. Family members feel they can't do enough for the person. They think if they're not washing or feeding or making the person better, they're not doing anything. I say, "You've done the most important thing that anybody could do, and that's to be here. Every time your father woke up, he saw that there was somebody in here who cared."

Dying patients can be hard on the nursing staff. When we have a lot of cancer patients on the floor, some nurses become really upset. Not so upset that they cry or stop functioning, but they dislike dealing with patients who don't get better. These patients are often irritable and demanding. They're not easy to take care of. Sometimes the nurse will ask for a different patient assignment after a few days. When that's possible, I'm perfectly willing to make the change.

Many of my staff members are very young RNs who don't feel

comfortable with the dying. There's no question that the first few times you see somebody die, the first few times you see family members stand at the bedside crying, it's very, very hard. That's true whether you've come to care about the person or not. Some of the middle-aged nurses who have seen a lot of dying have built in a type of relief system for themselves, good or bad. But a few of the older nurses still feel uncomfortable with death.

A lot of times, I think, nurses try to keep those feelings in. They believe they should be able to deal with them by themselves. Once or twice when there has been a particularly heavy oncology load, we've had conferences with Sandy Nichols, and we've all had a chance to ventilate. I would like to do more of that. Or sometimes I'll put articles on death and dying on the bulletin board so people will read them and perhaps talk about the subject a little.

When nurses do let their feelings show, I try to support them. That's another lesson I learned from Katie. After Tony Seletti died, I went into the nurses' lounge on the floor and cried. I overheard another nurse say to Katie, "Mary's crying." Katie said, "Sure, she's crying. There's nothing wrong with that. She'll probably be crying all day. Other people are probably crying too."

Not long after I came to Eight Cook we had an 18-year-old boy on the floor, Danny Dawson, who had cancer. We grew very attached to him, and everybody cried when he died, including Linda, a young RN I had thought of as aloof. When she reported for work on the evening shift, and somebody gave her the news, Linda went into the nurses' lounge and shut the door. I heard her burst into tears.

After a few minutes I knocked and went in. She was shaking with sobs.

"I shouldn't get so upset," she kept saying.

I put my arms around her. "There's nothing wrong with crying," I said. "It means you're a caring person. It's good to cry when someone you care about dies. It means you've invested something in that person's worth. If you were a patient, wouldn't you want that for yourself?"

The day after Virginia Medlock died, I met Jackie Neill for lunch in the Cook cafeteria. When we had started in on our sandwiches, I gave her the news. Jackie was relieved. Since she had been hearing me talk about Virginia's suffering for weeks, she knew how I felt about her dying.

Jackie also had death on her mind. One of her favorite patients, Mrs. Fritz, had just died the week before; another was on the way out. Jackie is three years younger than I am, and sometimes she questions me about experiences I've had as a way of sorting out her own experiences, I guess.

"Tell me something," Jackie asked as we ate our lunch. "When somebody dies, and you've grown to know the family, and the family comes in to pick up the person's belongings, what do you say or do?"

"Well, I go up to the family and say that I know saying 'I'm sorry' isn't going to bring the person back, but that I hope everything works out as well as it can for them."

"And how does the family respond? Do they start to fill up?"

"Sometimes, yes."

"How do you cope with that?"

"Usually I put my arms around them and tell them that it's really important for them to cry and get everything out."

"Well, that's a problem I've encountered," Jackie said. "When Mrs. Fritz died, and her family came looking for me, all I could say was, 'I'm very sorry.' They just shook their heads. I did mail them a sympathy card from the floor. I wrote on it that knowing Mrs. Fritz was good for all of us. But I just couldn't express it more openly when they were in. At times like that, I can't help but think there's a part of me that's lacking."

Jackie and I have talked a lot about our backgrounds and how they have affected our attitudes. The kind of conversation we were having about death was a help to us both.

I said to her, "I don't think it's a question of something lacking; I think we each just have to find what's comfortable for us."

"Also," Jackie said, after considering my comment for a moment, "Mrs. Fritz asked me to pray for her. I believe in God, but I don't have any way of getting in touch with that God. I mean, I don't routinely pray. When she said, 'Pray for me,' I knew deep down in my heart that I wouldn't know how to do what she was asking, because I knew what was going to happen to her."

"Did you think about her?"

"Oh, yes."

"Then I think you're praying. When I believed I was an atheist and people said, 'Pray for me,' I would try to explain that I didn't believe in God. Try to explain that to an old Italian or Jewish woman. It really upsets them. They would try to argue with me. So I got to the point where I didn't tell people in the hospital that I didn't believe. When they would say, 'Pray for me,' I said to myself, 'Yes, I'll think of you.' I think that thinking of a person is remembering that person. And what more is a prayer than remembering somebody?"

Sipping our tea, we talked a little about Virginia's last days and Mrs. Fritz's last days. We got onto the subject of what we had said to those patients toward the end when we gave them pain medications. Jackie told Mrs. Fritz she was there to stick her. I talked to Virginia a little, or touched her. I think it's important to let dying patients know you're thinking about them, and I said that to Jackie.

"But you've already told me that ninety percent of the patients you've seen die have very little of their minds left," Jackie said.

"Well, they're not alert enough to carry on a conversation, no."

"But you think they are aware of your presence?"

"As far as knowing somebody's in the room, feeling a hand, I think most people are. I go on the assumption that they understand what you're doing. I can't guarantee they don't know. Maybe they're picking up more than you think. Every book I have read says, 'Stay with that person who's dying.' "

Jackie lit a cigarette. "If you have a really busy Saturday," she said, "it's almost impossible to sit by somebody's bed and hold the person's hand while he dies."

I agreed. "But," I said, "I still go in the room and say, 'Mr. So-and-so, I just want you to know that somebody's here checking on you.' And I touch the person and leave the room. I just know that's what I'd want for my mother if she were in that bed."

Jackie said, out of the blue, "Do you think you understand pain?"

"No. I've never been in real pain."

"That's one thing I wish." Jackie laughed. "I'm not saying it masochistically! But I wish I had some idea of what real pain meant. Haven't there been times when somebody has asked for pain medication, and you've said, 'Yes, I'll get it,' and then two or three other things crop up, and fifteen or thirty minutes go by and you still haven't gotten the pain medication?"

"Sure, that's happened."

"That happened to me today. When I got back there, the patient was sweating with the pain he was having. His face was all red. I felt so bad. I thought to myself, 'Gee, if I could only have some comprehension of what kind of pain this guy is going through, maybe I'd go a little faster.' The same thing goes with dying. Maybe if I had lost somebody I loved, I'd be a better nurse."

"I know what you mean."

For a few minutes the two of us just sat there at the table without talking.

Then Jackie said, "You know, when the resident pronounced Mrs. Fritz dead, her doctor had tears in his eyes. He was crying. That's the first time I have actually seen a doctor cry."

"I have seen several doctors cry when patients have died," I said, "and I've always admired them so much more afterwards. I've seen men sit and cry when their wives had died. I've seen Ron cry. Once when we were ready to break up, he sat down and cried. I think that's really fantastic. I think it takes more of a man to let yourself be that way than to try and hide it."

"Usually, though," Jackie said, "the doctors don't get as involved with the patients as the nurses do, and usually the doctor's reaction when a patient dies is to get very tight and angry and start cursing."

"I know," I said. "That's one place nurses have it over doctors. Nurses, being women, are allowed to show tears. The doctors just stomp off the floor."

That conversation took place on Sunday. On Monday, two days after Virginia Medlock's death, Maureen Shay and I went to her viewing.

I had never been to a patient's viewing before. There have been people whose viewings I wanted to go to, because I knew them over a longer period of time, and I wanted the family to know I had felt something for the person. But I thought the family might not want me there. Or I didn't want the family to think I came so they would make a fuss over me. Or a lot of times people associate you with the white uniform and the hospital, and people who are in shock might not connect you with that person, which might embarrass them.

But Maureen and I really wanted Virginia's mother to know that we cared enough to go. Mrs. Payne and Toni Gillette were going to the service, which was at 7:00 that same evening. Maureen and I deliberately made plans to go earlier, before the family would arrive.

While I was dressing, thinking of Virginia, I got to thinking of Joy Li, I guess because both had died of the same disease and because I had loved them both. When I left home to meet Maureen, I was wearing a bracelet Joy Li had given me.

I told Maureen about it as we walked. Joy had called me in one day and said, "I have a gift for you. This is something my family gave me when I was little. It's white coral. Not pink coral. I want you to realize what the difference means. White coral grows farther below the surface of the sea. When the Chinese women dive for it, they have to hold their breath longer than they do when they dive for pink coral. So the white is more expensive. I want you to have it."

I told Joy I couldn't take the bracelet.

"I want you to remember me by it."

"But I'll always remember you."

"But if you have this bracelet, every time you wear it, you'll think of me."

She was right. I love the bracelet and wear it a lot, and I never put it on without thinking of Joy.

Maureen and I were so engrossed in our conversation that we got lost and arrived at the viewing at about 6:30. Not many people were there. We were the only white faces in the place. We stayed only a few minutes, just long enough to sign our names and to look at Virginia.

I couldn't believe what I saw. The person in the casket had a wig on, two tons of makeup, lipstick, false eyelashes, and a long blue sheer dress, all fluffy and frills. In her hands was an orchid. I could not believe it was Virginia.

Outside, Maureen said, "That didn't look like Virginia at all."

I agreed. "The only thing that was Virginia," I said, "was the smell. It smelled like Virginia."

The woman's body had rotted from her illness. Nothing the undertaker had done could change that. The body smelled like Virginia's room.

The next morning I said to Mrs. Payne, "It didn't even look like Virginia."

"No," Payne said.

"The only thing that was Virginia. . . ."

Payne interrupted me, "Was the smell."

"Yes."

"I thought it was just me that thought that."

"No," I said. "Maureen and I both thought the same thing."

Ron and I have often kidded about viewings. I hate it when people go up to an open casket and say, "Oh, they made him look just like he did in life." I always think, "Hell, he didn't look like that in life. He looks completely unnatural." Ron says that before he dies, he's going to record a little tape to be placed in his casket that will say, "Hi! Don't I look like myself?"

But Ron and I have also talked seriously about our deaths. Somebody I told that to said, "Oh, that's horrible. You're too young to be thinking about that." I don't think so. I want to plan. You never know what can happen.

Both of us want to give our bodies to science. If my organs can be used for something, I want them to be. Both of us want to be cremated. We don't see any reason we should take up space with our graves. We don't want to waste the land.

And neither of us wants extraordinary measures. I'm sure that if it came to somebody in my family dying—my parents or Ron— there would be so much emotion involved that making certain decisions would be very hard. I hope I would get through it. I hope I would not allow the emotion to force me to choose to prolong the dying. If only blood was keeping my mother alive, I hope I would have the strength to say, "Stop the blood. If you don't, I will."

I think it would be really hard for me to have a terminal illness and know I was going to die. I just hope I would be able to go to somebody, talk to somebody, and learn to deal with what I had to deal with. I hope my family would support me through it. As things stand now, I have people to rely on. Ron. His family. My family. They're all very caring. I think they would accept whatever happened to me, even though they would be very upset. I think they would help me. If it happens to them first, I hope I can help them. I hope I have enough in me to do whatever I can to make the best out of what happens.

8

NEW CHANCES

On the first of December, several days after Virginia's funeral, Jennie took down the Thanksgiving decorations on Eight Cook, and Kelly O'Brien went home.

A cabulance was scheduled to pick him up at 10:00. Stephanie had asked to be assigned to Kelly that day. At a little before 7:00, as soon as she had gotten her coat off, Stephanie stopped in to see Kelly.

He wasn't there. He wasn't in bed, and he wasn't in the bathroom.

After a few minutes of looking, Stephanie found him walking by himself in the hall—or trying to. She got him back to bed and bawled him out.

"You're not strong enough to walk by yourself," she scolded. "If you want to take a walk, call one of us."

Kelly said nothing. Forty-five minutes later, when we came out of report, there was Kelly at the front counter of the nurses' station, kind of weaving.

Again Stephanie got him back to bed. When he was settled, she said, "What's going on, Kelly?"

"I wanted to see how I'd do at home."

"But at home you'll have support. Your wife will be there. You'll have some walls nearby."

Stephanie stopped by the nurses' station a few minutes later to tell me she thought that Kelly might be trying to fall so he wouldn't have to leave the hospital.

I really didn't think so. But it was true that almost from the moment Dr. Benson had first mentioned to him the possibility of going home, Kelly had gotten increasingly depressed about the prospect. He had been in the hospital three months. Naturally he was worried about how he would do without a whole staff to support him. No one knew better than Kelly how involved his care was. Of course he would have a visiting nurse. We had taught Mrs. O'Brien to irrigate his tubes. I think Kelly knew she was competent.

But he was aware that his being at home would be hard on her. He also knew he wouldn't be able to manage at home indefinitely. I think he wondered if he'd ever make it back into the hospital.

In the days before he left, we encouraged Kelly as much as we could. Even so, he started to get very anxious. He complained a lot. Not about the care we were giving—he had always thanked us for things we did for him, and he continued to be very appreciative—but like a lot of patients suffering from anxiety, he picked on little things.

Payne came to me one day and asked not to be assigned to Kelly.

"I really like Mr. O'Brien," she said, "and I understand why he is the way he is. But everything's getting on his nerves now. If you don't shut the door, you're letting in the noise."

Payne was right. Kelly was very edgy. One day after he had been fed, I went in to clamp his tube and couldn't find the clamp. When I asked him where it was, he said, "Somebody walked off with it. They're always walking off with my stuff." He started complaining that people made too much noise. A nurse went in to take his weight one morning, and he later said that the nurse had been "belligerent" with him. He acted like a man afraid. You could hardly blame him.

Yet I felt sure Kelly would live to be readmitted to the hospital. I don't think anyone on the staff thought we were sending him home to die. After all, Rose was expecting him to get better. Kelly knew that. Despite his anxiety, I think he really wanted to go home. His walking in the halls that morning struck me as an honest attempt on his part to test his ability to get around. He was still pretty weak.

Shortly after the breakfast trays had come up, Stephanie found me and passed on some good news. Kelly had eaten his entire breakfast—orange juice, farina, milk, and coffee.

"First he told me he wasn't hungry and couldn't eat," Stephanie said. "He said, 'Don't say, "come on, Kelly," because I'm not going to eat.' But I set him up and left to do something else, and when I got back in the room, the food on the tray was gone."

At about 9:30 I went in to see how things were going. Stephanie had just about finished Kelly's A.M. care. She was putting his stuff into shopping bags. Between his own belongings and the equipment and supplies we were sending with him, there was a lot to be packed. Kelly watched everything Stephanie did.

"Looks like you're taking half the hospital with you," I said. "Don't forget the pillows."

Kelly gave me a funny look.

I laughed. "Didn't I ever tell you about the patient I had at Metro who tried to take two pillows home with her? I walked in when she was getting ready to go home and found her trying to stick the pillows into her suitcase. From the way she was dressed, I knew she was from a posh part of town. I said to the woman, 'Excuse me. What are you doing?'

"She answered, 'Oh, aren't we supposed to take these when we leave?'

"I said, 'You don't take the pillows when you leave the Hilton, do you?'"

Kelly said, "She probably does!" He laughed. "From the posh part of town. That figures."

He really got a kick out of the story. I thought he seemed less depressed than he had for days.

Just then Bev Bowles, the social worker who followed a lot of the cancer patients, came in to say goodbye to Kelly. Bev's about 35, very efficient but also warm. She took her hands out of her skirt pockets, put them on Kelly's cheeks, and kissed him on the top of the head.

"I talked to your wife this morning," Bev said, "and she's there waiting for you. She's really glad you're coming."

Kelly didn't respond.

Bev asked him if he needed anything.

Kelly sighed. "No, I don't think so," he said. "These girls seem to be taking care of everything."

Then he said, "It's strange to be going."

"Three months is a long time," Bev said. "It's going to be strange for us too, not having you here. Everybody will miss you."

She squeezed his hand. "You be good."

When Kelly looked up at her, his face got suddenly sad, as if he were about to cry. "I will."

Back at the nurses' station, Bev and I talked for a few minutes about how depressed Kelly had been. Bev asked me if I thought he was afraid to die.

I didn't. "I think he's afraid of dying an ugly death," I told her. "Like anybody else, he wants to go peacefully when he goes. And he's worried about what will happen to his family. But I honestly think he has accepted what's eventually going to happen to him."

Bev had the same feeling. "When I talked to him last week," she said, "he told me about a roommate he had had who said he wanted to go home to die and then went home and died two days later. Kelly said he thought that wasn't a bad idea. When he said it, he was very calm. I think he's ready for whatever happens. Actually I think he's a lot more prepared than his wife is."

"Well, I think she's starting to understand that he's never going to get well," I said.

To me it seemed that Mrs. O'Brien had begun to resign herself. She was not as nervous about things as she had been. I could see in her face and in her mannerisms that she was more relaxed. I also thought she was more comfortable being with Kelly than she had been.

Bev said, "She sure seems to be coping well with the idea of having him home."

"She sure does."

At a little after 10:00, two hefty young men appeared on the floor with a wheelchair and said they had come for Kelly O'Brien. I took them into the room. Kelly was sitting up in his chair, ready to go. He had a blue jacket on over his hospital gown and was also wearing hospital stockings, brown slippers, and his horn-rimmed glasses. Considering what he had been through, I thought he looked good.

The cabulance men moved the wheelchair up close to Kelly. Without waiting for anyone's help, taking care to keep track of his catheter bag and the three tubes, he lifted himself to his feet and started toward the wheelchair.

"Kelly!"

Stephanie grabbed him under the arm. With her help, Kelly got settled into the chair. One of the men covered Kelly's knees with a folded sheet and strapped him in. Then he pushed Kelly into the hall and out toward the elevators. Carrying a shopping bag in one hand, pushing a pump for Kelly's stomach tube with the other, Stephanie followed. Walking with her was the second cabulance attendant, carrying three more shopping bags.

For some reason the nurses' station was full of people—doctors, nurses, technicians of various kinds. Most of them knew Kelly. When they saw him, everybody had something to say to him.

"Kelly! Good luck, Kelly! Oh, good luck to you. You take care of yourself, now, okay?" And Dr. Benson's loud voice, "See you, Kelly."

Kelly's face remained serious, the sides of his mouth drawn down, his jaw firm. Without a word, he slowly raised his hands, clasped them over his head, and saluted his friends with a kind of victory sign.

The elevator came.

Stephanie went with Kelly as far as the street. When she came back to the floor, I was at the desk.

"I can't believe he's gone," she said.

She stood there a moment, then went into Kelly's room to strip his bed. I passed her in the hall as she came out with her arms full of linen. She stopped me.

"He was so sad," she said. "When we got to the door, I said, 'Well, see you Kelly.' He started to cry. I started to cry. He said something about his tubes. I said, 'Don't worry about that.' The escorts had to stand there and wait while we kissed each other."

Suddenly Stephanie stopped talking and walked off toward the dirty linen closet. She was really walking fast.

I just felt glad that Kelly was going to be home with his family for a while and out of this horrible hospital situation.

The morning passed fairly quietly after Kelly had gone. Since I had not talked with Emerald Lynch for a few days, I decided to sit with her for a few minutes while she was having her lunch.

"Always like to have a visitor," Lynch said to me, chewing and grinning at the same time. Half the teeth in her mouth were missing. I sat down.

"Lunch good?" I asked.

Lynch poked at a heap of boiled carrots with her fork. "I've had better." She laughed. So did I.

Ten days had passed since Emerald Lynch had lost her second leg. Physically she was doing about as well as could be expected of a diabetic who had had two amputations in two months. Her stump was reddened and swollen. Drainage was oozing from the incision between the sutures. She was running low-grade temps and having some pain. None of these problems was unexpected. Wound treatments, a mild painkiller, and bed rest would probably clear them up before too long.

Meanwhile, Emerald Lynch was in fine spirits. The nurses kept saying, "I don't believe what a good mood she's in." Most people cry after they've had a part of their body amputated, or they become withdrawn for a while. Losing a limb or a breast is not the same as losing a gallbladder. Your body image changes. Most people fear that they won't be able to do the things they used to do. But Lynch was cheerful and mouthy. With the help of a trapeze apparatus over her bed, she was already getting on and off the bedpan by herself. Most amputees would have put the light on for help to do that. Lynch didn't put the light on till she was ready to have the bedpan emptied. She was really a spunky lady.

"How's everything else with you?" I asked.

"Well, somebody stole my Cadillac, but I got it back."

"Your Cadillac?"

Lynch looked at me as if she couldn't believe my ignorance and nodded toward an oversized wheelchair in the corner.

"One thing," she said, tossing her salad. "That juice I get in the afternoon. That's vile. Any chance I could get something different?"

"Sure. Gin and tonic? Bloody Mary?"

Lynch hooted. "Nothing like that!"

We settled on lo-cal ginger ale. I wrote that down on a note pad I keep in my pocket. When I looked up, I saw Lynch wrapping her entire lunch pork chop in her napkin.

"Saving yourself a little snack?"

Again she grinned. "This is for my cats. I raise cats. I don't know if you knew that. Some Angoras, some Persians, but I like almost anything in the way of cats, except I had this one declawed male, awful-looking thing, and I had to get rid of it."

Lynch set the wrapped pork chop on her bedside table. "Now these friends of mine have found me a new black and white," she went on. "I told them to take some pictures of it and bring them in. My nephew's going to keep it for me."

"Is your nephew coming in to pick up your pork chop?"

"No. Larry'll take it."

I had a feeling that Larry was also going to eat it. Larry was Lynch's boyfriend, a skinny thing who swaggered in every evening bringing something in a brown paper bag. I assumed it was food for Lynch. The two of them lived together on welfare.

From what I could see, Larry didn't talk that much. Emerald bossed him around like Big Mama. She was always reading him things out of a big notebook, wetting her thumb in her mouth, turning the pages, reading aloud, and every so often you'd hear her all the way out at the nurses' station saying to Larry, "Oh, don't give me that!" God knows what their relationship was really like. But I was glad to see she had somebody who cared enough about her to visit her every day.

"Okay, Mrs. Lynch," I said. "I've got some other patients to see, so I'll let you have some peace." I got up and went to the door.

"Okay, Miss Efficient," said Lynch with a toothy grin. "Don't take any wooden nickels."

I had lunch myself with Jackie Neill, and when I came back to the floor, I had a message to call Miss Craig, the director of nursing and a vice-president of the hospital.

A call from Miss Craig isn't that unusual. She's a strong presence for the nurses at Central. I talk to her on the phone and usually see her a couple of times a week. Often she comes up to the floor and says, "Hi, Mary, how are things?" When I first came to Eight Cook, Miss Craig's visits made me a little nervous. One day I jokingly said, "What are you doing up here?"

She said, "Every time I come on the floor, everybody thinks there's something wrong. Sometimes I just want to see how people are."

I've had only two jobs as a nurse. I don't know what most directors of nursing are like. But the director at Metro was nothing like Miss Craig. The one at Metro had had very little floor experience. From what I could see, she was more interested in pleasing the doctors than supporting the nurses. She made it clear to the nurses that she wasn't one of us. She was an administrator.

As soon as I got to Central and saw supervisors answering lights, putting patients on bedpans, and in other ways helping the floor staff with the physical care of patients, I knew I was in a different atmosphere. I never saw supervisors at Metro doing those things. I never saw the director of nursing there do anything that could be considered floor nursing. But right after I started on Eight Cook, when I was passing meds one Saturday, I pushed the cart around a corner and saw a woman in a white jacket bending over the linen cart, picking up linen outside each room and taking it toward the laundry room. It was Miss Craig.

I think the woman is fantastic. She's a small thing, but she was an Air Force nurse, and when she gets off the elevator with the two associate directors of nursing, who are both bigger than she is, you know who's in charge. She really sticks up for her nurses. It isn't that she lets you get away with murder either. I have a great deal of respect for her, and I don't get nervous when she calls me on the phone. I called back.

"Hello, Mary. How's everything on Eight Cook?"

"Fine, Mr. O'Brien went home today."

At Metro I wouldn't have bothered to mention the departure of a long-term patient. Miss Craig likes to keep track of such things.

"Good. I guess you've heard by now that we're thinking of opening an oncology floor at Central Hospital."

"Well, I had heard that Dr. Rose wants one." A couple of the residents had mentioned that to me some months earlier.

"He wants one," she said, "and we're thinking about it. We want you to think about it too, because Dr. Rose wants you to run it."

"What?" Inside, I was thinking, "Oh, no." I felt torn already.

"Can you come down to my office at 3:00 and talk about it?"

I said I could.

I was not, I admit, totally surprised. It seemed to me that Rose had been putting on a big act with me, and I had had a feeling that he was buttering me up. He knew I was interested in oncology. I had never made any secret of my interest. Although he hadn't said anything to me about working on the floor, he had been talking to me more in previous weeks than he ever had before. He had told me about Kelly's surgery, for example. After that he told me twice that he liked putting his patients on Eight. He knew they got good care, he said.

The meeting that afternoon was short. Ann Sullivan, my supervisor, was there, but Dr. Rose and Miss Craig did most of the talking. First Craig outlined what would happen if Central's administration decided to go ahead with an oncology unit. The plan was simple. A floor that was already functioning would simply be turned into a CA floor. All cancer patients would be admitted to that floor. This way the transition could be made without building a staff from scratch. The cancer unit probably would not be in full operation for about a year.

Then Rose started talking. Ideally, he said, the floor would be Eight Cook. The staff would be basically the staff already on the floor. Rose would head the cancer unit, and Ed Lefcourt, a former chief resident who would be returning to Central when he had finished an oncology fellowship in Atlanta, would be the second in command. I knew Lefcourt.

Miss Craig stressed that the plan was tentative. Some of the doctors had reservations about the idea. They didn't necessarily want a floor marked ONCOLOGICAL CENTER. If, for example, on a given day all the beds in the hospital were taken except for ten on the cancer floor, five new orthopedic patients and five new gynie patients might be admitted to those empty beds. Seeing the sign, they might conclude that they had cancer and that their doctors had lied to them. It might be difficult to get these patients to accept that they did not have cancer.

Rose and Craig wanted to know what I thought.

I had to admit that my reactions were largely negative.

"I'm interested in oncology," I said. "I think you both know that. But I do have reservations about running the floor. I'm worried myself about the idea of a floor marked ONCOLOGY. Also, some of the people on my staff are not very comfortable with death and dying, including some of the people I rely on most, like Mrs. Payne. I'm afraid I'd lose some of those people if Eight Cook became an oncology unit. I'm just beginning to feel good about the way my staff is working now. I don't think I'm particularly ready to start over with a lot of new people."

I also said I thought an oncology staff should include a psychiatric nurse and maybe even a psychiatrist who were both interested in death and dying. Craig agreed with me but said the floor would not be that well staffed at first.

I had some other concerns, a couple of which I was willing to raise in front of Rose.

"I'm just getting to the point where I'm feeling confident about my own job," I said. "I'm interested in what I'm doing. I enjoy it. Though I do want to work in oncology someday, I'm not sure I want to do it now, and I've never thought I wanted to do it as a head nurse.

"Besides, Ron will be graduating from medical school in a couple of years. We want children. I don't think it would be fair for me to take over a new floor a year from now if I'm not going to stay long enough to really make it work."

Craig shook her head. "I think I'm going to make every nurse who comes to work in this hospital sign a paper saying she won't have babies for ten years," she said.

We all laughed.

"Any other reservations?" Rose asked me.

"Since you asked," I said, "Ed Lefcourt."

Rose smiled ironically. "I know Ed has had his problems with the nurses," he said, "but I think he's going to be a good oncologist."

"He may be," I replied, "but he's not my favorite person."

That was putting it mildly. I thought Ed Lefcourt was a conscientious doctor, but as a person, he was a holy terror. Some people called him a little Napoleon. He was sarcastic and nasty, always ranting at somebody, always hanging up on people, always complaining about the nurses. "They let this patient get the wrong tray! They didn't send this person to the OR properly! This I&O is crummy!" He was always saying he was going to push some nurse's face in or beat the shit out of some nurse.

He also often made sexual remarks and rubbed up against people. One day when I was in the cafeteria line, he sidled up in front of me with his back to me and pushed me against a wall with his body.

"Boy, did that feel good!" he said when I finally got free. "Now I have two holes in my back!"

I just passed that off as another example of Ed Lefcourt the turkey. His behavior was so outrageous it would almost have been funny if he weren't also nasty to patients.

Lefcourt had such a bad reputation among the nurses, in fact, that when Craig heard he was coming back to Central, she told the chief of surgery that Lefcourt was a problem. The nursing director at Metro would never have done that. But Craig told the chief that a lot of nurses couldn't stand working with Lefcourt and that they ended up in tears when they dealt with him.

According to Miss Craig's report to us later at a staff meeting, the chief of surgery wrote Lefcourt telling him that if when he returned to Central he continued to treat the nurses as he had treated them before he left, he would be asked to leave. I knew Lefcourt couldn't ignore the warning. Even so, I was not pleased at the thought of working closely with him.

"Well, think about it," Rose said. "Will you?"

I told him I would think about it.

Rose left the meeting. When I heard him shut the outer office door behind him, I looked at Craig and said, "He's my real reason."

"What do you mean?"

"I don't like Dr. Rose as a person, and I don't like the way he deals with patients. I've seen him be really nice to people, but he can also be crude and flip."

Craig said, "Maybe that's his way of dealing with all those patients dying."

I nodded. "Maybe it is. I know everybody needs an escape valve. But I'm not comfortable with that kind of behavior. Rose *or* Lefcourt would be bad enough. But both?"

Craig seemed sympathetic. We talked a little longer. I said that I really did like oncology, but I wanted her to know that I thought it was unlikely that I would take the floor. Craig urged me not to be in a hurry to make up my mind.

"I'd prefer you to think about it seriously for a while," she said.

"Okay," I said. "I'll think about it seriously."

9

THE PROBLEM OF SEX

The morning after Kelly O'Brien went home, James, the Admissions clerk, called me with the news that Judd Nicolai was returning to Eight Cook.

"Oh, god," was all I could say.

James wanted to know why.

"Don't you know about Nicolai?" I said. "Well, never mind, you're too young. Do me a favor next time, though, and put him on somebody else's floor, okay?"

I was only half-joking.

Judd Nicolai bothered me more than any other patient I have ever had in my care. He is a white male in his late twenties who had lost his right leg in a motorcycle accident about two years before I came to Central. He came in, had an amputation done, was fitted for a prosthesis, learned how to use it, went home, got on his motorcycle, and had another accident.

This time he injured his spinal cord and became a paraparetic. That is, he has decreased use of and sensation in his body below the waist. He's impotent and incontinent. He also weakened his abdominal aorta in the second accident. Nicolai had been a patient at Central half a dozen times before I ever met him and had also been a patient in another hospital. My first contact with him was when he was admitted to the floor to have an incontinency device inserted, a sort of trapdoor gadget that would allow him to control his urine output.

I felt uncomfortable with Judd Nicolai from the first moment I laid eyes on him. He was physically dirty. His hair was down to his shoulders and looked as if it hadn't been washed in two years. Really greasy. His fingernails were about an inch long, with dirt underneath. When he would slip these dirty hands through his greasy hair, it turned my stomach. I have a thing about dirt anyway. He looked like a real motorcycle dreg.

Right from the start I thought that he was odd sexually. When I first went in to say hello, he had the sheet pulled down to the nipple line, and what I could see of his body was bare. Partly as a result of using crutches, his muscles from the waist up were really developed. He seemed very concerned with what his body looked like. Very proud of it. Some concern would have been natural under the circumstances, but his seemed excessive. I guess his idea of masculinity is different from that of most men I've met. The men I know are concerned about being in shape but not about developing or showing off muscles. He was. To me he was completely repulsive.

A day or two after Nicolai had his incontinency device inserted, I began to think there was something really strange about him. I was in the hall giving out medications when I heard him call, "Nurse! Nurse!" I went into the room.

"Mary," he said, "shut the door and pull the curtain and come here and look at my catheter."

I left the door open, but I drew the curtain. He pulled the sheet entirely off himself. He was naked.

He said, "Look at me and make sure my tubes are all right."

I felt myself getting pink. I've seen fifty million patients naked, but something about this seemed abnormal. I put the sheet back over Judd's body, adjusting it so I could expose only the catheter, which of course was attached to his penis, and checked to see that everything was all right. Everything was.

Judd turned over onto his stomach. "I think I've had a bowel movement," he said. "Look at my rectum."

I had a weird feeling that what was going on was sexual, that what he was doing was trying to see what my reaction would be. I exposed enough of his backside to see that he had not had a bowel movement, then covered him again and said,

"Everything's fine." I pretended I was being very professional. But I was thinking, "Oh, god, what am I doing here?" I couldn't believe he was saying these things. I didn't know whether he was crazy or I was.

Other nurses began having trouble with Nicolai too. He would call somebody in and say, "Look at my rectum. Look at my anus. Check me. Do a rectal on me. Give me an enema." With paraparetics and people who have had the kinds of problems he had, there is a real problem with the bowels returning to their normal function. Constipation is common, and he did need enemas from time to time. I understood that. But when the nurse would insert a gloved finger or an enema tube, he would say, "Push it up higher."

I had only been head nurse a few months when this happened. I was new to the hospital, and I wasn't as sure of my role as I am now. I wasn't prepared to deal with Judd Nicolai. When I was a student, I had worked in a rehabilitation unit. There, patients' patterns of sexuality were changed because of what they had undergone, and certain patients would say things to the students to shock them, but I had never had such encounters. Then when I worked on a regular medical floor at Metro, none of the patients said those kinds of things. Or if they did, I was too naive to pick them up.

I had become a lot less naive since leaving nursing school. But at the time Nicolai was on the floor, I was still making my way as head nurse, and I didn't feel as strong as I do now.

I had a hard time dealing with Nicolai. I could do what I had to do for him, but I went in the room as little as possible. That made me feel bad. I would think to myself, "You're mature. You're a nurse. You're an adult. You should be able to deal with what this guy is. *He* has the problem."

But I had a problem too. And my staff had a problem. I didn't know what resources were available to me, and I didn't know whom to depend on, and I didn't confront the problem.

The one thing I did was to try to get help for Judd Nicolai from the residents. They didn't even want to listen to me. It was a Saturday morning, I remember, because the floor was rather quiet. Two urology residents who had been making rounds came into the nurses' station. Because the residents rotate so often, I never get to know any of them very well. When I approached these two and asked to talk to them about Nicolai, I was really embarrassed. I took them to a place in the hall where we wouldn't be overheard by patients. I said, "You know, something is really strange with Judd Nicolai."

They asked me what I meant.

I tried to explain.

They interrupted.

"Awwwww, that's nothing compared to what he did up at the other hospital!" one of the residents said. "Up there he would ask the nurses to come into the room and jerk him off!"

I began to feel I was going to get nowhere in the conversation.

"Well," I said to the residents, "before it gets to that point, I don't exactly know what should be done, but has anybody talked to him?" I had the feeling that because they saw him as an outpatient, they could steer him toward sexual counseling or a rehabilitation situation better than I could. I said this.

They laughed it off.

"He's a useless case," the second resident said. "He's hopeless. He's just a jerk."

End of conversation.

I was really bothered by their reaction. I thought they were being crude. They obviously didn't want to deal with Judd Nicolai either. I should have known that, because when they came up on the floor, they were in and out of his room in two seconds.

Nicolai was on Eight Cook about twelve days that admission. Though he was a problem for all of us, I also came to feel sorry for him. I thought, "Things must be pretty bad for you if you have to get your kicks by trying to shock a nurse." He could have been up and around, but he lay in bed all day just listening to the radio.

Once I said to him, "What do you do at home?"

He said, "Oh, I lie in bed and watch TV and smoke cigarettes and drink a few beers."

He lived with his mother on public assistance. He had had some kind of blue-collar job, but he wasn't even trying to work, though I'm sure there are kinds of work he could have done. He had never married. The only person I ever saw visit him was a black woman who looked to be in her late thirties. She came in one Sunday afternoon with a young son. Apparently Judd knew the father and the family. He seemed good with both of them. They sat there and talked. But that's the only normal interaction I saw him have.

Six months after Nicolai left Eight Cook that time, we heard that he had been admitted to Seven Cook. His incontinency device had become infected. The doctors took it out. To give the infection a chance to heal, they inserted a suprapubic tube into his bladder, which drained the urine out through a hole in his abdomen into a bag he could wear under his clothes.

We also heard that Nicolai was making his peculiar kind of trouble. At the time, there were male nursing students working down on Seven, and whenever a student went in the room, Judd would ask him whether he had been out on a date the night before. If the student said yes, Judd would ask very personal details about what had happened. The students didn't know how to tell him this was none of his business. Whether the head nurse on Seven Cook solved the problem, I didn't hear.

Now, a few months later, James was telling me on the phone that Nicolai was being readmitted to Eight Cook because he had been dribbling urine from his penis. The doctors were going to do tests to see if he could have another incontinency device inserted.

Nearly a year had passed since my first encounter with Nicolai. I was no longer green.

When I got off the phone with James, I looked around to see whom I could share the news with. Mrs. Dixon, a middle-aged LPN with a reddish Afro and a sassy mouth, was sitting at a desk writing nurses' notes.

"Wait till you hear who's checking into this fine hotel again," I said to Dixon. "You'll be thrilled. None other than Judd the Man Nicolai. In person."

Dixon stared at me. "He's too late," she said. "I'm getting married to somebody else." She broke up.

Nicolai came up to the floor while I was down in the cafeteria on one of my rare tea breaks with Jackie Neill. When I got back upstairs, I went into the room to say "Hi, how are you?" He was lying in bed with the sheet pulled down around his waist. I had exactly the same feelings I had had about him when I first saw him.

An hour later when I was working on charts at the nurses' station, his light on the floor monitor went on. The staff was all busy doing patient care. I answered the light.

Judd was lying naked in bed, completely uncovered.

"Can I help you?"

"I need to get up to go to the bathroom."

I left the room and came back with a gown from the linen closet.

"Here," I said, tossing it to him. "Put this on."

"I don't need a gown to go to the bathroom."

"Yes, you do." I pulled the curtain around his bed. "Put it on, and I'll help you get up."

He put the gown on. I helped him into the bathroom and waited for him and helped him back to bed. When I left the room, I headed straight for the telephone.

"Before things get bad this time," I was thinking, "I'm going to call Sandy Nichols."

Sandy had heard of Nicolai. Apparently his various escapades had made the rounds of the hospital. I told her on the phone what my experience with him had been. Sandy confirmed my suspicion.

"Yes, from the way you're describing it, it really sounds like abnormal sexual behavior," she said. "It's not a normal way of reacting to the situation." Sandy offered to meet with my staff to discuss Nicolai. I accepted the offer. Early that same afternoon, when the last nurse had gotten back from lunch, I got everybody together in the nurses' lounge and stated the problem.

"I got you together so we can decide how we're going to handle Judd Nicolai," I said. "Frankly, he bothers me and upsets me. I felt uncomfortable with him the last time he was in too, and I thought there might be something wrong with me. I know some other people on the staff felt the same way. Sandy has convinced me that there isn't anything wrong with us. What's wrong is wrong with him. If you're getting creepy-crawly feelings about Nicolai, it's not because you're strange. It's because he's adapting poorly."

I told the staff I wanted to work out a unified approach to Nicolai so he wouldn't get away with his behavior and so he wouldn't be a problem the whole time he was in.

Sandy started talking. I listened with admiration. Sandy was almost always helpful, always willing to help people work through these rough experiences. An interesting person too. She had just gotten back from a white-water raft trip on the Amazon.

"It's important to remember that a lot of people who have been through what Judd has been through physically do make successful sexual adaptations," Sandy said. "It's also true that a lot of people without physical problems get their sexual satisfaction from the rectal area. Male homosexuals achieve orgasm that way. So do some heterosexuals."

I glanced around the lounge in time to see a couple of the new kids do a double take. I felt sympathetic. Initiation is hard. I doubt that they had ever heard a talk like this in nursing school. I certainly hadn't.

"But," Sandy continued, "just because that's where he gets his sexual pleasure, and just because he wants to see your reaction, doesn't mean that you have to participate in any way. You don't have to subject yourselves to being his personal prostitutes."

With guidance from Sandy, we talked about specific solutions. We decided we could make things a lot easier for ourselves if we simply didn't do for Judd Nicolai the care he could do for himself. A lot of paraparetics give themselves enemas. A lot of paras do their own rectal checks too. In fact, though it sounds gross to say it, people who fail to regain control of the sphincter muscle around the anus not only do their own digital checks but also take the feces out of their rectum so they will be continent the rest of the day. We decided to remind Judd of this when he asked for rectal checks.

"Ask him what he does at home," Sandy suggested. "If he says, 'My mother does it,' just say, 'Well, you can do that for yourself. A lot of people do. It doesn't take a nurse to do that.'"

When he was home, Judd got himself on a bowel program. He would eat bran and take milk of magnesia and mineral oil, and he would have a bowel movement every day. In the hospital, however, he would try to get us to give him enemas by complaining that the regime wasn't working. From now on we would refuse to give him enemas.

"You don't have to be nasty," Sandy said. "Just say, 'If we give you enemas, it's going to destroy the program you had at home. You should wait and see how things go while you're in here.'"

From the way people participated and let out their feelings, I could see that everyone found the meeting helpful. At the end of it I told the staff that I would start the new approach by confronting Judd myself about his unwillingness to keep himself covered.

I got my chance before I went home that day. When I went into the room to give a shot to Judd's roommate, a nursing assistant was trying to help Judd out of bed. I went to assist her. As we maneuvered his leg over the side, the sheet pulled away from his body. He was naked.

I covered him. "Wait a second," I said. "I'm going to get you a gown." Before he could protest, I was out of the room.

When I came back with the gown, I said, "You know, it really bothers me that you don't keep anything on. If you want to go naked at home, fine. But in the hospital there are dietitians walking around, families, people who have no connection with nursing. I consider it disrespectful for you not to keep a gown on."

I was uncomfortable saying this to Judd, but I felt strongly that he should not be allowed to get away with his crude behavior.

Nicolai got very defensive. "I didn't mean any disrespect to you," he said in a strained voice.

"Well, I just want you to know that I consider it disrespect. I'm not used to having people stand in front of me with their clothes off. I don't like it when you do that. It makes me very uncomfortable. Not so uncomfortable that I'm not going to come in the room, but uncomfortable. I think out of respect for me and the other nurses and the other women who work here, you should keep some clothes on."

"It's too hot."

"Then just keep the gown at the foot of your bed and put it on when you get up."

Lo and behold, our new techniques paid off. Nicolai stayed on the floor five days, and after the first two, he more or less behaved himself. He began to put his gown on when he got out of bed. When he asked for enemas, we told him that that part of his care was his responsibility, and he stopped asking. He continued to ask us to check his rectum and his catheter, but we were less bothered by it. We simply told him that those things, too, were his responsibility. We made it clear to Nicolai that he couldn't manipulate us into his problems.

When he saw he wasn't going to get anywhere with us, he began to amuse himself by watching what we did for other patients and making suggestions as to how we could improve our nursing care. This was annoying, but it wasn't nearly as bad as what he had been doing. I felt good about the way I had handled the situation. I felt I had matured a lot since my first encounter with him, when I couldn't see the forest for the trees.

But I didn't feel completely happy about what happened to Nicolai that admission. The nurses solved him as a problem for ourselves. We didn't solve his problem.

A day or two before Nicolai left, I made another attempt to get a doctor to help him. Herb Weston, one of the two residents I had talked to previously about Nicolai, was now a staff man, and one morning when he was on the floor with a new resident, I got them aside.

"Something's really funny with Nicolai," I said to Weston. "He's dealing very poorly with his sexuality."

Weston said, "Look, I have enough problems with my own sex life!" They both started laughing, the turkeys.

I was mad. For god's sake, the doctors were men, they were doctors, and they were the logical ones to handle this situation.

"I'm not interested in that," I said, "That's your problem. I'm talking about him. Do you know whether he's seeing a psychiatrist now?" I had heard that Nicolai had seen a psychiatrist right after his second accident.

Weston only knew that the chief urologist was seeing Nicolai as an outpatient in the office.

"Well, he needs something," I said. "I've seen people in wheelchairs who are living the same type of life he is but dealing with it well. He's dealing poorly. Maybe he needs to get into a rehab program or at least have this option suggested, so he can start being around people in the same condition he's in who are coping."

The two of them listened and even agreed with me.

"You're right," they said. "That's what he does need."

But then they went back to joking about their own sex lives. I couldn't get them to take the problem as seriously as I was taking it. Before I could come up with another strategy, Nicolai was discharged. The tests had shown that he could not have another incontinency device put in.

Maybe the doctors had tried to do something about Judd Nicolai and just ended up thinking it was useless. Some rehab units kick people out for not going along with the rehabilitation, and maybe Nicolai's attitude was just too poor.

But from what I saw, the residents didn't even make a try. They just laughed the whole thing off. I thought that was wrong. My feeling is that if doctors don't want to get involved with patients, they shouldn't be doctors. I know they're busy. But a doctor doesn't have to meet a patient's needs all by himself. He only has to see that they're met. Write a consult to the social worker. To the psychiatrist. To the psychiatric nurse. Whatever.

I guess I should have said something to Nicolai myself. Maybe if he had been in longer, I would have. But I didn't know him well enough to sit down and say to him, "Look, Judd, you're really screwing up your life. Why don't you get off your ass and start doing something for yourself?"

On a rehab floor, nurses sometimes try these tactics. But on a rehab floor, everybody gears up to support the patient afterward. You don't devastate somebody and then walk off. Central isn't set up for that kind of tactic. There would be no support for what I said, and no follow-up.

Still, as Sandy says, unless Nicolai gets help, he'll only get worse. So if he ever comes back in, I won't wait for the doctors to talk to him about the possibility of a rehab program. I'll do it myself.

Not long ago I attended a conference run by a nurse who heads the rheumatoid arthritis floor at another hospital. Rheumatoid arthritis afflicts women in particular, and sometimes the women are quite young. When patients come to her floor, this nurse told us, they are asked to give a sexual history, including positions during intercourse.

"You'd be surprised how many doctors and nurses are really

afraid to ask those questions," the nurse said. "Many of them only know the missionary position. But these patients are never going to be able to use that position because of what has happened to their joints. Yet doctors and nurses don't talk to them about alternatives. Either they don't think to do so or they're afraid."

She's right.

On a floor like Eight Cook, the question of how to help patients adjust sexually to major physical changes rarely arises. That's usually the business of a rehab floor. Judd Nicolai was one of a kind.

But this does not mean that patients' sex lives should be a matter of no concern to the staff of a general surgical floor. Most patients who have surgery face at least a temporary interruption of their sexual activity. It's logical for them to wonder when they can return to their normal patterns. It's logical for them to expect this information from a doctor or a nurse.

Yet from what I've seen, doctors and nurses are often uncomfortable talking to patients about sex. I've watched a doctor go through the whole routine with a post-op patient—no climbing, no driving—and never mention intercourse.

Or I'll go into a room after a doctor has left and ask the patient, "Did the doctor tell you when you could resume intercourse?" and the patient says, "Oh, I was too embarrassed to ask." Patients assume that if the doctor doesn't bring it up, they shouldn't. I don't know how many times I've had to go back to the phone, call the doctor, and say point-blank, "So-and-so wants to know when she can have intercourse again."

Sometimes doctors and nurses avoid mentioning sex because they don't want to interfere in what they consider a patient's privacy. But I think a lot of times they just don't know what to say.

If everybody's background was like mine, I can see why. Maybe nursing schools just weren't dealing with such matters when I was a student. Maybe sex was discussed and I missed it. But if anyone at Metro even mentioned that impotency is often a problem for diabetic males, or that hysterectomy patients can't have intercourse for so many weeks post-op, I don't remember it.

I came out of nursing school very naive about sex. I guess a lot of that was my upbringing. It wasn't that my parents hid anything from me. These things just weren't discussed.

I didn't have a lot of dating experience. In high school I stayed away from parties, because I didn't like to drink and didn't like having the boys quote survey the meat. I felt insecure and uncomfortable in those situations. I should have been able to say "the hell with it" and gone to those parties feeling comfortable. Instead I removed myself. I did go out, but I wasn't experienced in long-term relationships.

After high school, I moved from my Catholic home to a dormitory at Metropolitan Hospital. Metro was strict. No jeans or pants outside of the dorm, mandatory study hours, in at 10:00 every weeknight, and no men above the first floor. We couldn't sneak anybody in because there was only one entrance to the dorm and one set of elevators. Ron couldn't believe it. Nobody could.

The lack of freedom was good in some ways. It gave you an excuse. If a creep you met at a frat party said, "Stay with me tonight," you could say, "I can't because I'll get kicked out." But maybe a different kind of situation would have broadened me more. Liz and Maureen, who got their nursing degrees at a university, had their own house with a gay guy their second year in school. I'm sure that's a broadening situation. I was a lot more sheltered.

My first sexual partner was Ron. I didn't start dating him until my last year in nursing school. We didn't marry for another three years. So I graduated without having a good understanding of what husbands and wives begin to mean to each other, or what any two people in a long-term relationship mean to each other.

As a nurse, I was not prepared to deal with certain things. I became embarrassed relatively easily. I was embarrassed the first few times I saw young guys, patients, walk around with hardly any clothes on. I remember my face getting really flushed. I remember my face getting flushed the first few times I handed a male patient a washcloth and said, "Okay, now wash between your legs." When I told that to Katie later, she said, "Oh, I had the same problem at first. What I thought a nurse did was give out pills and make people better. I didn't know you gave a man a bath!"

That kind of embarrassment is often cured by experience.

Certainly mine was. But length of time on the job doesn't necessarily make it easy to talk to patients about sex. Neither does getting older, and neither does getting married. I know. Now that I'm married and five years older and more experienced than I was when I graduated, I'm still not completely comfortable discussing patients' sex lives.

I am, however, a lot more comfortable than I used to be. I owe that mainly to a three-day Sexual Attitudes Reassessment conference I attended with Ron after I had been at Central for about a year.

The conference, sponsored by Rehabilitation Hospital just outside the city, was for health care professionals. Ron had seen a notice at school. Since anyone who attended was supposed to bring along a "significant other," he suggested we go. I was sort of curious. We both felt the conference could be useful.

The first day was unbelievable. We were bombarded with what I can only describe as porno films. Three or four going at once. They left nothing to the imagination—dogs, pigs, two women, three women, four women, two men, husband–wife, boyfriend–girlfriend, and a couple on a motorbike. We were told that the purpose of these films was to knock us down to a base level so that nothing about the conference from there on in would shock us. A couple of times I sat there with my hands over my face thinking, "Oh, god, this has got to go!" I felt I'd been put through the wringer.

But the conference really helped me. The part I found most valuable was on physical handicaps and sex. First we saw a film in which a married couple, both with cerebral palsy, showed how they gratified each other sexually. The film also showed how a man confined to a wheelchair and his wife, who was not handicapped, had gotten around the limitations of vaginal intercourse. Since he couldn't have an erection, she stimulated him anally with her tongue, and he aroused her through cunnilingus or manual stimulation.

After the film, we broke into small groups. In our group there were two young people in wheelchairs—a young man who had been paralyzed in a car accident eleven weeks before and a young woman who had been crippled for a number of years. Both were married to spouses who were not disabled. The two talked about their lives and relationships. Listening to them was great. They seemed so comfortable with themselves and with the role sex played for them. They didn't say sex was the greatest need in their lives. They just made clear that it was part of their lives. Their perspective actually gave me a sense of well-being.

I don't think I'll ever feel the same again about people who are disabled. Before the conference, I actually felt pity for people in wheelchairs. I still think it's a shame that they're in that situation. But I came away much more aware of how strong some of these people are, of how much the body can do, and of how much a strong person can do even when something terrible happens.

I also came away from the conference realizing for the first time how very important the question of sex can become to a person in the hospital.

In our small group we started talking about how soon a patient begins to wonder about the effects of his condition on his sex life. The young man in the wheelchair said, "I came to in the intensive care unit. The first thing I thought about was, 'Will I ever be able to have intercourse with my wife again?' Every doctor I met steered away from that question. Every nurse did. Even when I came right out and asked doctors if they thought my sexual ability would return, none of them gave me a clear answer. I thought about it all the time. Until I got to the rehab unit, nobody told me anything."

A couple of days after the Sexual Attitudes Reassessment conference, I started talking about it with Dean Marco, the stoma therapist who comes to see colostomy patients on Eight Cook. Dean, who's young, has a colostomy himself. After I had told him a little about what I had seen and learned, I said, "Can I ask you something? Do you ever discuss sex with the patients?"

"The ones I see on a long-term basis, yes," Dean said, "because I've established a relationship with them."

"What do you tell them?"

"I tell them that everybody has his own little routine for getting ready for sex, and that when you have a colostomy, you keep the same routine you had before you had the colostomy. People without colostomies go into the bathroom and empty their bladders. People with colostomies go in and empty their colostomy bags.

"I tell patients that they might have to change their positions or think about doing things a little differently, but that if they had a good sexual relationship before the colostomy, they'll have a good one after. A colostomy shouldn't curtail your sex life."

Dean then told me that once when he and his wife were really going at it, he got on top of her when his colostomy bag was full. It broke. The contents splashed all over both of them.

"It was a little embarrassing," Dean said, "but it was also kind of funny. My wife didn't get too upset." Dean sometimes tells that story to patients. So do I.

A few days after my talk with Dean, I got a chance to start putting my new awareness to use. A man came in to Eight Cook to have an impotency device inserted. The doctors placed a water pack in his abdomen and a tiny pump in his scrotum. By manipulating the pump with his hand, the man could force water from the pack in his abdomen to a tube in his penis, thereby stiffening the penis.

The patient was a quiet person, married, not too old, with multiple sclerosis. He went through his procedure well, and his post-op period was really good. On his discharge day, I asked him when the doctor had said he could go back to having intercourse.

"Go back to it?" the man said. "I haven't had intercourse for twelve years."

Before the sex conference, I might have just let that comment pass. But I said something that I guess must have made me seem receptive, because the man started to talk to me. Since getting MS, he said, he had not been able to sustain an erection. Now he could. He wasn't to have intercourse for a week, and at first he would have to practice to learn how to use the device properly. But he was really looking foward to going home.

"I'm so excited!" he said. "It's going to be like a second honeymoon. You don't know what it's like for a man not to be able to have intercourse for twelve years."

Once the initial barrier was crossed, talking this way did not seem uncomfortable to me. I relaxed to the point of thinking, "Hmmmm. Let's not leave the women out of this." So I said,

"Well, I guess it must be hard on anybody." I teased him about the male ego. We continued to talk. It was a conversation I know I would not have been able to have before the conference.

I have also started asking patients questions for my own information—questions I wouldn't have asked before. We had a young kid on the floor named Hap Callahan, a 23-year-old who had been born with his bladder outside his abdominal cavity. When he was young, the surgeons had put the bladder back in. But Hap still had trouble controlling his urination. He had to wear a rubber clamp on his penis to keep himself continent. He had come in to have an incontinency device put in, but because of infection, the device had to be removed. He spent a couple of weeks on the floor, during which time I got to know him a little. I had noticed that he was often visited by a young woman.

One day while I was taking care of Hap, I just matter-of-factly came out and said, "Given the problems you've been having with your urine, have you had any problems having erections?"

Hap said there were no problems.

I asked him what he did about the clamp when he wanted to have intercourse. He told me he opened the clamp and emptied his bladder beforehand, just as he did when he took a walk, except that for intercourse he didn't put the clamp back on. Talking about this didn't seem to faze him at all, and it helped me.

I've come to believe that nurses and doctors have to think about these things when we're dealing with patients. Sex is part of somebody's life. With some people, the sexual urge may be very strong; with others it's less strong. But I think if people have had good sexual relationships before their illness or injury, they want those relationships to continue if at all possible. I'm not just talking about younger people. I'm surprised at the number of 70-year-olds who want to know about resuming intercourse. It's so important. From what I can tell, it's on the minds of most people who come into a hospital. You can't ignore it.

I'm not saying I get into it that often. I can't talk with just any patient about sex. Sometimes I have to force myself to do it. But the more I use the word *intercourse* in front of people I don't know, the easier it is.

Of course there are patients who aren't the least bit interested in talking about sex and aren't concerned about sex after hospitalization. A certain hysterectomy patient was going home. I went in and started asking her my questions. "What instructions did the doctor give you? When can you start housecleaning, walk up and down steps, move furniture?" Then I said, "When did the doctor say you could have sexual relations?"

She looked at me as if I were crazy. "Sex! Who the hell cares about sex! Hell, at my age, I only care about cleaning the house."

The woman was 45.

I thought, "To each his own!"

Then, of course, there are patients who don't need to wait for doctors and nurses to get comfortable enough to raise the subject of sex. They raise it themselves.

"When can I screw my wife?" one man asked me as he was leaving.

"Tell him he can do it this afternoon, if he's that horny," Dr. Benson told me when I asked. I put it slightly differently to the patient: "The doctor says you can have intercourse this afternoon if you want to."

My coolest moment after the sex conference came when a gay guy who had had hemorrhoid surgery asked me when he could have rectal intercourse again.

I said, "I don't know, but I'll find out for you," and though the doctor giggled when I asked, I never batted an eye.

I don't work nights at Central Hospital, but occasionally when I worked nights at Metro and would go in to check on a patient, I could see from the way the bed was moving that the patient was masturbating.

Whenever the aides noticed this, they would come out and say in a joking way, "You know what *he's* doing!" Because I was uncomfortable with the aides and uncomfortable with the situation, I said nothing.

Now I would say, "Well, what would you do if you were in the hospital over a long period of time and didn't have any way to relieve yourself sexually?"

I think it's important for those of us who work in hospitals to be aware of the sexual needs of patients as patients. Some people are in the hospital for weeks at a time. How do they get through this period sexually?

Lots of patients are so sick that I'm sure sex is the last thing on their minds. I'm sure all they're interested in is getting out. But some patients are well enough to enjoy physical contact with a husband or wife who comes in to visit. Yet most of them are too uncomfortable to display affection in front of other people.

A woman comes in to see her husband, and now here's this person she loves lying in a big white bed with a bunch of nurses around. That woman feels uncomfortable even going over and touching her husband. The person she has had the most intimate relationship with is now removed from her. People in the hospital don't have a chance to kiss each other or hold each other or even cry together if they want without the whole world walking by, without a nurse walking in and sticking a thermometer in somebody's mouth.

I solve this on my floor when I can. I suppose that according to hospital rules people aren't supposed to be lying on a bed together. I don't know that there is a rule like that, and I don't intend to find out. A couple of times when we have had young patients, a boyfriend or spouse will draw the curtain and get on the bed with the patient. I remember one kid especially whose girlfriend used to come in, and they'd pull the curtain around them and lie on the bed and kiss. Certain staff members would say to me, "What do you do?" I'd say, "Just pretend they're not in there."

I mean the kids weren't doing anything wrong. They weren't going to set the place on fire. The boy didn't have an IV in. Even if he had had one, hugging and kissing weren't going to hurt anything. So I would say to people, "You don't need him for anything. He's all right. I'm sure she'll come out and get you if he isn't."

Once again, this is something I learned from Katie. When Ted Roger was a patient at Metro, he became friendly with another patient, Maury, who had had a kidney transplant. Maury had a private room. Often he let Ted and his wife use it. While they were in there, Maury would walk around the halls or go into the solarium and smoke his pipe. Katie suggested that he put up a DO NOT DISTURB sign on the door, so Maury would do that. Katie would say, "Put up a sign that says SEX IN PROGRESS!" Maury would reply, "I hope they put clean sheets on the bed!"

Maybe the Rogers were only hugging and kissing. But it was a chance for them to be alone. And where in the hospital do you get that? A patient can't even be alone with his or her own thoughts. When Joy Li wanted to shut out the world and die in her own way, the only thing she could do was close her eyes.

I think it's unfair for a couple to lie in bed and kiss if there's a roommate who is confined to bed and is embarrassed by what's going on next to him. That doesn't give the roommate much choice. But if the roommate is out of the room or doesn't care, and the couple has the curtain pulled, I don't think lying on the bed and kissing is out of place in a hospital.

Once at Metro a supervisor disagreed with me on a similar issue. We had a young teacher on the floor who was dying of leukemia. The doctors couldn't get him into remission. He was in the hospital a long time, in a private room. His wife used to stay all night with him. They didn't have any kids, so she would be with him all day, helping him get washed in the morning, getting him ice, bringing him yoghurt and other kinds of food, helping him pass the time, staying by him. Then at night she used to sleep in a big lounge chair in his room. Maybe because the couple was kind of hippie-ish, some of the nurses thought it was wrong for her to stay with him.

One night a supervisor came on the floor and said, "That's disgusting. She should be made to leave."

I said, "If it was my husband or my boyfriend or somebody I loved, and I knew he was dying, I'd be right in there too. If you want her to leave, you go down and tell her."

I don't know where I got the courage to say that to a supervisor. But I just refused to believe that the hospital couldn't accommodate to the fact that the guy was going to die. He was getting comfort from the person he loved and cared about. That may have been more important than any medication they could have given him.

There are no private rooms on Eight Cook. There aren't even any lounge chairs. But I try as much as I can to encourage the closeness that is possible. Often I will ask a spouse to help me turn a patient or help me sit the patient up in bed. I figure that that enables the two to touch, and that maybe if spouses do these things with me and see that they're not hurting the patient, they'll do them without me.

Or I'll say, "You know, you can go over and touch the patient. You're not going to hurt him. That's what he needs. He needs to be touched." I think that's something nurses really have to stress. Touch could make the patient feel more like a human being than anything else could.

I learned my first good lesson about this from a little old Russian couple in their eighties. She was very sick. She had a big bedsore on her rear end, and we were always turning her on her side, keeping the covers off, and putting the heat lamp on to dry the sore out. Her husband would sit in the room serenading her with his mandolin. One day for some reason I asked him to step out in the hall while I got her ready for treatment.

Instead, he came over to the bed and put his hand on his wife's buttock. He said to me, "I've seen that *tuchis* many, many times over the years. I've touched it many times. And I'm going to keep right on touching it and looking at it while she's in here."

I thought, "He's right. This is part of life. It doesn't stop being part of life just because a person is in the hospital."

10

WEAK LINKS, TOUGH DECISIONS: THE TRIALS OF RUNNING A STAFF

I was off the day Mrs. Jackson got the bad news. Thank god. I was dreading the meeting. Ordinarily I would have been in on it, but apparently Jackson got wind of what was going to happen and told someone she had heard rumors. So the nursing office decided to talk to her right away.

Jackson would not be fired outright. Miss Craig would give her several choices. She could step down and become a nursing assistant. She could stay on in her present position for a month while she looked for another job. Or she could hand in her resignation.

Mrs. Jackson was a black LPN on my staff who had worked at Central for sixteen years. For most of that time she had worked nights. Then she had asked to rotate again, which gave me a chance to watch her on days. I discovered that she really wasn't capable of doing her job. I began keeping careful records of her poor performances. I gave her one below-average evaluation and then another. She received several warning notices from the nursing office. She didn't improve. By the time Kelly O'Brien went home, Craig had decided that Jackson would have to leave.

At Central, the nursing office takes care of hirings and firings. Because of Craig's schedule, no meeting had been set up with Jackson. But three days after Mr. O'Brien had gone, Craig called me to say that since Jackson had heard rumors, the meeting would have to be held the next morning.

"I'm off," I said. "Do you want me to come in? I'd be glad to."

As I'm sure Craig knew, I wouldn't have been glad to come in at all. But I would have done it.

"No," Craig said. "Don't worry about it. The supervisor will be there, and I think we can manage, don't you?"

I laughed. But the next day, as I walked around the stores getting started on my Christmas shopping, I felt pretty uncomfortable about the whole thing. Even though Jackson had been prepared for what was happening, I knew she wouldn't be happy about it. I dreaded the aftermath as much as I had dreaded the meeting.

Jackson's case was tricky. What I considered to be her problems were not concrete. She didn't perform as an LPN should perform. Getting her to do anything was like pulling teeth. She was just not assertive. I guess that's the way I put it in the documentation. Nothing extra, and sometimes not enough.

Either she didn't care enough or she didn't know enough. She was older, in her late fifties. She had had a different type of education from the younger LPNs. She had not kept up with things. She was just not able to deal with the kind of sick patients we're dealing with. A nurse has to be able to notice changes in these people. You can't be oblivious to them or ignore them.

Or laugh at them, which she seemed to do from time to time. She didn't really treat patients as people. Her attitude was poor. She was fresh to patients and made unpleasant comments to them. I'd hear her from out in the hall. When I'd walk in the room, she'd laugh and say to the patient, "I was only teasing you." Hell, she wasn't teasing. She only said that because I walked in.

How do you tell somebody she has a nasty or destructive attitude? What makes up a good attitude? Everybody's idea is different. Jackson's tone and mannerisms were hard to document. If there had been numerous patient complaints, that would be one thing. But patients rarely complained about Jackson. All I could do was try to write down her way of talking to patients.

Over a period of several months, however, there were several specific incidents. The first involved a patient with a neurological disorder. I can't remember exactly what was wrong with the woman, but she had a lot of problems and was very, very weak. The incident occurred while I was in the patient's room with Mrs.

Viola, one of the supervisors, who was making rounds. Jackson was also in there.

Apparently she was having trouble getting the patient to do something. I heard her say, "You're just lazy. If you would help yourself, you could do things better. We mustn't baby ourselves."

I couldn't believe it. Right in front of a supervisor.

As soon as I could, I took Jackson aside and said, "Mrs. Jackson, I don't think it was such a good idea to say that to the patient. How would you like it if you were sick and somebody said to you, 'We mustn't baby ourselves. We're being lazy'?"

"Oh," she said, "I was only joking."

I said, "I don't think the patient took you to be joking, and I didn't."

"Well, I don't understand why you're making such a big thing out of it."

"I would not want somebody saying that to my mother," I said. "I don't think you would want anybody saying that to you. And I don't want to hear it again."

The second incident involved Virginia Medlock. One day I went into the room and found Virginia's colostomy bag hanging off her body. Virginia had been draining blood into the bag. Now blood lay in a pool all around her. When I looked at it, I was sick. I can take mistakes in I&Os, but I cannot tolerate somebody lying in dirt or blood or excretions. To me that is absolutely inhuman.

I also knew that Virginia hadn't been turned. She was too out of it to move on her own, and she was lying in the same position I had seen her in earlier.

I quietly went out and got Mrs. Jackson.

"When was the last time you changed Virginia Medlock's position?" I asked her.

"Oh, I just changed her a little while ago."

I said, "Well, she hasn't been changed since I last saw her, and she's lying in a pool of blood. I want you to come in there with me. I'm going to help you change her."

Jackson was really in a huff. But we went in and washed Virginia and got her straightened up. Then I said to Jackson, "This bag didn't look too good this morning. Now it's leaking. Why wasn't it changed?"

"I didn't know how to change it."

"That's no excuse. Why didn't you come and get some-body?" I was very upset.

In addition to these incidents, there was the problem of Jackson's parking. She had been accustomed to leaving her car in the garage across the street from the hospital. When the rates went up and she decided it was too expensive to park there, she started parking her car at a meter. Every two hours she left the floor to put money in. That meant she was off the floor when she should have been working and worrying about the meter when she should have had her mind on the patients.

As soon as I found out what the situation was, I informed the supervisor and told Jackson she would have to make other arrangements for her car. She didn't. Again I spoke with her, and so did Ann Sullivan, the supervisor. This incident, like the others, was carefully documented.

Furthermore, Jackson was often late to work and frequently called in sick. Apparently she did have medical problems. She was not a young thing. I don't mean that 57 or 58 is over the hill, but I'm sure it's hard on somebody that age to put in long hours and switch shifts.

When you take a job, however, you're supposed to live up to the responsibilities of that job or get out. I'm not saying that Jackson was abusive to patients. She didn't hit anybody. She just wasn't together.

I did not find it easy to take the necessary steps to have Mrs. Jackson relieved of her responsibilities. I worried a lot about her reaction. I worried about the reaction of the rest of the staff. But making her leave was not nearly as difficult for me as it would have been a year earlier.

Anyone who watches television might have the impression that when a head nurse ends up with her stomach in knots, a doctor is usually the reason. That is rarely true for me.

For one thing, doctors and nurses don't see nearly as much of each other in a real hospital as they do on television. For another, even when I have a problem with a doctor, it doesn't usually bother me unless it's on a day when Dietary is giving me grief, the ORs are coming back late, and the supervisor can't find a replacement for somebody who calls in sick on the three-to-eleven shift.

My staff is what sends me home with my stomach in knots. Considering all the people who have worked on Eight Cook since I started as head nurse, I really haven't had that many problems. Most of my staff members are good people and conscientious nurses. But as in any factory or government agency, there are a few people on the floor who need to shape up and don't do so unless they're told. With these people, I find I have to follow through on just about everything. I just didn't believe that people like that went into nursing. But they do. Getting staff to perform is the hardest part of my job. I don't mean perform like good Fido. I mean all of us working together.

I had no preparation for administering a staff. We had no management courses in nursing school, and though I sometimes acted as charge nurse at Metro, I wasn't responsible for reprimanding people or telling them what to do. In terms of dealing with people, I was basically unprepared for the role I took when I came to Central. I was going on instinct. Instinct wasn't nearly enough to get me through what I found myself going through.

Central did give a two-day management course for new head nurses. Later I attended a two-day conference on leadership skills at a nearby university. These were certainly better than nothing. After Jackie Neill and I had both been head nurses for about a year, we took a course in management at another university. We were the only nurses there. While the course was disappointing, we did find it profitable to listen to other people. Experienced managers were having the same kinds of problems we were. I came home realizing that telephone company management isn't much different from hospital floor management and that if you deal with people anywhere, you're going to have problems.

I started this job with the feeling that if I was very nice to the people on my staff, showed them I was willing to work along with them and help them, that I cared about patients, they would care about patients too, and they would do everything they could to make sure patients got what they needed. I wouldn't have to go after the nurses and correct them. I hoped that if the weaker people saw by the look on my face that I was displeased, they would respond accordingly.

Instead I learned that I had to confront things. When I started as head nurse, I noticed that people were straggling in to work ten minutes after the shift began. I thought they could tell that I wasn't happy about this. But it kept happening. Finally I had to say something. The staff seemed surprised.

"Oh," they said, "no one ever told us before to come in on time."

Problems with staff made my first six months at Central the worst work experience I've ever had. That might not have been true if I had gotten my own floor to begin with. But because of major renovations, construction delays, and various personnel considerations, I was assigned as acting head nurse on three different floors in four months. I constantly had to deal with a new staff. While I had head nurse responsibility in one sense, in another sense I didn't have it.

Oh, god, I was overwhelmed. The first floor I was on was the worst. To begin with, I was the first RN who had been on Three Warren in six months. LPNs had been in charge. My arrival meant that they were no longer running things. There were a lot of bad vibrations. It didn't help that I had come in from a different hospital.

Furthermore, I was the only white person on the staff. I felt uncomfortable in that situation. Occasionally a patient would ask for me specifically, and one day I overheard a staff member say to another, "The only reason this patient likes Mary is that she's white and we're black."

I felt I didn't have any peers. This was as much because of my age as my color. I wasn't married then, while all the others were. The only person I felt I had for support was Mrs. Bird, the supervisor, who was a few years older than I and who had been there a while.

Of course since I came to Central not knowing any of the people on my staff, I didn't know who was good. I didn't know whom I could rely on. I was struggling to get used to being in charge, struggling to learn my boundaries. I was intimidated by the staff. I found I did not know how to deal with people who weren't performing. Maybe because they sensed my insecurity, certain staff members resisted cooperating with me. I'd try to get them together for a conference, and they'd throw their eyes to heaven.

I began to fully grasp what I was up against as a staff administrator when I had my first actual confrontation with a staff member. I had been on Three Warren for about three weeks. A very heavy patient was brought up from the OR one afternoon. She had to be moved from the stretcher to the bed. I was on duty, and a nursing assistant named Sheila was on. A third person was off the floor at the time. An LPN, Marie, was eating lunch in one of the conference areas. The patient was too big for Sheila and me to lift by ourselves.

I went in and said to Marie, "I hate to bother you while you're eating your lunch, but we don't have anybody to help us get this patient off the stretcher. Could you come help us?"

Marie looked straight at me and said, "No."

My heart started to pound. I was shocked at her response, and I was too new to react. I just stood there with my mouth open. Finally I said, "I really need your help."

"I don't care. Go call one of the supervisors to help you. This is my lunch break."

It seemed to me that I had no other choice. I got a nurse from another floor to help with the patient. Having no idea what I should do about Marie, I called the supervisor, Mrs. Bird, who came right up.

"What do *you* think you should do?" she asked me.

"I don't know. I'm really upset."

"Why exactly are you upset?"

I thought a minute. "Well, I think it was very unfair of her to refuse to help. I'm very disappointed in her."

"Then I think you should use those words when you talk to

Marie," Mrs. Bird said. "You have to talk to her—and now. You can't take that, Mary. You can't ignore it, because it will only get worse."

Mrs. Bird left the floor. I called Marie aside. I was so afraid that I was shaking inside.

"You know," I said, "I was very disappointed with you today."

"Why?"

God, she was a tough cookie.

I said, "I wouldn't have come in there and bothered you for something trivial. That was very important. Sheila and I would have broken our backs trying to lift that lady by ourselves."

"What would you have done if I had been eating lunch down in the cafeteria? That was my lunch break. I'm not to be disturbed during my lunch break."

"Well, obviously if you had been off the floor, I couldn't have gotten you. I would have had to do what I did do. But you were here, and I'm in charge, and I asked you to help me. If somebody had come in and asked me to help, I would never have refused, whether it was my lunch break or not. I would have gone out and helped. It would only have taken a few minutes."

"It would have broken up my time."

I was mad. I hadn't planned to say what I said next, but I was so angry that the words just came out of my mouth.

"All right," I said, "if you feel that way, then you're not to eat lunch on the floor any more. You're to go off the floor so I won't be able to get you."

"All right," she said, "I'll do that."

Afterward I felt pretty good about the way I had handled the situation with Marie. I think she realized she was lucky not to have gotten a warning notice for insubordination. We treated each other coolly but courteously. What would have happened between us or how she would have performed in the long run I don't know, because I left Three Warren two weeks later.

My days at Central got worse. The problems I was having adjusting to staff were complicated by other problems. I didn't know where to find things. I didn't know which supervisors I could rely on, which dietitians and escorts were conscientious, whom to call in Central Supply, which social workers I could trust. I knew none of the staff doctors, none of the residents, none of the interns.

Surgery was new to me. I had never even seen a dental extraction. It had been so long since I had worked with surgical patients that the thought of doing so scared me. I had never dealt with surgical complications, rarely with wounds. It took me quite a while to learn what responses were considered normal, to learn when to worry about temp elevations, to get used to the equipment and techniques used in various post-op treatments.

Perhaps the worst thing was that I felt I was being used. I'd be trying to get certain people into a certain routine, and then I'd be moved. It was all extremely frustrating.

I dwelt on these problems. I'd be home ironing or watching TV and thinking about my job. Sometimes I'd come home and cry. I kept thinking I had made the wrong decision. Maybe I had taken on more responsibility than I could handle. Maybe I couldn't play the role I'd been hired to play.

I gave very serious thought to quitting. I'd go home and say to Ron, "I don't need this kind of shit. I'm a good nurse. I'll find a job in a dialysis unit or someplace else where I don't have to be held accountable for other people's mistakes." For a while, I was a pretty uncomfortable person.

But I didn't really want to quit. I'm not a person who quits easily, and I don't think it looks good to job-hop. I kept saying to myself, "I'll stick it out for a year." Ron urged me to stay on. We both felt sure that things would be better after I got my own floor.

The first weeks on Eight Cook were no better.

The layout was different from the layout on Three Warren. I had to learn all over again where to find things. The patients admitted to the Cook Building were sicker than the Warren patients. My timing was bad. I started on Eight Cook in July. The annual crop of new residents comes in July. So does the annual crop of new nursing school grads.

I had eight or nine people per shift to deal with, as compared with four or five on Three Warren. The floor supervisor,

Betty Fillmore, was a perfectionist. I was very unsure of myself and felt I couldn't equal her. It took me six or seven months just to get used to Betty.

To top things off, a serious problem developed almost immediately between me and one of the part-time clerks, Jeannette. She and I just couldn't work together. There was never any outright fighting, but some days it was like ice between us. Reaching a truce took weeks of hashing-out meetings with the unit manager who supervises the clerks in the Cook Building. In one of those confrontations, I ended up crying. I was very upset with myself for losing control. My crying, however, may have been a turning point, because my relationship with the clerk improved somewhat. But a real barrier remained between us.

Fortunately, all these problems were not the only things happening to me those first months on Eight Cook. Some good things were also happening. I was becoming familiar with the floor. I was growing more comfortable with surgical patients. I was learning which people in each part of the hospital I could rely on. By the time Jeannette and I had agreed to start over on a new footing, I had begun to believe I could handle the position of head nurse. The longer I stayed, the more I came to enjoy what I was doing.

By the end of my first year at Central, I no longer felt I was sticking it out. I was feeling better about my job in general than I had since before I left Metro. I was increasingly confident that I was capable of orchestrating a staff.

There are still days when that orchestration breaks down. Some weeks I'm ready to pull my hair out. But I can see more continuity. I also think I have more control over myself and my emotions than I did when I started. That pleases me.

It's still hard for me to talk to a staff member when there's a problem. I sometimes have to say to myself, "Get yourself together and go talk to that person." I may walk around the hall once and think, "I'm going to say this, I'm going to say that." Then I'll walk in and say it. I rehearse.

Keeping staff working well and working together is not as hard as it used to be, but it is hard. Deep down inside of me, I think to myself that if people are conscientious, they should want to do their jobs as well as possible. If they're getting paid, they should do what they're supposed to do. Unfortunately, some people don't have that motto. When this becomes the problem it became with Mrs. Jackson, I feel I have no choice but to get the person off the floor, however hard that may be for everybody concerned.

Mrs. Jackson was the third person to be let go on Eight Cook since my arrival. The other two were white RNs. All three of these dismissals were traumatic for me.

The first RN, Alice Patrick, was asked to leave because she made a lot of medications errors. Most were errors of omission. Though there were no serious repercussions, there was a consistent pattern. Alice was really not safe for patients.

I had a lot of trouble confronting Alice with that fact. Katie used to say, "When you tell people the truth about their performance, you're not telling them anything they don't know. They know. They just don't think you know." Yet I felt guilty about saying anything to Alice about what she had done and not done or about the fact that her job was on the line. I kept thinking that if I had been a better administrator, Alice might have been a better nurse. I thought the fault might be mine.

The process of getting her out was as hard as convincing myself that she should be out. I was amazed to discover how difficult it is and how much documentation is required to get rid of even somebody who makes consistent medications errors. I was in Miss Craig's office for an hour or two a day over an entire week. My stomach really gnawed at me while all this was going on. I got to be a bundle of nerves. I didn't even want to go to work. Ron kept saying to me, "You can't keep people like this in a hospital." I knew he was right. But I was depressed about the whole thing.

Maggie Foster was an even more difficult case. If patient care had been the only consideration, Maggie probably could have stayed on. She cared about patients and was good with them.

But she couldn't take charge. She had failed state boards several times. A year after becoming a graduate nurse, she still was not licensed as an RN and therefore was not permitted to serve as charge nurse on nights, evenings, or my days off.

Maggie did eventually pass boards. But even though she was technically qualified for charge, she still wasn't qualified emotionally. She had a difficult time just being a team leader. She was flighty and unsure of herself. She had the maturity of maybe a 17-year-old. She came across as a little girl. Simply having to ask a question made her flustered, and when it came to handling a situation, she completely fell apart. Once she was in a room when a patient stopped breathing. Instead of calling a code immediately, Maggie left the room and asked somebody else to go in and look at the patient first. Luckily, the person survived.

I think Maggie had probably been pushed into nursing. Her father, uncle, and grandfather were doctors. Her mother was a director of nursing. Apparently her mother was also very stern. Maggie was living at home, and we heard that she had many family problems. One was that her parents disliked her boyfriend. I always had the feeling that Maggie became a nurse to please her family, not herself.

The whole thing was a shame. She was a good, good person. Though people on the staff found her really immature, they liked her a lot. They were motherly toward her. "Look, Foster, you've got to do this or that." I mean if she had been nasty and acted as if she didn't care, she would have been out on her ear ages before.

She also really tried. One thing in her favor was that when she was unsure of something, she would always question. She would never do something to a patient and then tell you what she'd done. On weekends she came in half an hour early to get things going. If some of the people who had it all together in terms of organization gave as much as Maggie gave, you'd never had to worry about anybody.

But Maggie was hired as a staff nurse. A staff nurse at Central has certain responsibilities. One is charge. Maggie couldn't fully carry out the responsibilities for which she was being paid. Nor could she be counted on in an emergency.

That wasn't fair to the other staff members. It affected the organization of the floor. I had to adjust my assignments according to Maggie's weaknesses. Though none of us wanted her to go, clearly she could not continue to work at Central Hospital.

I broke the news when I gave Maggie her semi-annual evaluation. The evaluation was bad, no better than the previous one had been. After going over it with Maggie point by point, I told her as gently as I could that while she was a good person and not a bad nurse in certain circumstances, a busy floor in a city hospital was not the right place for her.

Maggie started to cry. "I'm no good," she said. "I'm a horrible, rotten person. I'll never be any good in this world." She went on in that vein, being really hard on herself. I felt so sorry for her.

"Maggie," I said, "a lot of us have failures in life. That doesn't mean we're failures as people."

"I'm going to be a waitress."

"Maggie, for god's sake. You've been in nursing school. You've spent three years getting a diploma. You're taking courses to get your B.S. You've given so much to this. Why be a waitress? That would be such a waste."

"I can't make it."

"Look. You're having problems being a staff nurse on an acute floor. That doesn't mean there aren't places for you. You could work in a nursing home or in community nursing, where acute situations aren't happening but patient care is important."

She kept talking about how she wasn't good enough to make it in this world. It was really sad. I seemed to me that she probably needed some help. But I didn't think I knew her well enough to say so, and it's probably the last thing she needed to hear from me. So I just listened. At one point I did ask Maggie if she had anybody she could really talk to.

"My boyfriend."

"Anybody else?"

She said there were a couple of people. I said, "Maggie, I think you ought to sit down and think about yourself and about what you want out of life. Then maybe it would be good for you to talk to somebody." I didn't say "professional." Hinting was all I felt I could do.

Maggie wasn't fired. She was asked to resign. On her last

day, I gave her some perfume and wrote her a note wishing her the best of luck. She wrote back thanking me for being considerate and for treating her well. Later we heard that she had gone to work at a smaller hospital near her home. A lot of middle-aged RNs are in charge. With luck, they'll mother her and help her gain confidence. Maggie functions there in patient care, and I'm sure she functions well.

I was very upset about the whole episode with Maggie. I felt sorry for her because she was such a misfit in her chosen situation, and I liked her. Knowing she shouldn't be at Central didn't make it easy for me to get her out. Having hospital backing didn't make it easy. The director and associate directors of nursing all felt something had to be done about both Maggie and Alice. I knew that. I knew Miss Craig wasn't blaming me. But I was blaming myself. I kept thinking, "It's my fault these people are the way they are."

These experiences helped me grow as a person. I came out of them feeling stronger as a head nurse. Though I didn't like being part of the decision-making, I realized that I couldn't let things go on as they were. I had to do something, and I did it. Maybe I became slightly hardened to the fact that I was hurting a person, because I could see that the greater good was the good of the patients.

The good of the patients is what I try to keep uppermost in my mind when I'm having problems with staff. That to me is the only thing that makes it possible to go through the hell of disciplining a co-worker.

I first learned about that kind of hell when I was a staff nurse at Metro and reported an LPN for the way she was treating patients. Talk about trauma. Mrs. Paulson was a big black woman who worked the eleven-to-seven shift. She would get patients on and off the bedpan very roughly, as if she were turning a sack of potatoes or moving a sack of garbage. She would leave people on bedpans for hours. When patients wet the bed, she yelled at them. In fact, she yelled at patients for many things. They could be terminal patients, senile patients, anybody. I never saw her hit a patient, but she sure as heck yelled at them.

I saw all these things whenever I rotated to nights. I wasn't strong enough then to say to Mrs. Paulson, "You're too harsh with patients. I want you to do it this way." I was afraid.

Instead, every time she went to do something in a patient's room, I would go in and help her so she wouldn't yell at the patient. I would compromise by saying to myself, "Maybe if I show her the right way, she'll do it the right way. She won't go on treating patients as she has been."

That didn't work. I don't think Paulson had it in her to realize how harsh she was. I don't think she had the motherliness, the compassion, the feeling of warmth necessary to understand that she was hurting patients.

One or two of the other nurses must also have seen that there was a problem, because they would answer patients' lights themselves rather than let Paulson go in. None of us had the courage to do anything.

The incident that finally pushed me to report Paulson was hearing her yell at a patient who had asked for a bedpan.

"You're always on the bedpan!" Paulson exploded. "What do you want the bedpan for again?"

By this time I was fed up with having to watch her constantly. So I went to Katie, and then to the supervisor.

Katie supported me. But even so, the aftermath was extremely uncomfortable. I had to sit in a meeting with Mrs. Paulson and say in front of her what I thought she was doing wrong. The union got in on the whole thing. So did the National Association for the Advancement of Colored People. Katie and the other administrators had to deal with those groups. I had to deal with Paulson. She accused me in the meeting of being prejudiced against blacks. The next time I worked nights with her, she found the occasion to jab me hard in the ribs with her elbow.

"Oh, excuse me, I didn't mean to do that," she said. She meant it, all right. She really hurt me. Unfortunately, I guess my complaint wasn't documentation enough to get Paulson fired. So far as I know, she's still there.

It was very hard for me to go through all that. It's hard for me now to give a bad evaluation to somebody who isn't doing well. It would be much easier to smile and say, "Yes, yes, you're doing a wonderful job."

But it's not fair for people to stay in institutions forever and time after time receive good evaluations they don't deserve. If the nursing administration doesn't know that certain nurses are not doing their jobs, the patients suffer.

People scream and cry about the necessity of good health care. I want to see patients get good care. As in any job, there are a few people in nursing who are cruel. I don't know what makes them cruel. But I'm not there to be a psychiatrist, and I'm not there to tolerate people being cruel to patients.

The morning after Mrs. Jackson got the word from Miss Craig, I returned to Eight Cook with my stomach full of tension. I expected that Jackson would fight the decision. I was also apprehensive about the rest of the staff. An associate director of nursing had warned me that some of the other long-time employees might be wondering where they stood themselves, perhaps thinking, "If Mrs. Jackson could be let go after so many years, what about me?" I expected some tension from the staff.

But I honestly didn't expect anything worse than tension. I think people sense who's good and who isn't. No one on the staff had gotten bad evaluations except Jackson. Several people, including Payne and one or two other black staff members, had received excellent evaluations. They knew they were functioning well. They knew I knew it.

I made up my mind that if anyone came to me and asked me why Mrs. Jackson had been asked to leave, I would be as truthful as I could. But I wasn't going to hold a general meeting and tell people why.

When I got to the floor, Sharon was standing at the nurses' station. I went up to her. Quietly, I asked, "What happened with Mrs. Jackson?"

Sharon answered me with surprise in her voice. "She came up after the meeting, cleaned out her locker, and left."

"What about the others?"

A slight smile. "You could have cut the tension with a knife."

Things were somewhat touchy that day. When Mrs. Payne came on duty and said hello to me, she was cool. The atmosphere in general seemed subdued. But the only person who mentioned Mrs. Jackson to me was Stephanie. As we stood at the meds cart doing the change-of-shift narcotics count, she mentioned Jackson in a whisper and said, "That needed to be done, but I don't know how you did it."

I said, "It wasn't very easy."

No one else said a word, not that day and not afterwards. We never heard a sound from Mrs. Jackson.

11

KELLY O'BRIEN RETURNS

"Obviously the nurses on this floor don't have enough work to do. I'll have to see about getting some more patients up here."

The comment came from behind me in the nurses' station. It was clearly intended for my benefit. I was sitting at the desk, where I had just taken information on a new admission over the phone.

"Well, if it isn't!" I said without turning. "The boy groom, back from his honeymoon."

"Right, and the whole place falls apart when I'm gone."

I gave Dr. Sam Polen the dirtiest look I could. He laughed. He was looking up from a chart he was writing in to watch Jennie, who was balancing on a chair taping a MERRY CHRISTMAS sign of red, green, and gold metallic fringe over the clock.

Polen said, "You call this nursing?"

"It's my lunch hour!" Jennie wailed. "I've done it all on my lunch hours!"

All is right. There was a tiny tree with wrapped presents underneath on the back counter, a plastic Santa Claus on the front counter, two green paper trees hanging from the light fixtures, and decorations all over the walls. Fringe. Sateen balls. Icicles. Sleigh bells. A big sheet full of Santa heads with the name of an Eight Cook nurse written on each beard.

"You've got to admit we have the best decorations in the

177

hospital," I said to Polen. "More patients want Eight Cook than any other floor."

"You've done a study?"

"While you were gone."

Polen had been married in Connecticut and then gone away for two weeks. I hadn't seen him to talk to him since he had come back to the hospital.

"So how was the wedding?"

Polen got a big grin on his face. "Well, there was a big party Friday night, and Saturday morning there was a brunch, and we got married late Saturday night, and there was another brunch Sunday morning at this classy hotel."

"Oh, isn't that nice. Sounds like there's a little money somewhere."

Polen ignored my sarcasm. He started telling me he had worn his tallith, a shawl that many Jewish men wear at services.

"I wore it when I was bar mitzvahed and when I got married," Polen said. "The next time I'll wear it is when I'm in the coffin."

"You should start going to services," I told him. "How do you expect to stay good?"

"Awwww, it's a bunch of baloney. Rabbis are all con men. They're all politicians."

"Some are, some aren't. I have a lot of respect. . . ."

"You would."

"There are some good ones," I said, "just as there are some good doctors and some bad doctors. Now you and I know there are a few bad doctors walking around!"

"Not in this hospital," said Dr. Paul Darnell, ambling into the nurses' station.

Darnell was Central's chief of surgery. He had a reputation for being temperamental in the OR, but I had never seen him act that way on the floor.

"How's Emerald Lynch doing?" Darnell asked Polen.

"Better today. The debridement seems to be doing some good. Her temp's down, and the wound looks as if it's beginning to heal."

Debriding Lynch meant cutting away dead tissue along the edges of her incision once a day, after giving her a shot of Demerol.

The doctors had begun the debridement because Lynch was still not healing properly.

"She still in a good mood?"

Polen gave Darnell an ironic look. "She's sassy, if that's what you mean."

Darnell smiled. He hoisted a hip onto one of the desks and lit his pipe. "You should have seen the way she treated Ed Lefcourt when he was here. She'd tell him to get his ass the hell out of the room. She'd say, 'You think you're so smart because you're chief resident. Shit, that don't mean a thing to me!' Lefcourt gave it right back to her. 'Emerald, shut your mouth!' "

Darnell took a long, slow puff and added, "Lynch is one of the few people who really get along with Ed Lefcourt."

Polen and Jennie and I all cracked up.

After a moment I said to Darnell, "You asked about her mood. I don't believe her mood. She keeps saying, 'I'm going to lick this thing. I'm going to make the best of it.' She's incredible. I keep wondering when she's going to crash."

"I know," Darnell said. "One of these days she's going to have to come down."

Since Darnell seemed especially relaxed at that moment, I decided to see what I could find out about Emerald's boyfriend's brown paper bag. What I had learned so far was that the bag contained not food but money. According to the night nurses, Emerald and Larry sat and counted bills all evening.

Darnell knew about the money and smiled when I brought it up. "Yeah," he said "they're into numbers or something. I think they're part of the Black Mafia."

The phone rang. It was James in Admissions. He told me that Kelly O'Brien was being readmitted to the hospital that afternoon.

The only thing I was surprised about was that Kelly had stayed out as long as he had.

"He wants to come back to Eight Cook," James said. "I know he's a lot to take care of both physically and psychologically. I'll give you a choice. Are you people fed up with him? Do you want him back, or do you want me to send him to another floor?"

In all my months on Eight Cook, James had never asked me that about a patient. I guess he really did know how much was involved in Kelly's care. All James would have had to do was tell the O'Briens there were no beds on Eight. Kelly would never have known.

I said, "Well, as far as I'm concerned, he can come back. But let me ask a couple of other people, because they take care of him more than I do."

So I found Ann Sullivan, the supervisor, and I asked a couple of nurses. Everybody said, "Oh, bring him back."

I called James and told him to send Kelly to Eight.

Kelly had been home just five days.

Kelly O'Brien returned to Eight Cook at 1:30 that afternoon. He was brought up in a wheelchair by his son, Mike. Kelly seemed scared and really upset about coming back in. But I think he also felt reassured to be back in familiar surroundings, because he smiled when I went up to him.

"Look at that smile!" I said.

"I have to smile when I see my girl!"

"You are so full of baloney!"

We put Kelly in 841, the room closest to the nurses' station, with Robert Shorey, also a retired policeman, also a Rose patient. Mr. Shorey was a few years older than Kelly. After having had a colostomy some months before, he had gone home and received radiation treatments as an outpatient. Then he became very weak, couldn't eat, and started having a lot of diarrhea. He was back in the hospital to be stabilized.

Mr. Shorey was very feisty and sarcastic. He'd complain so he wouldn't have to do anything. "Ohhhh, my back. Ohhhhh, I can't walk. Just let me go back to sleep, girls. Come on, go away. Let me go back to sleep." We'd have to say, "Mr. Shorey, for god's sake, stop your carrying on. You're going to get up and walk. Come on. Let's go." None of this was very serious. He was an old man. He had a couple of sisters who came in quite frequently, but his wife had been dead many years. For a while he had lived with a house-keeper who had also died. In the last year he had gone progressively downhill. I felt sorry for him.

When we took Kelly into the room, I introduced him to Mr. Shorey.

"Just call me Kell," Kelly said.

"Just call me Bob," Mr. Shorey said.

I said, "I know the two of you are going to get along well, because you both listen to the same music station."

I didn't say that Ron calls it "dentist's office music." Kelly played this station all the time. You could always hear the music floating out to the nurses' station.

We got Kelly into bed and got an IV started on him. Then I took his son down the hall to talk.

"Dad had a few good days, but then he got pretty sick," Mike said. Mike had Kelly's bushy eyebrows and his sort of teasing smile. "For the first few days, he was really in good spirits. He was sitting up, watching TV, talking to everybody. He was part of the family. Then he began to get very weak. All he could do was lie in bed and sleep. He started having diarrhea and vomiting. It got really bad."

Later I found out that Kelly's hemoglobin had dropped to 8. It had been 11.4 when he went home. It should have been up around 13 or 14. Apparently the radiation gastritis was still causing him to lose blood, which was why he had become so weak.

He was bleeding everywhere. Not frank blood. You couldn't look at his stool and say it was bloody. But minute amounts of blood were continuously seeping out as a result of the irritation. Over a period of time, the minute amounts added up to a lot of blood. When the hemoglobin is that low, the body doesn't get good oxygenation, and the person grows very weak.

About an hour after Kelly came back to the floor, we had to get him and two other patients downstairs for a chest X-ray. One escort arrived for the three of them. They were all in wheelchairs. I decided to go along. With one of us holding the elevator door open, the escort and I could easily manage the three patients.

As things turned out, I was glad to be along. One of the patients was suffering ICU psychosis. She was very paranoid. When we arrived in X-ray, she said to me in a very loud voice, "I'm first. I want you to know that I go first to get the X-ray, and then I go right back upstairs."

A couple of visitors looked at the woman, and the people at the desk glanced up. I went over to them and said, "Look, that lady wants to go first, but this guy"—meaning Kelly—"is really weak. If you take him first, I'll take him right back up." They did.

In the elevator, Kelly said to me, "You take good care of me."

"That's because you're special."

"That's my girl."

There was a liveliness in Kelly, I thought. He had been so depressed before he went home that he hardly spoke to anybody. He was much perkier now. The few days at home had done him a lot of good. He looked weak, but not as bad as I expected him to look. In fact, he looked better than he had when he went home.

As I was getting on the elevator at the end of the day, I heard Kelly and Mr. Shorey talking back and forth about a football game they were listening to on the radio.

On the street a few minutes later, something Sharon had told me earlier suddenly registered. She had been talking to Kelly shortly after he had been readmitted, and in the course of the conversation, he said to her, "I'm not going to make it out of here this time."

I had a funny feeling that Kelly knew what he was talking about. It seemed to me, as I thought it over, that he had probably made a decision.

12

RON

December had turned gray and bitter. Sitting at our favorite table in the front window of Mort's Deli, waiting for our order to arrive, Ron and I warmed our hands on our cups of steaming tea.

Mort's is a fairly new place about seven blocks from our apartment. Whenever we're both off on a Sunday, we walk over there for brunch. It's nice, because it's time we set aside for ourselves when we don't do anything else. Usually we try not to talk too much about work or medicine at Mort's. But this particular Sunday was different, because I was facing the need to come to some decision about the oncology floor. I needed a sounding board.

Ten days had passed since the meeting with Miss Craig and Dr. Rose. Although Ron and I hadn't had time to talk the subject out, I'm sure I had brought it up with him at least once a day. I was turning the whole thing over in my mind a lot. More than I had expected to, given my original reservations. I really didn't know what to do. That's how I opened the conversation over brunch at Mort's.

"Ron," I said after we had started in on our usual lox and bagels, "I called this meeting because I can't decide about the oncology floor."

Ron handles my decisions by staying out of them. However, he's always ready and willing to help me clarify things.

He said, "Tell me what's been going through your mind."

183

For the next half hour it all came pouring out—everything I had been thinking about a floor marked ONCOLOGY, about Rose, about Lefcourt, about Ron's and my future, about my staff. I talked especially about my staff. I knew I'd lose some of the best people on the floor, I told Ron, if all the patients on the floor had cancer. I didn't want to start over with a new staff.

"How do you know you'll lose them?" Ron asked.

"I just know how they react when we have several people dying."

"Why don't you ask them whether they'd leave or not? Maybe if they got excited about being part of a new project, they'd stay."

I hadn't really thought of it that way. What Ron said made sense. I sat there a minute and considered what I would say to Payne and the others.

Finally I said to Ron, "It's funny, because you're right that maybe they'd stay, and yet that doesn't seem to solve things in my mind."

Ron said, "I have the feeling that the staff's objections are not the problem. I think the problem is the objections you have yourself."

That struck home. I began to look at the situation in that light.

Ron ordered us some more tea. "Just what exactly is your main conflict?" he asked.

It was a question I found I could answer with no trouble.

"My main conflict is that I'm interested in oncology and I want to work with oncology patients, but I don't want to work with Rose and I don't want to be head nurse."

It was amazing how clear the whole issue had suddenly begun to seem. I couldn't help smiling.

"What's funny?" Ron asked.

"I'm just thinking how useless it always is for me to talk to you. You never say anything helpful."

"Thank you." He smiled back.

We talked some more. We had some more tea.

Mort's was filling up, and when at last a line started to form at the door, Ron and I paid our bill, bundled up again, and went back outside into the freezing wind.

Half a block later, when we could finally get our breath, I said, deadpan, "Now let me ask you a question. What should I do about the oncology floor?"

Looking straight ahead, Ron hunched deeper into his jacket and replied, deadpan, "You should figure out what you would feel most comfortable doing and do it."

He bolted. I chased him all the way home.

When Ron told me he was going to be a doctor, I cried. I did not want to marry a doctor. My dream was to marry a Ph.D. in English or history, settle down in an ivy-covered environment, and raise children with a man who could spend some time being a husband and father.

Right or wrong, I had the idea that divorce was really prevalent among doctors. That upset me. So many married doctors I knew were running around. No matter what anybody else feels, I don't consider that a sign of a happy marriage. I don't want that for myself.

My mother says if people want to run around, they can, no matter what their occupation. But I think it's easier for a doctor to have an affair than, say, a construction worker or a cook in the local diner. Doctors have more money. It's feasible for a doctor to support two families. Doctors have more opportunity, because they have more control over their schedules than other people and because of all the women they meet in a day's work, a lot of whom would like to land a doctor.

I also wanted a husband who had a nine-to-five job. A lot of the doctors I knew came to the hospital very early and left very late. I don't know what their home lives were like, but it looked to me as if they were devoting all their time to the hospital. I thought they were fools. A lot of my friends had poor relationships with their fathers. I wanted children. I didn't want a non-father for a husband.

When I met Ron, he was a biology major. This was at the end of my second year in nursing school. June. At about 10:00 one Sunday night, my roommate Rebecca, who had just been talking on the telephone to her boyfriend, Bruce, invited me to go over to his apartment with her. I had my hair in curlers and didn't feel much like socializing.

I was still getting over my one big love. He was a med student, older, about twenty-five. Very sophisticated. He had his own apartment. He was into dance and would cook for me when I went up there. We had gone out for about three or four months. I was so infatuated with this guy I think I would have done anything. But I was more involved than he was. One weekend he went to New Hampshire to visit his parents, and after that I didn't hear from him. I sulked for a month. Stayed in my room and cried.

"I'm going to bed," I told Rebecca.

"Oh, come on," she said. "Joe is going to be there."

That interested me. Joe was Bruce's roommate. Both were freshman med students. I had met Joe a couple of times and kind of liked him. So I went.

Bruce had invited a few other people over. Ron was one of them. He was a friend of Bruce's from high school and was home for the summer from the University of Michigan. When Rebecca and I got to the apartment, Ron was sitting in a corner talking with another girl. We were introduced. Then I just started teasing Bruce and carrying on with him and Joe. I didn't really say anything to Ron at all.

A few days later when I was in the dorm studying, Rebecca came in from seeing Bruce and said, "Guess what? I have a date for you!"

I thought, "Oh, good, Joe!" I said, "With whom?"

"Ron."

"Who's Ron?"

"The guy you met at Bruce's apartment."

"Oh, dear god," I said. "I'm not interested in going out with him." To me Ron had looked like a twerpy little kid. He was just my age, and I had been going out with guys four or five years older. At that time, he weighed less than I did. He was short. I just wasn't interested.

"For god's sake," Rebecca said. "It's only a blind date."

I let her talk me into it. The four of us went to a movie and then out to eat. At the end of the evening, I invited Ron to a coffeehouse affair at school the following week. I wasn't interested in him, but I needed a date.

We started going out. Almost every time we went out, we went to a movie. Or we went to a concert. Ron was interested in classical music. I wasn't. I was bored. At the beginning I went out with him only because I didn't have anything else to do. For the longest time—most of the summer, I guess—I just considered him a friend.

But then things began to go really fast.

By the time Ron left to go back to Ann Arbor for his third year of college, things were hot and heavy between us. I was very upset about his leaving.

We wrote every day. Sometimes I wrote twice a day. I'd enclose crushed flowers from the garden in the envelopes. I thought our letters were so romantic. When I look at them now, I can't believe them. They're X-rated. We'll never be able to show them to our kids.

Ron teased me about my letters. He couldn't read my sentences, he said. I didn't put my periods in the right place. I was pretty hurt. English had never been my strong point, and I wasn't particularly proud of that in myself. I was so hurt by Ron's teasing that I took a grammar course. But a grammar course couldn't begin to solve the really serious problem of communication that began to develop between us.

Ron and I knew each other for four years before we were married. For three of those years—the first three—we lived hundreds of miles apart. Ron was at school in Ann Arbor; I was at Metro.

Things between us were off and on those three years. We had a lot of problems. Ron would come home for his breaks, and in between his breaks I would fly out there, but most of our relationship was conducted through letters and telephone conversations. We limited our talks on the phone to five minutes. Ron kept a timer going. His parents were supporting him through school, and he felt guilty about using their money for that kind of stuff. We'd be talking along, and I'd hear DING!

I didn't have much money either. To earn student air fare to Michigan that first year while I was still in school, I worked every other weekend at Mother of Mercy. When classes were over on Friday afternoon, I'd take a bus home to my parents' house, sleep for a while, then work the midnight-to-eight shift and the eight-to-four shift. At midnight I'd go back for two more shifts.

I got to Michigan four or five times that year, but it wasn't enough. It seemed to me that one of us was always coming or going. I'd see Ron and get to know a little more about him, and then we'd be separated for six weeks. We had fights. Not yelling fights, but clashes. I'd be crying on the phone, saying, "You don't love me!" I didn't see how I fit into his life. Things were blown out of proportion because we were constantly moving in and out of each other's lives.

Uncertainty about Ron's future added to the problems between us. During his first two years at Michigan, he had been considering a career in genetics research. In his junior year, he was having second thoughts about that. One of the alternatives he considered was medical school. When he told me this, I really didn't say anything. I wasn't that upset about it till Ron started applying to med schools in his senior year. By this time I realized that we were getting very serious.

That's when I cried. Just once, and not in front of him.

Ron applied only to medical schools here in his home town. One by one, they turned him down. The question of what Ron was going to do with his life was very much up in the air.

My life, on the other hand, was more or less set. I had graduated from nursing school and was working as a nurse. Curiously enough, none of the pressures of my relationship with Ron affected me at work. There I could ignore them. My mind was caught up in other things. I was working a lot of nights and evenings then, and I was very dedicated. The other nurses—and one in particular—teased me a lot about that.

"Stop running around here!" she'd say. "Doing this. Wiping that. Reading the Kardexes. If you don't sit down, you're going to kill yourself. I wish your man would come home and use up some of your energy so you'd stop running around like a nut!"

If Ron was in town, she'd say, "Your man is here and you still have all this energy? I don't know what the two of you do when you go out, but it must not be anything good!"

What was good, for me, was that year. I liked my job. I had my own apartment and liked that. I saw a lot of my friends. Despite the problems between Ron and me, knowing he was in my life meant I didn't have to worry about going out and finding other men. I could devote my energy to other things.

Ron was taking genetics courses that year. Shortly before

graduation, a genetics professor learned that Ron had not been accepted to med school. He said, "If you don't have anything to do next year, why don't you apply and get a master's degree in genetics while you're waiting to get into med school?" Ron did apply and got in.

That summer between his fourth and fifth years in Michigan was a bad one for us. Ron was working three-to-eleven as a stock boy in a pharmacy. I was rotating and working some weekends. I asked to work three-to-eleven as often as possible, but by the time we both got off work, it was midnight or later. We were so physically exhausted that we fought all the time. Sometimes we saw each other during the day, but this was long before I had begun to think seriously of converting to Judaism, and Ron didn't want his parents to know how serious we were about each other. Things were really tense.

By the end of the summer, I was pretty upset. Ron and I had been going out for two years. I loved him. I wanted us to make a commitment to each other. The class behind mine at Metro had graduated. Most of those kids with steady boyfriends had already begun to realize their dreams of getting married and setting up housekeeping. They kept saying to me, "Well, what about you?" I got to the point where I was ready to pop the next person who asked me when I was getting married.

I was just very frustrated by what was happening. I didn't *know* what was happening. I didn't even know whether Ron wanted to marry me. I had the feeling that when he got accepted to medical school, that was going to be the end of me.

The night before he left to go back to Michigan, we had a big blowup. We were lying on the floor at his parents' house, watching TV, and we started talking. Suddenly I got very upset and hyper. I started yelling at him. I had never done that before. It wasn't really yelling, because Ron's sisters were upstairs, and we were trying to keep our voices low. But I was being very dramatic and really giving it to him.

"You son of a bitch, you're using me!" I said. "You want all the good parts of the relationship, but you don't want to make a commitment." I got up and ran out of the room. I was crying.

Ron came after me. He tried to put his arm around me and comfort me.

I said, "Get your hands off me! Take me home! I don't want to have anything to do with you ever again!"

He said, "Don't you think I'm frustrated too? Don't you realize that I feel like a failure for not getting into medical school? I don't know what's happening with my life at all. Your life is already set. You can make plans for the future. I can't make any plans."

Of course I felt horrible about what I had been saying. I felt very sorry for Ron. I also felt I was being selfish. He told me that in addition to everything else he was worried about how to let his family know that he wanted to marry me. They knew I wasn't Jewish, but he hadn't let them know we were as serious about each other as we were. Because his parents had always been very nice to me, I hadn't realized how concerned Ron was about their reaction to us.

Ron and I put our arms around each other. We stood there in the kitchen, both of us crying, and made up. The next morning he left for Michigan. That night I called him. Somehow or other, as Ron started his fifth year of school and as I started my second year as a staff nurse at Metro, we had made a commitment to each other.

Long before the year was up, Ron was accepted into the medical school he wanted, which is not far from Central. Despite the concerns I had had about marrying a doctor, I was happy. I knew that was what he wanted. In June he came back to town to stay.

Because we had known each other under such stressful situations, Ron and I both felt it was necessary for us to get to know each other on a day-to-day basis before we took the final plunge into marriage. At the time I was living with a friend, Joyce, who was also a nurse. Ron took an apartment a few blocks away. He and Joyce's boyfriend spent so much time at our apartment that it was almost as if the four of us were living together. It was fun.

Everything else worked out well too. My rotating was good for the relationship. Ron got a lot of studying done while I was at the hospital. In addition to going to school, he had a parttime job, so we didn't see a lot of each other during the week, but we saw each other weekends, and the time we spent together was reasonably relaxed. We lived so close that we could walk back and forth very easily. With very little difficulty, we established the continuity we had often wondered if we would ever have.

Ron started medical school in September 1974. The following February I left my staff job at Metro to become a head nurse at Central. In March we became engaged. In October, four years and four months after we had met in Bruce's apartment, Ron and I were married.

One day at about the time of our first wedding anniversary, I called my mother to cry on her shoulder.

"I'm so upset!" I moaned. "I never see my husband! I might as well be divorced."

My mother has a cool head, and she really likes Ron.

"You've got to realize that he's got it really hard," she said. "You have to be good to him. You have to be understanding."

"I am understanding. But I want to see him."

"I almost never saw your father," she said. "Some weeks he worked seven days double-shift."

"Yeah," I said, "but I don't want that kind of marriage."

My mother said, "The two of you have to be thankful that you get along as well as you do."

I knew she was right. There's nothing I can do about Ron's schedule anyway. I just have to make the best of it. Everybody else who's married to a medical student goes through exactly the same thing. You just have to keep yourself active and your mind on other things.

So that night, because Ron was on call, I stayed up until 3:00 in the morning making a quiche, a stew, and a cake. Meals for half a week.

I've missed Ron since we got married. A med student's schedule is rotten. Depending on what rotation he's doing any given week, Ron may be on call Monday night till 9:00, Wednesday night all night, Saturday all day and all night. By the time he gets home Sunday morning, chances are I'll have gone to work already. On the nights he's not on call, he'll get home at about 5:30, and I'm usually in bed by 10:00 or 10:30 because I've been up since before 6:00 A.M. Considering that in those five hours we cook and eat dinner, clean up, and then I may do chores while he studies for an hour or two, we're not really spending much time together.

And what time we spend is likely to be tired time. At home in the evening, I may sit on the couch and read while Ron is sitting over his desk reading. There's companionship, but there isn't a lot of talking.

Such a marriage.

The situation is better now than it was. When we got married, I had been on Eight Cook only three months. I came home at night exhausted from the emotional stress. Ron was beginning his second year of med school. His schedule wasn't that bad. He'd be full of energy. Weekends when I'd work, he'd want to go out to a movie at night. I'd say, "Look, I really don't enjoy it because I'm so tired. I keep worrying about the fact that it's getting later and later and later."

I knew I shouldn't be that way. I wanted to enjoy the time. But usually the movie didn't end till 10:30 or 11:00 and we didn't get home till 12:00. I still had to get up by 6:00.

Ron kept saying to me, "I don't understand why you're so tired. You'd better make an appointment for a complete physical. Maybe you have mono. Have a CBC." That's a complete blood count, a diagnostic test for anemia and other conditions.

Then, nine months after we were married, Ron started his first rotation. It was surgery, one of the rougher rotations. That was Ron's learning experience. He had to get up at 5:30 in order to get to the hospital by 7:00 so he could make rounds with everybody before they went into the OR. When he came home at 5:30 or 6:00 at night, he looked dead. A couple of times when I got home late from work, I found him asleep on the couch.

"Poor baby!" I'd say to him. "Are you tired? I can't imagine why you're so tired. You should have a complete physical. Have a CBC. Maybe you have mono."

Ron is less tired now that he's accustomed to the rhythm of school. I, too, have more energy than I did when we were first married. Things have been pretty good on the floor. When I'm not depressed, as I was those first months at Central, I don't get nearly as tired.

Still, our schedules do cut down on our conversation time, and we both think that fatigue is a factor in our intimacy.

"We played more before we got married than we do now," I've jokingly said to Jackie Neill. "If it's once a week, I'm lucky!"

Ron and I have a real closeness, a physical need or desire to touch and be near one another. We do not like being separated. But from the standpoint of intercourse, neither of us is that gung-ho. Sometimes I'm so tired at night that all I want to do is sleep. I'm just not interested in anything more than kissing and holding.

We have talked about that. I keep reading books to see how we compare to everybody else. Whether or not we're normal. The books say that on the average, people our age who have been married a couple of years have intercourse two or three times a week. I really think the fact that Ron and I have intercourse less frequently has to do with our jobs.

Other people I've talked to with schedules like ours seem to have the same pattern. My friend Rebecca, whose husband is a surgical resident, said to me, "We haven't screwed in a month! He's on call every other night, and the nights he's home, he falls asleep in a chair at 9:00."

Or when Ron and I get together with our friends Steve and Susan, the four of us will joke about it. Steve is in Ron's class. Susan will say, "I could walk in front of him completely naked, and he wouldn't do anything because he's so tired!"

It's a comfort to know that they're going through the same thing we are. Actually, I think I'm more concerned because of what the books say is considered normal than I would be if I just paid attention to our own situation. Ron and I have a lot happening in our lives right now. With sex as with other things, we do what is comfortable for us.

Too little time together when we're both rested is the bad side of our schedules. There are some positive things. I really have the best of two worlds—married and single. I have Ron, and I have my nights when I don't have to cook dinner and can sit around with my hair in rollers and read or watch TV.

When Ron's on call all night and I'm off the next day, I'll usually call June Fong, a good friend from nursing school. Sometimes we'll go out and eat. Sometimes we go over to another friend's and just sit and talk. The first year Ron and I were married, a girlfriend and I got tickets to the ballet. Ron doesn't like ballet. I've always loved it. Because of Ron's schedule, I could do something I enjoy and he doesn't.

June lives next door. Jackie Neill is my best friend at the

hospital, and sometimes I do things with her after work or on our days off. But in a lot of ways I'm closer to June. We've gone through a lot together.

My best friend of all is probably Rebecca, my nursing school roommate who's now living in Ohio. I don't think a person has that many close friends. To me a friend is somebody to whom I can tell my gut feelings and who will support me. If I need something, that person is going to be there and really care about me, no matter what I say or do. A close friend is someone you don't hide your feelings from. I consider Ron's mother my friend, as well as my own mother. I can say a lot of things to them, and both are very supportive.

When Ron and I go out together, we often go with Steve and Susan or another couple who are both in Ron's class. Sometimes we'll all go to a movie. Sometimes we'll eat dinner in. Sometimes we'll go out to a restaurant. Before I met Ron, I thought going to restaurants was a waste of money. My parents never went to restaurants. Ron's always did. When he started taking me out to eat, I realized how nice it is, and how much you learn about food and different approaches to food.

I don't socialize with people from work. If I was not a head nurse, I wouldn't care. But being quote an authority figure, I feel that if I mingle with the crew, I wouldn't be able to be as impersonal an administrator as I try to be. If certain doctors or nurses were known to be my friends, other people might think I was giving my friends special treatment sometimes. That wouldn't be fair.

My main extracurricular activity is reading. I really enjoy reading. If I am not reading, I feel I'm not doing anything for myself. My tastes are pretty varied. Recently I've read books on the Swedish social system, on homosexual adolescence, on telling children about death, on Marie Antoinette, and on runaway wives.

I also enjoy cooking. Since Ron is at the hospital so many evenings, I get out of the habit of wanting to cook when I get home. So often I'll spend an evening or part of a day off cooking for the week. I'll make out menus first, then put together some meatballs and roast a chicken and perhaps make other dishes.

The first year we were married, Ron was cooking as much as I was. At least three nights a week he would have dinner ready when I got home. He could do it because he was getting home himself at about 3:00 or 3:30 in the afternoon. He doesn't make cakes or anything fancy, but he'll do roasts and steaks. He enjoys cooking.

He helped with lots of things that first year. I don't know many guys his age, but compared to the husbands of my mother's friends, he was helping out a lot. He didn't like doing laundry, but he did it.

Since that first year, though, he has had very little time to do anything around the apartment. He usually does the dishes, but he's really not home much, and I'm doing just about everything.

Sometimes that becomes annoying. One day he said to me, "I'm running out of undershirts." The next day he said it again. I felt like saying, "If you're running out of undershirts, go to the laundromat and wash some."

Okay, he doesn't have time right now. He's putting in a long week. But when his schedule is lighter, I will expect him to help out a little. If two people are sharing a house, one shouldn't be stuck with all the chores just because she's a woman.

On the other hand, Ron has helped me a lot with things connected with work. I talk with him about things at work fairly often. Sometimes I want his opinion; other times I just want him to listen. Sometimes he acts as devil's advocate. If I describe something I don't like, he'll say, "Well, think how you would feel if you were a supervisor." That always makes me think.

A couple of times in the beginning when I had a very difficult evaluation to write, I asked Ron to look at it and tell me how it sounded. "Does it make sense?" I'd say. "If you were reading that, would you understand what I mean?"

Now that I feel more comfortable in my role as head nurse, I no longer ask him to look at evaluations. But I may still ask for his help when I'm working on one. When I want to use a certain word, but I find from the dictionary that it doesn't have quite the meaning I'm looking for, I'll say to Ron, "If I want to say such and such a thing, what's another way of saying it?"

He also supports me when I'm giving a poor evaluation. Doing that always makes me feel bad, even though I know the person doesn't deserve a good one. Ron will say, "If someone is goofing off, it would be unfair to the patients to give that person a good evaluation." I know that's true, but I feel stronger having heard another person say it.

From all the books I've read on marriage, you're not supposed to unload your problems at work on your spouse. I think, too, that that's unfair. I really like it on the days when Jackie Neill is on, because I can get out some of my gut feelings to her and not have to batter Ron about them. Every once in a while I get on a kick where he and I are not going to discuss work or school at all. That usually lasts about a day and a half. It always helps me to talk things out with Ron. Unless he starts complaining, I guess I'll keep on doing it.

Lately we've been doing a lot of our talking at Mort's Deli. The whole situation is conducive to good conversations. It's a time of day when we're not tired. The place has a nice atmosphere. Butcher block tables, lots of light. It isn't very expensive. Sometimes when we go out for dinner, I come away feeling it has been a waste of money. If there's a lot of food, I feel like a stuffed pig when I walk out. That's not comfortable. At Mort's we eat lightly. Lots of different kinds of people come in there. I love to sit and watch them out of the corner of my eye.

Ron and I sort of catch up on each other at Mort's. We may sit and talk about his parents or mine. Mostly we talk about our plans for the future. What we're going to do after Ron graduates. When we'll be able to afford to have a child. What branch of medicine Ron will specialize in. Where we want to live. I call it daydreaming.

Ron's being a doctor doesn't concern me much any more. Knowing him better and myself better, I don't think things will be any tougher for the two of us together than they would have been if he had gone into genetics research.

I know his being a doctor will take time away from me and from what I imagine as the ideal family life. That bothers me. But Ron is an aggressive personality. He puts himself completely into whatever he's doing. I've come to the realization that he could stack boxes in a drugstore for the rest of his life, and I wouldn't see any more of him than I'm going to see when he starts practicing medicine.

I think Ron and I can adapt to each other's lives and aspirations. I don't know what will happen if, when we are thirty or forty years old, we tire of each other. But now when there's a problem, we discuss it until we resolve it. If we ran into a problem we couldn't solve, I think we'd both be willing to get help, to go to somebody to talk things out and try to reach an understanding that way. I think we each have a firm commitment to solving our problems. I think we'll make our decisions together. I think we have a good bond.

13

FAMILY MATTERS

"Nurse! Nurse! Help! Help me!"

I was in the hall, and I started running. The voice was Mrs. Whittemberry's. Her husband, a Peruvian physician, had been admitted a few days earlier with about ten things wrong with him, including Parkinsonism and diabetes.

I was the first nurse to get into the room. Dr. Whittemberry was sitting up in his chair, turning blue. His wife, who was from the United States, was bending over him, screaming. On the bed was a plate of orange sections. Mrs. Whittemberry screamed at me that her husband had a piece of orange stuck in his throat.

"My god," I thought, "he's going to aspirate and die right here."

I pushed past Mrs. Whittemberry, got behind her husband's chair, and started trying to lift Dr. Whittemberry up so I could get my arms around his chest from the back. Sharon came in.

"Stat-page Anesthesia!" I snapped at her. "And Ann Sullivan!" Stat means it's not a code, but get here quick. Sharon got on the phone.

I was having trouble. I wanted to force the orange out of Whittemberry's windpipe using an abdominal thrust, a new technique I had read about but never tried. It involves picking up the person from the rear, putting your arms around the rib cage, and hitting the mid–sternal area with your fist. It's like giving someone a sharp hug. This forces exhalation of breath, which the old

199

method of hitting someone on the back may not necessarily do. Whatever is caught in the throat is supposed to pop out.

But with the back of an armchair between us, I could not get a good hold on Dr. Whittemberry. I kept trying to kick the chair out of the way. Meanwhile, Mrs. Whittemberry was hovering over us, screaming, "Ohhhhhh! Ohhhhhh! He's gonna die! He's gonna die! He's gonna die!"

Sharon saw my problem and came to help as soon as she hung up the phone. She couldn't get to us. Mrs. Whittemberry was blocking her path. Sharon tried first one way around her, then another. She lost maybe two seconds. Seconds counted. Mrs. Whittemberry was making so much noise that she couldn't hear Sharon ask her to move. She kept screaming, "Ohhhhh, god, he's gonna die, he's gonna die!"

"OUT OF THE ROOM!"

The voice was mine. Never before in my life had I yelled at a family member.

For an instant, Mrs. Whittemberry looked at me with her mouth open. Then she turned and went out into the hall.

As Sharon grabbed the chair and pulled it aside, I grabbed Whittemberry and hugged, hitting my fist into his chest. The orange didn't come out, but it must have dislodged, because he stopped turning blue.

Just then the emergency team from Anesthesia arrived. Someone put a laryngoscope down Dr. Whittemberry's throat, located the orange section, and pulled it out with a pair of tongs.

My heart was pounding. My chest was pounding. Everything was pounding. But Dr. Whittemberry was all right.

His wife never said a word to me about my ordering her out of the room, and I never said a word about it to her.

Members of a patient's family don't often constitute a problem on a hospital floor. The occasional exceptions are usually hovering wives. Mrs. Whittemberry was typical. She was overly conscious of everything that was happening to her husband. She acted as if she thought the nurses weren't doing enough for him. She herself treated him with so much concern you would have thought she was his grandmother.

To me she just didn't treat him like a man. I walked into the room one day and said, "Good morning, Dr. Whittemberry. How are you?"

"He's fine," his wife answered.

I started to feed him. Because of the Parkinsonism, the man couldn't really talk, but he was capable of answering questions with a word or two, so I was trying to make conversation. I didn't want him to feel he was a blob lying in bed. I figured the man had functioning brain cells. Even if I'm only in the room a few minutes, I try to talk to people as though they're adults.

I said, "Can I ask you a personal question?"

He looked at me. I knew he was saying yes.

I said, "What kind of practice were you in?"

His wife said, "Oh, he was in general practice for many years and had a thriving practice right outside Baltimore."

I asked Dr. Whittemberry another question. Again his wife answered it. I made a shushing gesture to her. But she went on answering every question for him.

"God," I thought, "I hope I never do that to Ron."

Mrs. Whittemberry's hovering actually jeopardized her husband's life. That's the only time I've seen anything like that. But I often see women taking over for their husbands, especially when the man is very debilitated. The woman ceases to treat her husband like a functioning male. Instead, she becomes a mother, feeding, helping to wash the man's bottom, doing all the motherly, nursey things—and doing the talking. She treats her husband like a child. You look at the man's eyes, and he's saying, "Please. I can answer." It seems to me that the husband wants to answer, but he doesn't want to tell his wife to shut up.

This was really brought close to home for me when Ron's grandfather was dying. He was no longer the doctor, the strong one. His wife answered for him every time a question was put to him. I finally got to the point of saying, "Grandma, please. I'm talking to Granddaddy. Let him answer." I'd be thinking to myself, "This is the man you slept with. Had children by. He has led a functioning adult life. He's still a human being. Please. Let him answer for himself."

It's much more common for a woman to treat a man this way than the other way around. I've seen some men be very solicitous with their wives, and treat them with a certain kindness and warmth that I usually attribute, rightly or wrongly, to women. The solicitous man might offer to help you move his wife up in the bed. But it's rare to see a man put his wife on the bedpan. Mostly men fill the water pitchers. Men aren't used to being around people who are sick. I don't think they're used to cleaning rear ends or doing personal things to somebody, whereas women are. When a woman patient leaks urine onto the paper pad under the bedpan, the husband will find a nurse and say, "My wife is wet." If the situations are reversed, the woman will take the pad out from under her husband. Maybe women are more bred to being mothers. Maybe it's just that our society has taught women to be the doers, the givers.

At any rate, a lot of women get right in there and take over. They end up doing everything for their husbands. Maybe they think they're helping. Often they're not. Say, for example, a right-handed man has a major stroke, has partial return in his right arm, and can use his left hand. That man should be learning how to feed himself. It's fine if his wife wants to cut his meat. But often, because the man drops the meat on the way to his mouth or because he's sloppy, his wife ends up feeding him, which is the worst thing to do in a situation like that.

I have tried to nicely alert hovering wives. I usually wait till I feel comfortable and then say something like, "Look, the best thing for your husband is to let him do as much as he can for himself. If you talk about your grandchildren and let him answer you back, that allows him to feel that he's still important and still able to function on his own. We're really helping him get better if all of us don't answer for him."

But it's hard to convince some women, because they see themselves as martyrs and seem to get satisfaction out of mothering their husbands.

There's another kind of hovering wife who's harder on the nurses than on the patients. This is the wife who constantly pesters the nurses to do more for her husband. A lawyer, Mr. Fineman, came in recently for gall bladder surgery. A cholecystectomy is not a minor procedure, but it's routine. We never have any real problems with cholie patients. Well, according to this man's family, you would have thought he had been laid out already.

The wife was going around moaning, "Ohhhhhh, my poor

husband, my poor baby," wringing her hands. They had private duties on nights and evenings. The wife arrived at 10:00 in the morning. One of the new grads took care of Mr. Fineman post-op, and the wife really gave the kid a hard time. "When are you going to rub his back? When are you going to straighten his bed? When are you going to check his dressings?" It was the same thing every time I went in the room. "When are you going to get him some Vaseline for his lips?"

One day I went in, and the wife's sister, who was sitting there with the wife, said to me, "Ask him how he is."

I said, "What?"

"Ask him how he is, dear."

I thought, "I'm going to kill somebody." So just to placate her, I went up to Mr. Fineman and said, "How do you feel?" Since he was groggy, all he could do was groan, of course. I thought, "Oh, god!"

Mrs. Fineman was standing there wringing her hands. I said, "What are you so upset about?"

"Oh," she said, "he's so sick. Ohhhhhh. . . ."

I said, "I'm not being flip with you. I hope you understand that. But he is fine."

She looked at me in amazement. "Is he really?"

"Really. If he was not stable, they would never have sent him back to a regular floor after surgery. They would not be getting ready to take out his intravenous. He's going to be going home soon. He's just fine."

Mrs. Fineman wasn't nearly as bad as Mrs. Gresham. Judge Gresham came in and had a colectomy done for a tumor in the colon. He was a nice man, but his wife was a *nudj* first-class. She was aggressive, bossy, domineering—you name it, she was it. Unbelievable. A complainer from the first word. She was on the offensive even before she knew what the floor was like. Nothing was right. She complained that the place was dirty. She reported a nursing assistant to Miss Craig for not letting her stay beyond visiting hours without permission. She was having us page supervisors and doctors two or three times a shift.

Just before a weekend, Mrs. Gresham fired the private-duty nurse she had hired for days, then drove the supervisor and me both nuts because she was having trouble getting another for

Saturday and Sunday. Another day she kept calling people in to irrigate her husband's nasogastric tube. That only needs to be done a few times a day. One of us would irrigate the tube, then write down on the I&O sheet that we had done so and discover that somebody else had just done it. This wasn't dangerous, just unnecessary.

Dealing with Mrs. Gresham was so irritating that one doctor told me, "I refuse to go in the room while she's in there!" Everybody disliked going in the room. We all avoided it if we could. It was strange. The more attention she tried to get for her husband, the less he got.

But the main reason Mrs. Gresham was a problem was that she took up the nurses' time, time we should have been spending in more important ways.

As for whom I'd rather deal with, I'll take any patient's family over the Dietary and X-ray departments.

At least you can understand, to a certain extent, why families are the way they are. I've never run into what I would call an irate relative. Most families, even when they're worried, are pleasant. Some seem to really understand what nursing is and let you know that they appreciate what you do for them. Some go out of their way to let you know. They'll write the staff a letter or send us a box of cookies. It's not that we need the food; it's the thought that's appreciated a lot.

A few times I've gotten close to family members. Tony Seletti's wife was someone I was very close to. She kept a lot of things from Tony, then she'd come out of the room and sort of fall apart with me. Their 19-year-old son was a dope addict. Tony's wife would go home after visiting Tony in the hospital and find the TV or the radio gone—sold—and the kid zonked out on the couch. When she tried to kick the son out, he threatened the daughter, who was 16 and pregnant.

The Selettis didn't communicate the way Ted Roger and his wife did. I think Mrs. Seletti used the nursing staff for a sounding board. She felt a lot of guilt and frustration. This was at a time when my parents were having trouble with one of my brothers, who was selling pot.

So I would tell Mrs. Seletti I knew how hard it was for her, because I knew how hard it was for my mother. I just tried to let her know that other people were heartbroken by the same situation she was going through. It gave us common ground. After Tony died, she wrote me a couple of times. I wrote back. I told her about work and about Ron, and I also told her I thought her husband had been a really good man. At some point one of us stopped writing. She had her life, I had mine. But there was a real warmth between us while we were both taking care of Tony.

Most problems a nurse runs into with patients' families don't amount to much. Occasionally a relative will pose as Dr. So-and-so and ask to read a chart. Some families are sneaky and say they're going to visit Mrs. Jones when they're really going to visit Mrs. Smith, because they know Mrs. Jones doesn't usually have visitors, and they get themselves an extra visitors' pass that way. I can see three people in a room. But I think you have to be on the polite side. If you have a sick roommate, it's not fair to have four or five friends in there laughing and smoking.

Once in a while a visitor gets mad because he can't bring kids in. Visiting age is 16. If a patient is really sick, we ignore the rule. Otherwise we observe it, because kids get rambunctious, and it's not fair to the other patients. But I encountered a man recently who accused me of being a meanie because I wouldn't let him take two young children into their grandmother's room. She was fine. I suggested they visit downstairs.

The father got really loud, and one of the kids burst into tears. I felt like Scrooge. Later I felt mad. I thought the man was an ass, acting like that in front of his children.

An odd family situation comes up occasionally. I'm thinking of Jim Lloyd, a cancer patient in his early fifties. He was married, and he had a girlfriend. I don't know whether he and his wife had been living together or not. But when the doctors told him he was dying, the wife started coming in to be with him all the time, sort of taking over her wifely duties, and she yelled at him for letting the girlfriend visit.

Dr. Rose finally told Lloyd there was nothing more to be done for him in the hospital. He suggested to Lloyd that he go home and enjoy as much as he could the time he had left.

Lloyd wanted to go home with his girlfriend. His wife wanted him home with her. She started insisting that we teach her how to give his medication. He didn't want to be beholden to her. He wanted to learn to administer it to himself.

The nurses might have been caught in the middle of that battle, but one day Mr. Lloyd's daughter told me her mother wanted to speak to one of the doctors. I took the opportunity to ask where her father was going after his discharge.

The daughter said, "His girlfriend's. My mother's upset because she's his legal wife and she's legally responsible for him."

Which was true. So I called the doctor they wanted to see, and he talked things over with the patient and the family. I don't know what happened, but Mr. Lloyd went home with his girlfriend. We taught him to give his own medication.

Actually Rose had more to cope with in that situation than the nurses did. One morning he came in and said to me, "That Mr. Lloyd? You won't believe what happened. I was lying in bed, listening to my tapes, and at midnight I got a call from Mr. Lloyd's wife's cousin. He wanted me to tell Mr. Lloyd that he shouldn't let his girlfriend come into the hospital."

"What did you tell him?" I asked.

Rose laughed. "I said, 'The man's dying. I think he should have a right to see whichever one he wants to see. Don't you?' "

The cousin said he didn't. Rose told him he would take care of it in the morning and hung up.

"So," I asked Rose, "are you going to take care of it?"

"I am not!"

I listened to that story feeling glad that at least no family member ever calls a nurse in the middle of the night.

I've only had one really bad experience with a family member. This was after Ray Powell died—the fireman who had been so hostile at first, then finally broke down and cried.

Mr. Powell died during the day. His wife wasn't there at the time, which was a good thing. His death was horrible. There was so much blood all over everything that we really had a difficult time getting the room cleaned up so it would look all right when the family got in.

We were washing him, and as we turned him over, some blood oozed out of his nose onto the sheet. I remember it as being only a little splotch. Maybe it was bigger than I remember. I don't know. But because we had spent so long getting Mr. Powell and the bed cleaned up, and because we knew the family might arrive any minute, we put a pillow over the spot of blood instead of changing the sheet again.

From what I've seen, after a death most people want to touch part of the body of the person they cared about. If the body's covered, they're uncomfortable about reaching under the sheet. So when I help somebody wrap a patient, I usually leave an arm outside the sheet and make it look as natural as possible. We did that with Mr. Powell. We made him as presentable as we could and asked the patient in the next bed if he would mind sitting in the solarium for a little while.

The wife came in with Mr. Powell's sister, a nurse. The sister was a big woman who looked to me like a staunch, old-fashioned type. I had never seen her before. She had never been in. Mrs. Powell had told me that the only person in the family who was giving her any support was her father. The Powells had five children, Mr. Powell was dying, and nobody else in the family offered to make a meal for them or even drive the kids to Cub Scouts. So I was a little surprised to see this sister.

I liked the wife. I put my arms around her and went in the room with them. She held onto me and sort of cried. Then I left the room so the wife and the sister could be with the body in private.

A little while later, I saw them leave the room. I was giving out meds. The sister had her arm around the wife in a very protective way. The two of them came toward me. When they got in front of me, the sister raised herself up and said, "I've been a nurse for many years, and I've never seen a body left in such disgraceful condition."

I must have looked dumbfounded, because that's how I felt.

She said, "The blood under the pillow. That's a disgrace. I would never have left a body like that."

I said nothing. I was very upset. The whole staff really liked Ray Powell, and they had given a lot to him.

Mrs. Powell put her arm around me and said, "You girls did a good job for him. Thank you very much."

That helped. But the sister's words really stung.

Later I said something to one of the supervisors. "She's probably feeling guilty that she never did anything," the supervisor said. "She's taking it out on you. That's *her* problem."

Somehow it made me feel better to think the sister spoke out of guilt rather than out of anger with the nurses. I never did say anything to the staff about it. I thought they'd be angry, and I wouldn't have blamed them.

I'm sure the sister's comment would have bothered me under any circumstances. But I think it upset me more than it might have otherwise because she was not a regular visitor. I thought to myself, "You never even came in to see him, and here you are saying something like that." Nurses notice when family members don't visit patients. We think to ourselves, "The nurses are giving really good care, and the family never comes in."

That's being judgmental, because who knows what the family situation is? I say that because of a situation in my own family. My maternal grandmother has been in a mental institution since my mother was eight years old. Until she was sixteen, my mother visited her often. And then for years and years, because she could not bring herself psychologically to face my grandmother, she didn't visit. I know my mother feels very guilty about that.

Two years ago she finally went to visit her mother. I went along. I had not seen my grandmother since I was a toddler. She's in a state hospital several hundred miles from where my parents live. Because my grandfather was in the Army, the Army has been footing the bill all these years.

We found my grandmother in a building for incurables. We had to talk through one locked door, then another locked door. We went into a large sitting room. It was dimly lit, with a bunch of chairs against the wall, several big chairs in the center, an old beat-up piano in one corner, and a TV in another. All the women were sitting around in different positions. Some were half dressed. A couple of very dumpy-looking people were sitting there with their legs spread. None of them looked in touch with reality. They looked as if they had been in an institution for years and years. Very depressing. And I remember aides sitting around reading newspapers.

My mother picked out my grandmother. She was a very wizened-looking old lady with most of her teeth gone, no dentures, white hair cut very short, and a dirty dress on. She was just sitting there. She didn't remember my mother. When my mother mentioned the family's last name, my grandmother did start talking about some of her brothers with that last name. But she talked about them as if they were still children. My mother sat there and cried.

I found the nurses' station. A haggard, big-busted, prim-looking woman with a cap on was sitting there going through charts. Another nurse was behind her, pouring meds. I felt very uncomfortable under the circumstances, but I had to find out how my grandmother was doing.

I said to the nurse at the desk, "Can I ask you something about Mrs. Cole?"

She looked up as if to say, "Who are you?"

She said, "Who?"

"Mrs. Cole. I'd like to know how she is."

The two nurses exchanged glances.

The one at the desk said to me, "You never wondered how she was before. She hasn't had any visitors all these years. Why is everybody so interested all of a sudden?"

I pulled myself up and said, "I want you to know that my mother has not been able to accept what has happened to her mother. There were a lot of family problems. This is the first time she has been able to bring herself to come down here. I came with her, and I'd like to know how my grandmother is." Then I told the woman that I was a head nurse.

The nurse changed her tune. She told me respectfully what was happening with my grandmother.

I'm sure if those nurses cared about their patients, they felt the same indignation seeing me that I feel at times. I know I've come out to the nurses' station and said things like, "Hmph! That's the first time *they've* come!"

But because of the situation with my grandmother, I remind myself that when families don't visit patients, there may be extenuating circumstances. Maybe nobody can get in. Maybe there's some reason why they're not coming.

The situation with my grandmother gave me a different perspective on families. I have also gained a different perspective on nurses by being in the position of family myself. This has happened three times. The first time was when my mother was in the hospital for a hysterectomy. I'd see nurses go by laughing and carrying on when my mother would have her light on, and I'd think, "They're so crude. Don't they realize my mother's lying in there sick?"

Then I would think, "That's how all patients must feel. They're lying there. Maybe the nurse just got back from lunch, or she's having a rotten day. The patient doesn't see that. All the patient knows is that he or she is in pain, that the light is on, and that the nurse is standing out there carrying on."

Another time Ron's mother was in the hospital for a minor illness. I did private duty on her. I remember hearing some of what the nurses would say, and I'd think to myself, "They don't even care. They don't care whether the patient gets well or doesn't." Maybe they honestly did care, and their minds were occupied with something else. But I wasn't seeing that. I was seeing only the negative side.

Then when Ron's grandfather was in the hospital, and he had private-duty nurses, his grandmother would tell me that the floor nurses would refuse to help the private duties get my grandfather out of bed. One person could not do it alone, but the floor staff would say, "He has private duties."

I think Ron's grandmother is particularly hard on nurses. But what she said made me see things from a different point of view. I think it has made me a little more sympathetic to how nurses look to family members. I try to keep these things in mind, now, when I'm going around the floor. I try to treat family members as I would want to be treated if I were family. I always feel, "It could be me."

A really good family can help morale—both a patient's morale and the nurses'. But no family can keep up its own morale indefinitely. Even a family as supportive as Kelly O'Brien's.

The first few days after Kelly returned to Eight Cook, I saw that he was beginning to have problems with his family. First one of the people on three-to-eleven told me that Kelly's daughter, Pat, had said to the nurse, "I sure wish this would end."

Another day Mrs. O'Brien walked into the room, and I heard her say, "Kelly, I come in the room and you're asleep. I might as well go home."

He said, "Well, if you want to go home, go."

The next day while I was in doing something for Mr. Shorey, Mrs. O'Brien said to her husband, "Kelly, I come in to see you every day. I sit here all day long. You close your eyes, and you don't say anything to me."

He said, "Look, go home."

"Well, if that's the way you feel about it, I will."

She didn't. But you could tell they were getting tense with each other.

When you're in the situation Mrs. O'Brien was in, you can be a support just so long. There comes a time when you're running back and forth to the hospital, you know the person is going to die, and you have your own life. You think to yourself, "Why doesn't he get it over with?" I'm sure Kelly was intelligent enough to realize that his family was under a lot of strain.

It was as if they were going through an extended mourning period. If somebody dies very quickly, you don't have a chance to prepare for the death, but at least you don't suffer the physical drain, the long, drawn-out period of wondering, "Is he going to die today? Is he going to die tomorrow?"

People have lives outside the hospital. They have to get up, keep the house in order, buy groceries, eat, take baths, wash their hair. When somebody is sick as long as Kelly had been, the closest family members don't have even a few minutes to themselves. Everything's focused around the dying person. This sometimes goes on for months.

Most people I've seen do not begrudge the time. Yet it starts to show on them. It seems to show on women in particular. In the beginning, women come in, and they look pretty much together. Then as they spend more time in the hospital, the way they look becomes secondary. They stop having their hair done every week. They stop putting makeup on. They dress less carefully. I guess they figure they're just going to sit in the hospital all day long; nobody's going to look at what they wear.

They get circles under their eyes. They may lose weight. They've had time to prepare themselves for the patient's death, but in the process, their bodies have gone through hell.

That's what was beginning to happen to Mrs. O'Brien. She looked tired and haggard. No wonder. She was coming in at eight or nine in the morning and staying till ten at night. I think people have to do what they think best under the circumstances. Some family members cannot force themselves to sit in the room even if they love the person very much. But being in the hospital every day put a lot of strain on Mrs. O'Brien. She was worn out. She seemed to have so little push to her.

Pat really looked out of it too. I'm sure the whole thing was exacerbated by the fact that the Christmas holidays were coming up.

Bev Bowles had been talking with Mrs. O'Brien right along, but I decided I would try to have a little talk with her myself if things didn't seem to get better between her and Kelly.

As I had told Bev, I thought Mrs. O'Brien had begun to face the fact that Kelly was going to die eventually. Yet I didn't feel that the O'Briens were making plans. I didn't know what they had talked about at home. But it didn't seem to me they were using their time together to talk about things. Maybe Mrs. O'Brien didn't think Kelly was going to die any time soon. If Rose didn't think so, why would she? Rose was talking about sending Kelly home again in time for the Christmas holidays.

It seemed to me that Kelly was far too weak for Rose to contemplate sending him home. He was deteriorating. The first few days he was back in the hospital, he seemed in reasonably good spirits and better physically than he had been before he went home. Then he began to get depressed again. He became very demanding. Things he could do for himself, such as getting on the bedpan, he wanted the nurses to do for him. He began to vomit more frequently. He was losing blood all the time.

Rose couldn't understand it. He kept insisting that if we could just support Kelly enough through this period, he could get better for a while.

Rose certainly knew more about Kelly's internal condition than I did. But to me, Kelly no longer looked like a man who could get better.

One afternoon about a week after Kelly came back in, I was in the room hanging an IV bottle, and he said, out of the blue, "I just want you to know that I'm not afraid of dying."

I stopped fiddling with the bottle and looked at him.

"You know," I said, "I really don't think you are."

He said. "I've had seizures. I know what it's like to be out. You just close your eyes and go to sleep. I'll be glad when I die. Nobody has suffered as much as I have. I've been through hell. I want to die."

He spoke matter-of-factly. We looked straight at each other. I felt very close to Kelly at that moment. I said nothing. There was nothing to say.

Rose wasn't ready to make Kelly a no-code. I was beginning to think he should.

14

NURSES AND DOCTORS

Mrs. Dixon laid a chart in front of me. It was open to an input-and-output sheet. Tapping a place on the page with her finger, Dixon said in a huffy voice, "What's this all about?"

I looked. The chart was Al Moore's. Moore was a 23-year-old who had been admitted a couple of days earlier. The doctors thought he had a pancreatic cyst. We were supposed to measure and record Moore's urine output.

However, Moore had not been saving his urine. Although we had asked him several times to do so, he just wouldn't cooperate. So Dixon had finally just asked him how often and how much he had urinated. Then she had written on the I&O sheet, "Bathroom × 3. Patient states good stream."

What she was pointing out to me was something a resident had written next to her entry: "This is not acceptable. L. George." George had drawn an arrow to "Bathroom × 3."

Dixon was pretty upset. "What does he expect us to do if the man won't save his urine?" she grumbled.

I was upset myself. So were a few other nurses who happened to be in the nurses' station at the time. Instead of just writing a reprimand into the record, I thought George should have had the courtesy to talk to me or the team leader about the situation. If he had talked to one of us, he would have found out that there was an explanation for what Dixon had written.

Lee George was the same resident who had given me such a

hard time about getting Marshall the King off the floor. George has a foul temper. He flies off the handle easily. He comes on very defensive, which gets me defensive, and then I get upset with myself for not maintaining my cool. He really gets my dander up. I didn't know whether to call him about the Moore thing or not. I knew that no matter what I said I would get a ten-minute lecture. I thought, "Is it even worth getting on the phone and trying to explain this?"

But I didn't want to just let the thing go, and I thought I could stay cooler if I spoke to him immediately instead of waiting. So I called.

"Dr. George," I said, "what about this sentence in Al Moore's chart, 'This is not acceptable'?"

There was a sarcastic sigh. "I didn't want to make a big thing of it," George said. "That was just my lighthearted way of telling you that Dixon's entry wasn't acceptable. We want I&O on this man. 'Bathroom × 3' doesn't tell me how much he's putting out."

"Well," I said, "what you wrote really upset a few people."

"I don't care whether your nurses are upset or not."

I thought to myself, "You act as if you don't."

I explained the problem we were having with Moore. Then I said, "All I'm calling to say is that I would appreciate it if in the future when you have a comment to make, you either find me or talk to the nurse in charge."

George snorted. "Then a big stink would have been made."

"No, it wouldn't. If you had come to me, I would have tried to find out what was happening."

"I was in a hurry," George said. "I didn't have time."

I could just see his face. He gets so red.

I said, "I'm taking up your time right now. If you had come to me instead of writing that sarcastic little. . . ."

"It wasn't sarcastic. It was lighthearted."

"Well, nobody took it as lighthearted."

I realized I was taking the wrong tack. It's not worth arguing with George. He just doesn't understand. His priorities and mine are twenty miles apart. Besides, if you go out of your way to one-up George in one circumstance, he is childish enough to try to destroy you in another circumstance.

Yet if you back down, he bullies you. You have to stand up to him without giving him the idea that you're trying to intimidate him. Then he won't try to intimidate you. That's my gut feeling. Maybe that's why I've had to learn to be just pushy enough to find out what I need to know.

I said to George, "All right, forget what you wrote in the chart. How do you expect to remedy the I&O situation? What do you expect the nurses to do?"

George said, "I think the nurse in charge should go into the room every half hour and ask the patient if he has to pass his urine. The doctors certainly don't have time to come up there every half hour and do that."

I thought, "Mary, keep your cool."

I said, "Dr. George. This man is 23 years old. He's alert, oriented, up walking around, smoking cigarettes. When he came in, Stephanie went over the whole thing with him. She gave him a urinal and asked him to urinate into it. She told him to put his light on when he had finished so one of us could collect the urine. Since he hasn't been cooperating, we have asked him several more times to please cooperate.

"I don't think we should have to do more than that. I don't think it's up to the nurses to walk in there every half hour and try to convince an alert, oriented adult to save his urine."

I asked George whether he had talked to the patient himself about the problem. He had not, as I knew very well.

George hesitated. Then he said, "I do think it's the doctors' responsibility to do that." He sounded a little less sarcastic than he had.

"Well, I'm glad you do," I said. "You talk to him, and I'll talk to him, and let's hope that's enough."

Once Ed Lefcourt had left Central for his oncological fellowship, Lee George was the worst resident I had to deal with. Physically he was kind of attractive. He was tall, with broad shoulders, sandy hair, a fair complexion, and a deep voice. But his personality was rank. He was flip to nurses and flip to patients. I honestly don't think George wanted to be a doctor. How could you act as he did and like your job?

I didn't hate George. I'm not saying he was incompetent. I don't think he harmed any patients. After all, the chief resident and staff physician were over him, so his patients probably got decent care.

But he really did just the minimum with patients. He talked to them only long enough to find out what he wanted to know, never thinking about what they might want to know. No follow-through. Also, I don't think he took any nurse's view into consideration, and I don't think any of the residents could stand him either. More than most people, he needed to calm down a little and accept the idea that other people could help him. Instead, he made demands. Everyone was annoyed with him.

My idea of a good doctor to work with was Jon Benson. I respected him for the way he treated patients and the way he treated me. He was very conscientious, saw patients as human beings, and seemed more attuned to patients' needs, both physical and mental, than most doctors. When he talked to a patient, he looked him in the eye. While he may not have spent more time with patients than other residents do, the quality of the time he spent was better.

He talked about patients in a way I don't often hear from other residents. "Give the guy a break," he'd say about a patient who seemed uncooperative. "He's had a rough time." When Benson was taking care of patients who were dying, it bothered him a lot. He said so. I respect a doctor who cares that much. Benson told you quietly that he was depressed. He wasn't doing it to get everybody's attention. He meant it.

Unlike a lot of doctors, Benson never put nurses down. He'd take a suggestion from a nurse. If he knew you were trying, he gave you credit for what you were doing. I could always get a hearing with him. I could talk to him about what was happening to a patient, or I could just sit down and gossip with him a little.

I occasionally got into conversation with him about how medical science can keep anything alive. In that kind of discussion, you get a broader sense of what someone's personality is like. Some doctors wouldn't bother to have a conversation like that with a nurse. Benson took the time with us.

Maybe I was prejudiced toward Jon Benson because of the way he came across with me. Let's face it, that can interfere with your judgment. Somebody who comes across as flip in my eyes is going to have a tough row to hoe convincing me that he's a caring person. Whereas if somebody comes across as a decent human being, I may think he's better than he actually is. I know Benson was a good doctor to work with. I think he was a good doctor, period. But I can't be certain.

It's hard for nurses to judge doctors. There isn't much to go on. This is especially true of the staff physicians. If a staff person has two or three patients on Eight Cook on any given day, which is common, I might see him once each day for a few minutes. If he makes rounds before I get in, I don't see him at all.

I know from the residents what the staff doctors' reputations are. But I never see a surgeon doing surgery. I can't judge the progress of patients after surgery because I don't know what their condition was before surgery. I can judge wounds, and if the patients of a particular surgeon always had infected incisions, I would wonder what was going on. But I've never seen that kind of pattern. I don't see the surgeons talking to patients in their offices. Maybe they know patients better than I do. Maybe they don't.

I see somewhat more of the residents, but not much more. A resident might be on the floor for fifteen minutes in the morning and fifteen minutes in the afternoon. I wouldn't necessarily see that resident both times. If I see any doctor for fifteen minutes a day, that's a lot.

As is true of the staff doctors, I can't judge the residents' skills in the operating room. The one technical skill on which I can judge a resident is how he responds in an emergency. If there's a cardiac arrest or if a patient goes sour, you can tell if the resident seems calm and goes through the logical procedures in the logical order.

I've seen a few residents become really klutzed in emergencies and have to be told what to do. Once I saw a supervisor take over a code from a resident. The patient had gone suddenly bad. The resident, who was brand new, couldn't get the IV started. The supervisor kept making suggestions and finally stuck in the IV herself. The patient ended up in the cardiac care unit, but he survived.

Since I really don't know that much about the doctors' medical skills, about all I can judge them on is how they seem as people in their relationships with patients and nurses. That can mean two separate judgments. Doctors who are good from the patients' point of view may be bad from the nurses'.

That's true of Drs. Aubrey and Faust, two well-respected internists, associates who often have medical patients on Eight Cook. Most of their patients are upper-middle-class. Some are rich. Most of those I've seen are well educated. They have a good understanding of their diseases. They know what's going on.

Most nurses agree that Aubrey–Faust are very good to their patients. They sit and listen to them. They explain procedures more elaborately than most doctors do. When they write orders, they check more thoroughly than other doctors do to make sure the orders have been carried out.

But Aubrey–Faust can get the nursing staff pretty upset, because they tend to believe whatever their patients tell them without listening to the nurses' side. If Mrs. Jones says a nurse didn't give her a sleeping pill the night before, I've seen those doctors come out yelling, totally believing the patient. They expect a lot from nurses. That's all right, except that sometimes they seem to think we can be in all places at all times.

They come across as very uppity: "I'm the doctor. You're the nurse. You do what I say." They don't accept nursing judgment. I guess they've had some bad experiences with certain nurses and tend to judge other nurses on those experiences. They do have respect for a few nurses, and the ones they respect, they treat as professionals. Yet if you make one mistake, I think they remember that and put you down as somebody who doesn't care about their patients. That upsets a lot of nurses.

On the other hand, some doctors who don't cause trouble for the nurses aren't particularly good for patients either. I've seen doctors who stand and talk to nurses, play up to them, and act as if whatever the nurses thought was right *was* right. These same doctors spend no time with patients. If I were the patient, I'd judge such a doctor as bad. I judge him as bad myself. He may be a nice person, but I wouldn't go to him with a medical problem.

Sam Polen is one of these. I like Polen. But with patients, he seems to be somebody who's in there to get the job done and get out. I don't think he knows much about patients. The only time he gets to know anything more than their medical condition is when they're delayed getting out of the hospital for some reason.

Take, for example, an old lady who's had a foot amputated, lives on the second floor, and has nobody to take care of her. She's going to have to be stronger before she goes home than she would if she were going to live with a relative. But Polen usually doesn't know where the patient is going. He just makes plans to discharge her. Then one of the nurses has to say to him, "You know, Mrs. Johnson doesn't have anybody." When Polen is thinking of sending a patient home, I think he should have it in him to ask the person, "Whom do you live with?"

No matter how they treat patients, most doctors do not treat nurses as fellow professionals. I'm not saying they don't appreciate nurses. I think most of the doctors I deal with rely on me, value me to a certain extent, and consider me a good nurse. I don't think they view me as some dizzy little thing. I don't think I have any bad relationships with doctors. I think a few, like Benson, respect me and respect the role I play in patient care.

But from what I've seen, doctors who respect nurses are in the minority. I think it's traditional for the doctor to think he's better than the nurse. Some older doctors in particular have absolutely no respect for nursing. Most younger doctors have some. But it's a rare doctor of any age who even thinks of a nurse as a fellow professional, let alone treats her as one.

This message comes across in many ways. The only round-the-clock record of a patient's physical and mental condition—and usually the most complete record—is the nurse's note written into the chart once each shift by the nurse assigned to care for that patient. Most doctors don't read nurses' notes.

Nor do they ask nurses what's going on with their patients. Very rarely does a doctor come on the floor and say, "What's happening with Mr. So-and-so?" Nurses have to ask the doctors what's happening. It improves patient care when people discuss the patient, but if we waited for doctors to start those discussions, there would be very few. I would say that nurses initiate conferences on patients about 85 percent of the time.

I could count on one hand the number of times a doctor has asked me what I thought about something. Once Dr. Aubrey asked Jackie Neill what she would recommend for a patient who was addicted to pain medication—and then took her suggestion. Jackie couldn't believe it. I couldn't believe it when Aubrey took me aside a few days after Craig and Rose talked to me about the oncology floor and asked me what I thought of Dr. Rose. I was shocked.

Here was a staff man asking *me* what I thought of another staff man. That was a first.

My friend June, a nurse anesthetist in another hospital, says doctors do ask her opinion on things. Of course she's a specialist. On Eight Cook doctors might ask nurses about bedsore care, wound care, or drug dosages—especially sleeping pill dosages—but that's about all.

Even then the nurses will do the initiating. A doctor orders Valium. The nurse says, "I don't think that's good" and gives a reason—Valium makes some people more depressed than they already are, and a patient who's sleeping a lot anyway may not need it. So the doctor asks the nurse what she suggests. It's pretty rare for a doctor to come up and say, "God, we've got this horrible infection. What are we going to do about it?"

Since doctors don't often ask a nurse's opinion, I guess it's not surprising that when a nurse offers a suggestion, she sometimes gets a flip answer. A doctor may say, "What are you trying to do, teach me my business?" To me the biggest insult is a doctor saying, "Are you trying to be a doctor?" When a doctor says that, I'd like to pop him one. I say to a doctor, "This patient was put on Digoxin three days ago. Now he's having diarrhea. Do you want to get a Dig level?" Digoxin is a heart medicine, and diarrhea can be one of its side effects. The doctor says, "Where did you go to school?" or "Where did you get your degree from?"

In other words, where did you get the intelligence to think that up?

Which fits right in with what doctors started saying to one of the nurses on Eight Cook when she applied to medical school. "Good," they said, "you're too smart to be a nurse."

Which also fits right in with the astonishment some doctors show when they discover you're assessing patients. A nurse says to a doctor, "Mrs. So-and-so started running a fever. She's having chest pain and pain in her legs. Do you think she's having an MI?"

An MI, or myocardial infarction, is a heart attack. The doctor looks at the nurse with his mouth open. Nurses aren't supposed to know when a patient is having a coronary. We're supposed to describe what's happening. Only the doctors are supposed to say what it means. We're supposed to say, "Dr. Jones, Mr. Smith has ceased breathing." Christ, he's dead!

There are also doctors who aren't even satisfied to have nurses as handmaidens because what they really want is servants. I'll hear a doctor yell, "I need a nurse in here right now!" I run in and find he wants somebody to tear a piece of tape for him.

When this happens, I wait till the doctor leaves the room, then say to him, "Do you realize what I was doing when you called me in for that? Please. Don't ever do that again unless it's an emergency."

The truth is that the doctor probably had no idea what I was doing when he called me in to tear tape. Doctors don't know what nurses do. When a nurse says I'm a good nurse, I take it as a compliment. When a doctor tells me I'm a good nurse, I say, "What does that mean to you? What does a nurse do?" He can't answer.

A surgical resident once told me he considered a certain nurse especially good because her I&Os were always correct. Oh, god. I said, "You're cute."

I mean correct I&Os are important, but they're hardly the measure of a good nurse. Some doctors think you're a good nurse if you're quote a pillow-fluffer and a sweetie and you keep the patients happy. You're a good nurse if you follow their orders. You're a good nurse if their patients have no complaints. If their patients complain, you're a rotten nurse.

Many younger doctors, as well as some older ones, look for something more from nurses. When Jackie Neill asked a doctor why he referred to a certain nurse as good, he said, "Because I can count on her. I know when a patient is doing well or going bad. If there's something wrong with the blood values, she's going to tell me. She keeps me up to date on what's happening with the patients."

More commonly, doctors think a nurse is good if their patients are happy, like the floor, have their physical needs met, and if their temperatures stay down. We're good nurses if we take off orders properly, make discharge plans for patients, and follow through.

Fine. But doctors don't really have any idea what's involved in getting those things done.

Feminists say that our society makes women subservient to men. I think nurses put themselves in that position.

From time to time a doctor will walk out of a room and say to me, "Mr. So-and-so needs to be on the bedpan." That annoys me more than anything else. Hell, the bedpan's right there. The doctor can put the bedpan under that patient. I can see why he wouldn't if the patient is really sick and the doctor doesn't know how to lift the person properly. But sometimes all the doctor would need to do is hand the patient the bedpan. Instead, he comes out to find a nurse.

Usually, I'm stupid when that happens. I don't even stop to think that the doctor has two eyes and two hands and could easily give the patient the bedpan himself. Instead I think, "Oh, yeah, I'd better go do that," and I run and do it. What I should do is say to the doctor, "Next time I would appreciate it if you would give the patient the urinal."

The other day I asked Jackie Neill if anything like this ever happened to her. She laughed.

"Twice today!" she said. First, Jackie told me, she had walked into a room where one of the doctors had just finished drawing blood from a patient. The doctor was holding the patient's arm to put pressure on it. Instinctively, Jackie took over for him and held the patient's wrist herself. The doctor walked out. She stood there thinking, "Why am I standing here holding this patient's wrist when I have more important things I should be doing?"

Later one of the doctors was down on Six reading a chart and noticed that there was no space left for him to write progress notes. He said to Jackie, "Where are the progress note forms?" Instead of saying to him, "They're in the bottom drawer on the left-hand side," she got them for him.

Telling me about these incidents, Jackie said, "I don't feel as if I exerted any independence at all today. I don't feel I tested anything. I just played the traditional nurse role. Whatever the doctors wanted, I got for them."

When I'm thinking about what I'm doing, I won't play that role. I will help a doctor look for a chart as readily as I will help a nurse from another floor or somebody from Anesthesia. I won't be purposely ignorant to anybody. But I won't get up and look for a chart just because a doctor is looking for it. If a doctor asks me where something is, I usually tell him where it is instead of getting it myself.

That is, I tell him where it is unless the guy is feeble, like a couple of the old obstetricians are. They can just about take their hats off. You don't know whether you're going to code them or their patients. For them I get stuff.

I won't give my chair to a doctor. The only doctor I ever did that for was a 75-year-old man at Metro who walked with a cane. If a doctor takes the chair I was using, I'll tap him on the shoulder and say, "Excuse me. I was sitting there taking off orders." Or I'll glare till he takes the hint. I reason that if I don't think of myself as subservient, I won't be.

At first most nurses are intimidated by doctors. I certainly was. But the doctors don't intimidate me at all now. In dealing with them, I've learned to think about the patient, not about myself. If I have a question, I ask it. If I have a suggestion, I offer it. If I'm upset about something a doctor says or does, I confront that doctor. I think you have to let people know that you're not going to be stepped on or taken for granted. I don't think you should let people get away with certain things—even if they're doctors.

When I first came to Central, we had a lady on the floor who was completely out of it psychologically. She had been in and out of mental institutions for several years. She weighed about 160 pounds and was very dirty. Some people were upset by the way she smelled. I could see why.

One day a resident came out of her room and said to me, "Who could fuck her?"

Before I started nursing, I guess I assumed that crude people didn't go into the healing arts. Now I realize that some doctors and nurses are crude. I thought this resident's comment was incredibly crude. While I may make a gross remark or say something in poor taste, I hope I would only do it in front of Ron or friends who understand that I'm just ventilating, not expressing my true feelings. I would never make such a remark at a nurses' station in front of people who didn't know me.

At the time, I had only been at Central two weeks. I was still unsure of myself. But I said to the resident, "You have a lot of nerve. That could be someone you love. Do you know what that woman was like two years ago? I've seen her pictures. She was overweight, but she wasn't unattractive. You might change, too, if you were that sick. I think what you said was cruel."

He just looked at me. I don't know what he said to other people, but I never heard him make a comment like that again.

From time to time I have reported doctors. I've never reported a doctor at Central for incompetency, but I have reported Central doctors for being turkeys. For instance, I reported the infamous Dr. Lefcourt a couple of times for cursing and yelling at nurses and for slamming the phone down while a nurse was talking to him.

Once at Metro I reported an intern who refused to help me in an emergency. Two of the other nurses and I were getting a very obese lady out of bed when she almost completely gorked out. Some kind of failure. It wasn't cardiac arrest. She still had a pulse. She was still breathing. But she became red and sweaty and almost totally unarousable. When we pinched her under the arms, we got no response.

The other two nurses were very rotund themselves. Their heaviness interfered with our getting the patient back into bed. I went out into the hall, grabbed the first intern I saw, and said, "This lady is completely out of it. We need help getting her back in bed."

The intern took one look at the size of the patient and said, "Mary, I can't. I have a bad back."

Well, I stat–paged the night supervisor, and we got an orderly and the patient's resident to help us, and we finally got the woman back into bed and stabilized. But I reported the intern to the supervisor, who in turn told the director of nursing.

I never learned what happened. Reporting someone at Metro didn't get the results that reporting someone at Central does.

Once, just once, I yelled at a doctor. This was the day that Ray Powell died, the fireman who had been so hostile at first.

A resident named Stan Belsky was in Mr. Powell's room. I had just started my 10:00 meds when all of a sudden I heard, "Nurse! Nurse!"

I went running into the room. Belsky was standing there holding Mr. Powell, who had apparently been trying to get up when he collapsed and died in Belsky's arms. Blood was spurting from the man's face, from everywhere. He had spewed blood all over the place.

I burst into tears. I was so upset that all I could do was stand there sobbing.

Belsky lay Mr. Powell back down on the bed and started to leave the room.

I said, "Are you going to call the family?"

"No," Belsky answered, "that's not my job."

I was furious. Still crying, not having any idea how loud my voice was, I really gave it to Belsky.

"Your responsibility is to call that family!" I said. "You are the resident on the service today, and it's your responsibility to let that woman know that her husband has died. We need time to clean up. She may be on her way in here. What happens if she walks into the room and sees all this blood?"

Belsky turned to face me. "Listen, Mary," he said calmly, "I don't need to be yelled at by some nurse, and I don't need a nurse to tell me what my responsibility is."

He left the room.

I stood there shaking. I realized I had overreacted because I had been so attached to the Powells. Belsky, after all, was not the resident on the case. The resident on the case—as both Belsky and I knew—would be coming up on rounds any moment. Belsky obviously thought that the resident who knew the family should tell the family. I knew he was right.

I looked for Belsky and found him in the nurses' station.

"I'm sorry," I said to him. "I didn't realize I was yelling. I shouldn't have done that. I was just very upset about what happened to Mr. Powell."

"Don't you think I understand that?" Belsky asked.

When doctors yell at me, which happens often enough, I usually walk away. I won't yell back, because I will not stoop to that level. Instead, I might take a sickening-sarcastic tone: "Yeeeesssss? Is there anything else I can do for you?" Or I'll say, "Don't you have two arms on you? Can't you get up and walk over there and pick up what you want? That's what I would have to do. Thank you very much."

When I'm behaving maturely, I'm able to toss off whatever it is the doctors say or do that bothers me. I don't think sarcasm is a particularly adult way to handle situations. I've always been somewhat sarcastic. I try to be less so. For some reason it's the doctors who can still bring out the sarcasm in me.

Being sarcastic to a doctor once got me into a lot of trouble. This incident occurred at Metro. We had a patient on the floor who had had a renal transplant done by Dr. Colberg, one of the prominent staff doctors. The woman was transferred to our floor one afternoon from the intensive care unit. All transplant patients receive high doses of cortisone to minimize the possibility of rejection. This patient was supposed to receive so many milligrams of Imuran that afternoon.

However, the order was never taken off. The woman arrived at about 3:30, at change of shift, which is a very busy time. Since there was confusion on the floor at that hour, the nurse who ordinarily would have taken off the order apparently thought that somebody else had done it. The patient never received the dose.

The next day, Saturday, I had charge. I was down at the end of the hall giving meds when I heard Dr. Colberg stalk into the nurses' station screaming like a maniac.

"Where's the nurse in charge? I thought my patient was going to get good care on this floor! If you transfer a patient out of the ICU in this hospital, you might as well let her die!"

If the doctor had called me aside and complained, I wouldn't have gotten so upset about what he was saying. But there were visitors listening to this tirade, many of whom had family members on the floor who were dying of cancer. That he could make such a scene in front of these people made me really angry. I went to the nurses' station and said to him, very quietly, "Yes? Can I help you?"

Dr. Colberg nearly took my head off. "Mrs. So-and-so didn't get her Imuran yesterday! Why wasn't it given?"

I started to explain.

He interrupted. "This is not acceptable!"

I'd had enough.

"You know," I said to him, very quietly but sarcastically, "we all make mistakes once in a while."

Well, Colberg left the floor and called the director of nursing at home. He told her that she had a very flip nurse working on the twelfth floor. Early Monday morning the director called me into the nursing office and really laid it on me. She never even asked me what had happened. She just told me I had no right to talk like that to a doctor.

I should have said, "I wish you had gotten the two of us together, so I could have heard what he said about me." At the very least I thought she should have asked me to say why I did what I did. I thought she was being very unfair. I hadn't even said anything nasty to Colberg. I hadn't cursed. I hadn't told him to go to hell. I had just been sarcastic.

But I was too scared to defend myself. I just sat there.

When I left the office, and for a long time afterward, I felt traumatized by what had happened. It was as if the director of nursing had said, "Your side doesn't count." Her failure to support me was one of the reasons I left Metro. She lost a good nurse because she wouldn't stick up for me against a doctor. That would never happen with Miss Craig.

I'm not particularly proud of the way I handled Dr. Colberg. I do feel good about the way I handled a similar incident recently with Dr. Faust. Faust came on Eight Cook one day really angry. I don't remember the exact details, but apparently one of his patients had complained about some treatment not being done or not being done properly.

Faust was yelling and screaming about nursing care. He had an audience. The nurses' station was full of nurses, medical students, and surgical residents. After he had said what he wanted to say, Faust told me in a high and mighty way to check on what had happened and call him back before the end of the day. Without waiting for an answer, he stalked off the floor.

The nurses who had heard him were very upset. They felt put down.

"Maybe the whole thing was blown out of proportion," I said to them. "Just let me try to find out what happened."

So I checked on what had happened, and the facts were not what Faust had thought they were.

I called his office from the utility room. When I reported what I had found, Faust's voice changed. He said, "Thank you very much. I really appreciate your calling to tell me what did happen."

I wasn't finished.

"Dr. Faust," I said, "may I ask a favor of you? The next time you're upset, please call me aside and tell me. When you stand in the nurses' station and say the kinds of things you were saying, every person who hears you takes sides mentally. Doctors against nurses. Nurses against doctors. They don't hear the whole story. They just hear your complaint. That's bad for morale."

Faust wasn't saying anything.

I continued. "If you tell me something and I give you a flip answer, or if you don't get any response to what you need or what patients need, then I think you should go to my supervisor. But yelling just upsets everybody."

He answered, "You know, you're right. I shouldn't have done that. I won't do it again."

I had a lot of respect for Dr. Faust for responding that way. My confrontation with him has made a positive difference in how he and Aubrey treat me. Of course part of the reason this story ended differently from the Colberg incident is that Faust is a different kind of person.

But to me the Faust story is different from the Colberg story in two more important ways. One is a difference in situation—the support given nurses at Central Hospital. At Metro I might not even have tried to suggest to Faust that he change his behavior. If I had, I might have received a reprimand myself.

The other difference is in me. The Faust story ended as it did partly because I wasn't sarcastic with him. I'm more experienced now and—I hope—more mature.

I personally don't feel oppressed by doctors. I don't care what they think of me. I used to care. Now the way I look at it is that I'm a person too. I have as much right to say what I want to say as anyone else has. If the doctors don't see it that way, that's tough shit, in plain English. I'm not there to have them like me or decide whether I'm a professional. I'm not what the doctors think I am. I am what I am. I don't feel particularly put in my place by any doctor. If I do, I just ignore it.

I think nurses who stay in nursing either become disillusioned or develop a feeling of confidence about what they are. Maybe I'm patting myself on the back, but I've always considered myself a good nurse. I don't think I know everything. I have things to learn. Some days, when I go off on tangents, I know that other people could do a better job of organization than I do.

Still, I honestly know that I give a lot. I care about patients. I put long hours into the job. I can't give any more than I'm giving. So if the doctors don't like it, they can lump it. If they don't respect me, I can live with that.

The most serious trouble with the attitude some doctors have about nurses is that it affects patient care. I believe you have to think of patient care as a team effort. Each person in the system has something to give. Each should be respected for what he or she can do. I know people who say, "Oh, she's only a nursing assistant." I think that's horrible. If you're good, you do a good job, no matter what your title. If the cleaning lady goes into a room and says something that cheers a patient up, that's positive. It's one of the things that helps that patient get better.

Doctors who don't accept that, who don't see that anyone who's good in his or her field is helping the patient, are, in my opinion, very immature.

Unfortunately, there are also immature nurses and social workers. Some nurses are very negative about doctors. There's rivalry from time to time. My feeling is that if everybody would help each other out instead of worrying about who is taking over whose territory, everybody would be better off. Yet some nurses and some social workers, like some doctors, think their profession is the only one that makes patients better.

But only the doctors see themselves as doing everything.

Of course they don't do everything. They couldn't possibly. They don't have the time, the training, or the inclination. This isn't to criticize doctors. It's to say that patients need more than doctors alone can provide or are providing. It would be easier on the nurses—and better for the patients—if doctors would acknowledge that.

Sometimes it is difficult to get doctors to talk to the family of a dying patient. They go in and say, "We're doing this, this, and this, goodbye." If the doctor would just say that he's uncomfortable talking to the family, or that he doesn't want to do it or doesn't have time to do it, we could see that somebody else did talk to them.

If a patient is going home, it's rare for a doctor to ask a nurse, "What do we need to teach this patient before discharge?" The diabetologist makes sure to let us know a week in advance when a patient is going home so we can teach the patient about his insulin injections. That's uncommon. Usually the information isn't conveyed till the last minute. We find out that a patient is being discharged just a few hours before he leaves. Then a nurse has to ask the doctor, "Is this patient going home on Coumadin?"

Coumadin is a blood thinner. How many times have I gone up to patients the day they were leaving and asked them what they knew about Coumadin, and all they could tell me was that it was a pill? They knew nothing about side effects. The doctors hadn't told them. If I hadn't remembered to ask the doctor, the patient could have gone home without important information.

Some doctors think they can handle social services. I'll say, "How is this patient getting home?" A doctor will answer, "Her family's coming to get her."

"Where's she going to live?"

"No problem. Somebody will look in on her."

Then a few days before discharge I find out that the patient's daughter lives several hundred miles away and that the patient doesn't have any way of getting home. The doctor told me he was going to handle it. You can't trust that. You have to make sure it's done.

Occasionally doctors actually stand in the way of what I consider good patient care. Several times doctors have refused to let patients be seen by someone from Central's Social Services Department. Some doctors think social workers are meddlers. They'll call a social worker for cabulance service or for a hospital bed in the patient's home or for Meals on Wheels, but they don't want a social worker seeing a patient who's depressed or whose spouse isn't providing enough emotional support. When they see a social service consult, they get extremely agitated.

Technically, any nurse is permitted to put in for a social service consult without going through a doctor. However, the social workers have learned not to see the patients of certain doctors without checking with the doctors first. They know from experience that the doctors may object.

One doctor hates the visiting nurse. He yelled at me for having Central's visiting nurse coordinator come up to see a patient. He thinks social service butts in. He thinks he can take care of the problem.

Other doctors don't want their patients visited by a member of the Mastectomy Club. They get upset if you even bring it up.

"I'm going to teach her about it myself," they say.

I say flippantly, "Oh? And when did you have your mastectomy?"

They argue that it's possible to teach a patient about cancer without having had cancer yourself.

"Yes," I say, "but maybe the woman would like to talk to someone who has actually been through the experience."

The doctors just look blank.

Doctors would rather have social workers than a psychiatrist or the psychiatric nurse specialist. When we have a patient with behavior problems or psychological problems, it's very difficult to get support from certain physicians. Doctors don't want to deal with the psychological aspects of patient care.

Marshall the King was an example of this. Marshall was psychotic. The doctors thought he was funny. Judd Nicolai never did get psychiatric help. Some doctors feel negatively toward psychiatrists. They say psychiatrists aren't really doctors. They think they can solve the problems themselves. Trying to get a psych consult on one of their patients is like pulling teeth. I'll say, "You know, Mr. So-and-so is very depressed. Maybe one of the psychiatrists should talk to him."

The doctor will yell, "I don't think my patient needs a psychiatrist! I don't want any psychiatrist seeing my patient! What's a psychiatrist going to do? They're all full of shit!"

I've heard that often. In my opinion, these doctors are afraid that their patients will think that the doctors think they're nuts.

One of my more memorable attempts to get a psych consult on a patient occurred over a 28-year-old woman, very heavy, who came in with back pain. She said she had slipped on some ice and fallen. X-rays showed nothing. The neurologists found no pathology. The act this woman put on getting out of bed was incredible. I've taken plenty of people out of bed after major back surgery, and

I've never seen anyone fall all over the place as this one did. She was almost on the floor.

The woman's husband was on disability. The doctors began to think the woman was malingering to get on disability herself. So they finally told her they were stopping all medications.

I could see that the woman was very depressed. She didn't read, didn't do anything. Just lay in bed. One morning I went in and said, "I guess your husband will be glad to have you back home."

"No, he won't," she said, "because I have to stay in bed the whole time."

I looked at her. "Why will you have to stay in bed? The doctors want you to start getting up."

The woman seemed angry. "These doctors don't know anything. I'm having back pain. I'm going home, and I'm getting into bed, and I'm going to start taking my pain pills again."

"You know," I said, "I'm not feeling your pain. I don't know what it's like. You can go home and take your pain pills and ignore the world if you want to. You're a big girl. That's your decision. But lots of people have pain, and they don't shut off the world."

She said, "I don't care what you say. I'm having pain."

I thought the woman needed to talk to somebody. I called Sam Polen, who was following her, and told him about my conversation with her.

"Oh, she's such a turkey," Polen said. Speaking of turkeys.

I said, "Did you ever think that maybe she's depressed?"

"So?"

"So maybe she needs a psych consult."

"Hah!" Polen barked. "Psychiatrists don't do anything. They're all turkeys. Everybody in my class who went into psychiatry was crazy himself."

"Look," I said. "You're a surgeon. You can't solve every problem in your personal life. That doesn't mean you're a rotten surgeon. I'm sure psychiatrists have problems themselves, but that doesn't mean they can't help other people."

"Psychiatrists are only good for psychotics."

"That's not true. Sometimes people just need to talk to somebody."

"They're all turkeys."

"You're not speaking from personal experience. I don't think they're all turkeys."

Then, before I realized what I was saying, I jokingly said to Polen, "You should send her to mine."

"Yours!"

"Yes, mine. What's wrong with that?"

Until that moment, only Ron and my mother had known I had gone to a psychiatrist for a couple of months. I had been feeling generally depressed. Maybe I was more concerned than someone else would have been about keeping my depression under control because my grandmother is in a mental institution. After a few sessions, I realized that the depression was temporary. After a few more sessions, the psychiatrist said he felt I didn't need him any more. I agreed.

I hadn't told anyone about this because I hadn't been married long at the time, and I didn't want anybody to think I was having problems with Ron. I wasn't. But when Polen started sounding off on psychiatrists, I just blurted it out.

I was glad in a way. I think it made him stop and think. He finally agreed to put in a psych consult for the patient. As it happened, this was on a Saturday. You can only get a psychiatrist for emergencies on the weekends, if, for example, a patient is threatening suicide. On Sunday the woman checked herself out of the hospital.

When I think one of the doctors might object to a consult, I've usually tried to say to him, "I was talking to Mrs. So-and-so the other day, and she mentioned such-and-such a thing, and I thought I'd put a social service consult in," so the doctor is aware that somebody is going to be quote meddling.

If that doesn't work, I may manipulate the situation. If I know a patient is having a problem, and the doctor is one who gets upset about consults, I'll say to the patient, "You know, I think the Social Services Department could help you with that problem."

The patient will say something like, "Do you really think so?"

Then I go back to the doctor and say, "You know, Mrs. So-and-so was talking to me about social services. She'd like to see somebody."

I don't see that as lying; I see it as helping things along. Facilitating. That's part of my job, even if it involves a little cheating here and there. Anything for the patient's benefit! I think I have to help the doctors get over their little backward feelings about social services.

Jackie Neill thinks I have an easier time dealing with doctors than she does because I'm married. I think that's true. Because I'm married, and the doctors know I'm married, I think to myself, "I'm not playing up to you. I could care less if you jump in the lake. I'm going to say what I feel."

The fact that Ron is a medical student also has some influence. It has allowed me to feel more comfortable with doctors and to worry less than I might otherwise about what I say to them. Like who in the hell cares? So you're a doctor. My husband's a medical student, his grandfather was a doctor, almost all our friends are medical students. Big deal.

Jackie says she has elevated men—and therefore doctors—to a certain level. She thinks that because she hasn't lived with a man, she hasn't yet accepted that doctors are human beings with the same problems and frustrations anyone else has. That makes her vulnerable when a doctor yells and screams. She's apt to go into the nurses' lounge and start crying. Whereas the doctors have never had me crying yet.

Being married to a medical student also gives me more empathy with doctors than I might have otherwise. I don't say doctors are wonderful when they yell and scream. I think they should control their tempers. But sometimes I can understand why they behave the way they do.

Their hours alone explain a lot. One morning one of the chief residents at Central was really in a bad mood. He snapped at several of us over the phone. Then the supervisor told me that the resident had been up all night with a patient who had gone bad. Nurses just out of school don't have the slightest idea what kind of hours doctors put in. Only after you've been in a hospital a while and seen doctors wandering around at three in the morning, on two hours' sleep, do you begin to realize that a doctor's schedule is pretty rugged.

That's why I often try not to snap back at people. I've worked the night shift myself on very little sleep. I know how it feels. You may function well enough, but unless you have an easygoing personality, you snap at people more easily. So sometimes when I'm mad, I remind myself that there are going to be times when Ron will be up all night, and I hold my tongue.

Doctors have a lot of knowledge. They work for what they get. You hear about all the money doctors make. But most people are on salary from the age of 22. By the time they're 30, they're beginning to climb to the top of their profession. That's when most doctors are just getting started. Granted, nobody beat them on the hands and said, "You become a doctor." That was their choice. But it's still a hard life.

Doctors have to put up with a lot of crap at times. A lot is expected of them. A patient gets depressed at 10:00 at night. You call the doctor and say, "Mrs. So-and-so is very depressed." Well, the doctor may be very depressed too. Maybe his kids are sick. Maybe his wife is yelling because he's never home. Whatever. The more you see what doctors have to put up with, the more empathetic you can be.

You don't have to marry a medical student to learn to see a doctor as just another person. About half the kids in nursing school dated med students or interns or residents. You can get a more realistic view of doctors as human beings. All the time she was in nursing school and for six months after she graduated, my friend June looked up to doctors as if they were gods. It seemed to her that the doctors knew exactly what they were doing and that she herself knew nothing. When June began to realize that she knew a lot, she stopped thinking of the doctors as gods.

Maureen Shay arrived at the same conclusion by a more complicated route. Maureen was in a four-year baccalaureate program. The message she got there was that physicians were the enemy. The nursing instructors emphasized to the students that nurses were professionals in their own right. They had to stake out their own territory. They might have to step on doctors' toes to do it.

Maureen and the other students in her class also got the impression that it was going to be up to them as nurses to put warmth and feeling into patient care, because doctors were cold and unfeeling. These messages had social implications. According to Maureen, the ultimate degradation was to date a doctor.

It was relatively easy to avoid dating doctors, because women in four-year degree programs spend much less time in the hospital than we did and don't build the rapport with doctors that we did. Until she graduated and started work, Maureen thought doctors were just like the rest of the population.

Then Maureen entered what she calls the intimidation stage. She discovered that she and other new graduates considered it quite an honor to be asked out by a doctor. In her opinion, the doctors capitalized on the fact that nurses felt that way. As Maureen explained it to me, "Inside the hospital, you're subservient to doctors. You do what they want. Outside, it's extremely difficult not to do what they want. Doctors assume you'll go to bed with them faster than you might if you weren't a nurse." The social and professional relationships became so confused, Maureen says, that looking back at that period, she's upset for getting "sucked into the system."

Maureen feels she grew out of the intimidation phase as she progressed in her role as a nurse. After a year, she says, "you realize that doctors are no different from anybody else."

Unfortunately, not everyone arrives at that point. Liz Roberts doesn't believe she has grown out of the intimidation phase yet. Liz roomed with Maureen in nursing school. Like Maureen, Liz is an excellent nurse, sometimes dates doctors, and believes that outside the hospital, nurses and doctors are on the same level.

But inside the hospital, Liz still feels intimidated by doctors. It's very hard for her to talk to a doctor about a patient. She feels insecure. She lacks confidence in the doctor's willingness to listen. She's afraid the doctor won't respect what she knows or says. Liz is by no means the only experienced nurse who feels this way.

Miss Craig keeps telling us that that kind of fear restricts nurses as professionals. She believes nurses could do a lot more if they became more assertive.

I agree. Specifically, nurses have to learn not to be intimidated by doctors. We have to learn to ask the questions in our minds. I don't mean asking, "Why did you do that?" in an accusing way. I mean saying, "What is your plan for this patient? What are you going to do now?" If nurses are afraid to do that, patient care suffers.

The question is what will make nurses unafraid.

I think education will help. Nursing education is beginning to change the view young nurses have of themselves. The more that nurses view themselves as professionals, the more other people will be forced to view them that way. Right now an awful lot of nurses don't see themselves as professionals.

The attitudes of younger doctors will help. Actually, I think that some of the older doctors believe they have to play a certain role and would get out of it if they knew how. As they see more residents treating nurses with respect, more older doctors might do so themselves.

I also think hospitals could do something to improve the self-respect of nurses. They could eliminate special facilities for doctors. At the hospital connected with Ron's school there's no separate dining area for doctors. They sit with everyone else. But at Central, as at Metro, part of the cafeteria is partitioned off so the doctors can eat by themselves. Nurses are not allowed to sit there unless they're with a doctor.

I have never sat there.

I could count on one hand the number of times a resident has come out and eaten with me.

Maybe it seems small, but that separate room really annoys me. I could rip it out with my bare hands.

A postscript on the subject of the nurse–doctor affairs that are supposed to go on in hospitals:

Maybe they do. A lot of the married residents at Metro were running around with nurses or having affairs with somebody on the outside. I really don't know what the staff men were doing. They weren't part of the gossip. But when the married residents are trying to date your girlfriends, you know there's something going on.

I don't see this at Central. This may be because I don't really hear as much gossip as I did when I was a staff nurse and single. A lot goes on that I don't know about. One of the supervisors got a divorce, and I didn't find out about it till ages afterward.

Sam Polen told me recently that Central is the only hospital he knows of where the married doctors aren't sleeping around. God knows. They could all be sleeping around and just hiding it well.

I have heard that Dr. Rose, who's separated, had an affair with a nurse who was on my staff. I don't know. I've also heard that one of the other staff doctors is a great swinger at parties, has a few girlfriends, spend four nights a week at a Holiday Inn, and only goes home to his family on weekends. He says he stays in town because he has to make rounds at four hospitals every morning. Other people guess other reasons. I really don't know. I don't particularly care to know about the personal lives of the doctors. Knowing whom they're running around with would make me uncomfortable.

Of course there's a lot of teasing. One of the residents is always offering to have an affair with me, and a couple of the others carry on jokingly with the nurses.

But as far as I know, joking is the extent of it. I've never had to talk to a staff member about carrying on with a doctor. Of course I would only say something if I thought it was interfering with patient care. If a nurse was flirting with a doctor and a patient needed help, then I would say something. Katie had to do that once at Metro. But I haven't yet run into it.

As for linen closets, the only two people I ever caught locked in a linen closet were a young guy from Environmental Services and another young guy from Escort.

After I had had my conversation with Lee George about Al Moore's urine, I talked to the patient myself.

"Mr. Moore," I said, "the doctors want us to come in here every half hour and ask you if you have to urinate. You're an intelligent adult man. I don't think you need us coming in here every half hour. I think that would really begin to bug you. So could I ask you to just please save your urine?"

The man looked at me as if I were insulting him.

"I *was* saving it," he said. "Then I'd leave it in the bathroom and nobody ever came to empty the urinal and it got full and I had to urinate into the toilet. So I stopped saving it."

Sometimes, it's true, nurses do not get into the room as often as they should to empty the urinals. On the other hand, I think patients sometimes think we know when they've urinated. And I've seen men pass their urine and fill up the whole urinal in one shot. Women are always on the bedpan, but men are like camels. They wait a lot. Anyway, I was upset about what Moore was saying because I knew that at least three nurses had told him to let the nursing staff know when his urinal was full.

I told him again. "When you pass your urine, Mr. Moore, just put your light on so one of the nurses will know to come and empty the urinal."

That worked for two days. Then the man decided he didn't want the surgery George was proposing for him. He signed himself out of the hospital.

15

BROKEN TIES
TO THE BEDSIDE

In mid-December I told Miss Craig that I had decided to turn down the position of head nurse on the oncology floor. The reasons I gave were the same as the reservations I had expressed to her during the original meeting with Dr. Rose and after he left.

Craig did not try to get me to change my mind.

"Well, you're going to destroy Ken Rose," she said jokingly. "Here he pays you the high compliment of wanting you to run his floor, and you turn him down."

Craig said she respected my decision. I was glad she didn't press me further. If she had, she might have gotten out of me something I didn't feel ready to discuss with her. Trying to decide about the oncology floor had made me think about my career in general. That caused something very important to come into focus for me. I realized that the longer I spent in administration, the deeper in I got, the farther I would be from my ideal nursing situation.

Taking over a brand new floor would mean investing at least a couple of years. It would take that long to get it running smoothly. After four years in two head-nurse positions—two years on Eight Cook, two on the oncology floor—it would be very hard for me to become a staff nurse again. The most logical next step would be up to supervisor. In fact, the nursing office had spoken to me about the possibility of a supervisory position even before the position on the oncology floor came up.

I took that as a compliment. But I'm not interested in moving up. I take home too many of my problems now, with just one floor to worry about. If I were worrying about two or three floors, I'd go nuts. Besides, supervising isn't for me. I'm far enough away from patient care as it is. If I became a supervisor, I'd never give a patient a bath or get a patient out of bed or sit and talk to patients or do any of the other things I enjoy doing. Maybe I'll change my mind. But right now I don't want to be a supervisor.

I never wanted to be a head nurse. If certain things hadn't happened at Metro, I might never have taken this job. For nearly three years there, I felt very close to being in my ideal nursing situation. Katie was a big reason. She really built up my confidence, saying she thought my strength lay in emotional support of patients, which is where I wanted to be strong, and telling me I was one of the best bedside nurses she knew. Because I was doing bedside care, I got to know the patients very well. I learned a lot. I felt I was doing a good job. As long as Katie was head nurse, I remember being really happy most of the time.

Then Katie quit. After several years in the job, she felt she had learned as much as she could about it and had given as much as she could to it. I was very upset about her leaving.

Just after we got the news about Katie, we learned that she was being replaced by Marilyn, a nurse on the floor who had graduated the same year I did, had worked exactly as long as I had, and was known to be a pet of the director of nursing.

I could rationalize Marilyn's getting the job. She had a B.S. degree. I wouldn't have wanted to be head nurse at that point. But I was hurt that I hadn't even been considered.

Also I didn't like Marilyn. If I had respected her, it wouldn't have been as upsetting. But she was so task-oriented that it didn't seem to me she really cared about patients. In addition, she looked down on me and the other three-year nurses. She never talked to us. She was like the Great Stone Face. The prospect of working under her made me very upset.

At the time Marilyn was appointed, I was living with Joyce Duff, a friend from nursing school. Joyce had become head nurse on Four Cook about a year earlier. When she saw how unhappy I was about the situation at Metro, she suggested that I come to work at Central.

I wasn't ready even to consider it.

"No," I told Joyce, "I'm not going to have everybody saying that I'm a spoiled brat, that I'm leaving just because Marilyn got to be head nurse and I didn't.

I didn't want to leave Metro. Counting nursing school and my time as a staff nurse, I had been there nearly six years. I knew the place. I had good friends there. Except for Marilyn, I liked everybody I worked with. Also, since Marilyn had all new grads on the floor except me and one other person, I didn't think it would be fair to leave. I even thought that Marilyn might change enough, once she got into the job, that I would become comfortable with her.

Plus I kept thinking that another hospital wouldn't necessarily be any better. My friends at other hospitals kept telling me how rotten their jobs were. I thought, "Why should I go to another hospital where I may have the same or worse?"

Months passed. Things got much worse for me at Metro. Because of Marilyn, I felt a great deal of frustration. She was giving me more nights and evenings than anyone else. I had to pretend to like her when I didn't. To top things off, when I had the run-in with the director of nursing over my sarcasm to Dr. Colberg, I got no support at all from Marilyn. It got so I couldn't stand going to work.

All this time Joyce kept telling me how wonderful she thought Central was and what a fool she thought I was to take all the rotating at Metro. Every time I complained about something, she'd say, "If you were over at Central, things like that wouldn't happen."

Finally I said to myself, "This is ridiculous. You're complaining all the time. If you hate the job that much, get out. You're driving yourself crazy."

I was really scared about the change. I didn't know whether I could handle the head nurse position. But I did feel very strongly that I needed a different situation. This was all happening during Ron's first year in med school. I knew we would be getting married soon. Though I didn't mind rotating, I liked the idea of straight days for a change. My salary would increase from $10,600 to $11,900. That would help a lot, because my salary would be supporting us while Ron went through medical school on loans.

So finally I applied at Central and got the job.

If you're primarily interested in doing patient care, then being in an administrative position can be very frustrating.

I don't know from personal experience what it's like to be a supervisor. From what I've seen, the supervisors at Central have more patient contact than the supervisors at Metro did, yet Ann Sullivan seems to spend most of her time making patient rounds, calling the appropriate people when there's a problem, and helping out with the administration of a unit when one of the head nurses has a day off. You do talk to patients on rounds, but getting information from or about them in a brief visit is a lot different from getting to know them by doing physical care on them.

I'm able to do a little more direct patient care than Ann is. But not much more. Twice since I became head nurse I've given complete charge to somebody else and done patient care all day. I call that a play day. Other days I get into each patient's room once or twice at most, for five minutes at most. Usually it's only for two or three minutes. Unless it's someone who's very sick, I may spend no more than one hour with a patient during that person's entire hospital stay, whereas a staff nurse may spend an hour a day.

A head nurse can't really find out much more about patients than a supervisor can. You can read the charts and see what the doctors have said, what the nurses' notes say, and what the lab studies show. Ideally your staff will come to you, as mine does, and tell you things. If I had an uncaring staff, I wouldn't be able to do half the things I do.

But if I make rounds and spend fifteen minutes in the room, a patient is not going to open up about something unless he or she is really upset or particularly in the mood to talk. When a light goes on, I go in and take care of whatever it is, but I'm not getting to know that patient. Though I may know certain things, I don't have the continuity that somebody has who's taking care of that patient a couple of days in a row. All I know about the person is bits and pieces. I see this as unavoidable. There are only so many hours in a day. But I don't like it.

You build up a rapport by taking care of a patient. For the most part, the patients I have gotten close to are those I did physical care on. There's more time to get to know somebody, and a warmth develops when you do something physical for somebody.

What's frustrating for me about not doing direct patient care is that I miss out not only on getting to know different people and improving their care but also on the satisfaction of seeing results. When somebody is really sick, maybe to the point of being powerless, and I help the person do certain things or do them myself— brush his teeth, rinse out his mouth, shave him, wash his body off, put lotion on his skin, put a clean gown on him, put Vaseline on his lips, comb his hair, get him up or change his position, change the sheets—I feel really good.

If I do all that for a completely comatose patient who doesn't even respond to pain, I can still get satisfaction. Some people can't. Ron teases me at home about how much I like to clean and shine. I guess my enjoyment of direct patient care comes from the same impulse. I can look at the person and see what I've done. That's not true of most of my tasks as head nurse. I have to convince myself that making telephone calls or taking off orders is doing something for patients. Doing those things is a means to an end. Doing direct care *is* the end. I see that as the fruits of a nurse's labor.

Administration isn't difficult just because of what it is not. It's difficult because of what it is. Or at least that's true about the administrative position I know about from experience.

Miss Craig says that head nurse is the hardest job in the hospital. I'm sure there are people in the hospital who would disagree.

But I am the only person in the hospital directly responsible for all the patients on Eight Cook. Nurses on my staff are responsible only for certain patients for one shift. The supervisor covers several floors or units, so while Ann Sullivan has more patients to worry about, she is only indirectly responsible for each of them, and again, for only one shift.

A supervisor is not totally responsible for whether a unit works or fails to work. I am. My job is to direct, monitor, and evaluate all patient care on the floor. The supervisor will try to answer questions I can't answer or to solve problems I can't solve. Since these are the toughest questions or problems, I'm sure they must be frustrating for the supervisor to deal with. By the same token, the supervisor doesn't have to get into all the minor hassles that take up so much of my time.

The supervisor deals mainly with two or three head nurses. I deal with everybody. Every question or problem that arises on

Eight Cook comes first to me. That's policy, but it would happen anyway. Everybody wants to talk to the head nurse. They could ask anybody, but they ask me.

"I want the nurse in charge! Did Mr. So-and-so get such-and-such a pill?"

I could be giving an enema to somebody, and a clerk will call my name through the intercom, "Mrs. Benjamin! You're wanted on the phone!"

Some people think paperwork is the worst part of being a head nurse. While I'd like to get rid of all the paperwork, I'm used to it. What I hate is the telephone. When you're answering everybody's questions and straightening out everybody's problems, you spend a lot of time on the phone. Also, because of the way Central is set up, the person in charge usually is stuck with all the scheduling of tests and X-rays. Sometimes it seems as if I do nothing all day but dial or answer the phone.

I like least being on the phone to X-ray. Frequently they put me on hold and don't come back for fifteen or twenty minutes. It doesn't help to hang up and call back. They just put me on hold again. Now I work on charts while I'm waiting. But my anxiety level still gets so high that I feel like ramming the phone through somebody's head.

Maybe once a day we have a problem with Dietary. At 10:30 A.M. a patient will put the light on and say, "How come I didn't get a breakfast tray?" I call Dietary to find out what happened.

Dietary says, "We sent that tray up."

"I say, "But it isn't here."

"Are you sure? Did you check all the other rooms to see if the patients got the wrong tray?"

At that point I feel like screaming, "Lady, do you think I have time to go around to every room and make sure all the patients got the right trays?"

Instead, I'll say, "Maybe it was sent to the wrong floor." So the dietitian checks into the matter. But not before I take flak from the person on the other end of the line. Dietary yells a lot. Pharmacy yells. X-ray yells all the time. The nurses are always wrong.

Of course the nurses are sometimes wrong. When you consider all the details involved in getting just one sick person well enough to go home, it's a wonder everybody isn't wrong more often. But I don't think supervisors always realize how much time a head nurse can waste on phone calls and other chores that aren't really nursing.

Given that so few of those chores have visible results, it's probably understandable that I rarely have somebody come up to me and say, "You did a good job." Sometimes I need that. We all want to feel we're doing a good job.

According to several articles I've read, praise is a problem for many head nurses. Often head nurses end up getting their praise from doctors. That's not where we should be looking for praise. The head nurse who gets praise from doctors may be doing too much for doctors, buttering them up just to get praise. If Dr. Smith praises her, she makes sure that Dr. Smith's patients get the best nursing care, that Dr. Smith's blood studies get down to the lab on time, that Dr. Smith's orders get taken off right away. When Dr. Smith needs sponges, the head nurse runs right into the utility room and finds some sponges.

She's functioning as Dr. Smith's servant. That shouldn't be. A head nurse shouldn't need to seek praise in that way from doctors. She should get it from other nurses. From her peers. From nursing management.

That's fine in theory. I don't find it working in fact. Sometimes one of the staff nurses will compliment me on the way I've done something, and of course that pleases me. But usually the closest to praise I hear from the staff is, "Gee, I'm glad to see you back!" if I've been off over a particularly busy weekend. Betty Fillmore, who was my supervisor at Central for more than a year, never gave me positive reinforcement.

That was very hard for me. Betty was very conscientious and really cared about patients. There wasn't anything she wouldn't do for patients. But she was moody. I took her moods to be disapproval of me. I always felt I was doing something wrong. Until she gave me an evaluation that was above average, I never knew how she really felt.

The only outright praise she ever gave me was something she said one day when she was orienting a new supervisor. When she brought the man over to me, she said, "I want to introduce you to Mary Benjamin. She's an excellent head nurse."

I almost died in my tracks. She had never said that before. Oh, my god, here it is! Palpitations!

Before I knew how Betty really felt, I would say to myself,

"Well, I never praise or thank her either. Maybe she's the kind of person I am and finds it very difficult to praise someone." I don't have an easy way of praising people. It's one of my faults. My family isn't very praise-oriented, so maybe that's why I'm not. I try to praise people, but sometimes I don't feel comfortable doing it. It's hard for me.

So I started saying things to Betty every once in a while, when it seemed natural. "That's a really good suggestion," I'd say. "I never would have thought of that." She didn't respond in kind. After a while I got used to getting no praise from her. I accepted it as Betty and no longer blamed myself.

Now that Ann Sullivan has taken over for Betty, I feel a lot of support. Maybe that makes it easier for me to support Ann. Once in a while when we're both doing something in the nurses' station, I'll say, "Thank god you're here today, Ann. Makes the day a little better."

Someone else will jokingly say, "Why are you thanking her for being here? She's getting paid."

I'll say, "Well, nobody else pats us on the back. I think we have to be nice to each other."

When doctors do praise us, it's hard not to be pleased. Recently a hysterectomy patient—an obese woman who had developed a big pus pocket at the bottom of her incision, right above the pubic area—was transferred from the gynie floor. She was running 102° temps. Twice a day we had to put on sterile gloves, draw up pHisoHex in a sterile syringe, put the tip of the syringe into this golfball-size opening, squirt out all the pus, then pack the area with gauze and cover it with a 4 × 4 gauze pad. The treatment took fifteen or twenty minutes.

One day I picked up the woman's chart and saw that in the progress notes a doctor had written, "Wound looks good. Nurses obviously doing good job irrigating wound."

I mentioned this in report. The people who had done the irrigating really perked up. After report they looked at the progress notes for themselves and went around saying, "See! There it is! The doctor did write that!" I was as happy as they were.

Or sometimes a doctor will say, "This is a good floor. I really like having my patients up here." Ron says that on the days I hear something like that from a doctor, I come home bubbling.

But I consciously try to get most of my praise or input from patients. This can be done fairly easily by doing little things for them. I like it when patients say, "I want to speak to Mary." This happens most often with patients who've been on the floor a while. It's not that they want me because something is wrong. It's that they think I'll make things a little bit better. That makes me feel good. Or I'll do something for a patient, and the person will say, "Thank you, doll. That was really nice of you." It's said honestly. That also makes me feel good.

Of course since I am able to spend so little time with patients, that kind of praise doesn't come along very often.

Sometimes I get very frustrated with my job. There are days when I come home with my stomach in knots, really keyed up, unable to relax. I tell myself that I should divorce myself from what's happening at work. Sometimes I'll rush home and bake a cake. Clean. Take out my frustrations and anxieties that way.

These tricks don't always work. Sometimes my frustrations set a tone at home that Ron notices. These are usually the times when I'm depressed enough to say to myself, "What else could I do?" I'll sit and daydream about a time when I can sit home and do macramé and make pottery and go to temple bazaars. Of course I argue with myself that maybe I wouldn't like staying home at all.

Being a head nurse certainly doesn't account for all the frustrations I feel about my job. A lot of it is my personality. I'm very hard-driving and fairly aggressive. I was that way as a teenager. Also, I was always taught that you don't goof off if somebody's paying you. So it's not just the job. I think I would suffer a lot of work-related tension if I were employed as a secretary.

Yet I think I would prefer the frustrations of a staff nurse to the frustrations of the job I have now. If Ron and I could afford it now, if I could get a staff job for the money I'm making as head nurse, I'd do it.

At least I say I would.

But I wonder, sometimes. Could I really go back to a staff position? Maybe I'm not as idealistic as I'd like to think.

I could get back into rotating, I'm sure. Though I don't like it, I don't think it would bother me that much. If the head nurse were a little older than I—a year, even—if there were a real peer relationship between us, and if she ran a well-organized floor, then I'm sure I'd love it. But what if I got onto a floor and thought to myself, "The running of this floor is crappy. I could do a much better job of it."

For now, the question is academic. No staff nurse earns a head nurse salary. At this point, I can't go back to a staff nurse salary. Our income would be cut by at least $2,000. We could afford to stay in our apartment, but we would have to change our life-style. There would be no way we could even plan to have a home.

From a monetary standpoint, I'm not in a position to move. At least till Ron graduates and starts bringing money in instead of putting money out, I have to stay where I am. I couldn't become a staff nurse. I have to go on being a head nurse.

I try not to dwell on that. There's nothing I can do about it. I have to make the best of the situation.

When all is said and done, I have to acknowledge that even with the frustrations, I basically like my job as head nurse. I learn a lot. Something new happens each day. It's interesting and satisfying to handle new situations. Whenever we get a new patient or a new staff member, we have to learn appropriate ways of dealing with these people. A young man came in recently with Hodgkin's disease. Since I don't know much about Hodgkin's, I got out a book and read enough to feel confident about having the patient on the floor.

It's a challenge to get different kinds of cases and to see different kinds of surgery. It's a challenge to have a really sick patient to take care of. It's satisfying to straighten out mix-ups.

It also makes me feel good to think I've helped staff members develop in certain ways. Liz and Maureen, for example. They were good people to begin with. They came with high ideals. But maybe I've made it easier for them to grow than someone else would have. Seeing the way they function now makes me feel good, because I think I had something to do with the change.

I hope what I've encouraged in staff is a general feeling for patients. I believe deep down that a nurse who wants to can learn to do anything for patients. People like Mrs. Payne, Toni Gillette—these people basically care about patients. They both have a lot to give. I hope I've helped them keep giving it. God, I hope I'm not stifling people. That, I think, is a crime.

Of course I also get personal satisfaction from what little bit I am able to do for patients in the way of physical care. We had a patient on the floor who wasn't eating. Nothing we tried was working. Finally, I spent a morning with him. I went in there thinking, "I'm going to keep at this man until I make him eat." I did. He got down everything on his lunch tray. That made my day. When you feed a person and the person does eat, there's a good feeling.

So despite the drawbacks of my job, I'm happy in what I'm doing. But I can say that because I've learned to see myself in a different light.

I guess from a patient care standpoint, it doesn't really make any difference what level you're on. If you're good, whether you're a director of nursing or a nursing assistant, you're influencing patient care. You can say to yourself, "I'm in nursing. I'm doing a good job. Therefore, I'm giving nursing care."

But on the days when I have very little patient contact, I have to reassure myself that nursing is what I'm doing.

Those are the days I become upset.

16

IN SICKNESS AND IN HELL: HUMAN RESPONSES

Christmas was a week away. The stack of mail delivered to Eight Cook each morning grew thicker and thicker. Many of the cards were addressed to the nurses. Ruth, the clerk on days, taped the cards to the edge of a long shelf along the back wall of the nurses' station. Most of the cards were from the nursing staffs of other floors: "To Eight Cook from Six West."

A couple were from doctors. The rest were from patients or their families. On a few of those were notes: "Many thanks for the care you gave my husband." Most of the people on the staff took a look through the new cards every time they came on duty.

The floor seemed very Christmasy. A relative of one of the patients brought in a small tree, which we put in the solarium and decorated with ornaments from home. There were poinsettia plants in a dozen rooms. In the nurses' lounge, Jennie's Christmas party list was filling with written promises of cookies, sandwiches, or punch. From Kelly's room across from the nurses' station came a background of Christmas music from morning till night.

Kelly was not in good shape. For about a week after he returned to the hospital, he had had good days and bad days. Then his days started to be almost all bad. He was constantly losing blood. Every time he vomited, he brought up blood. Every time he had diarrhea, minute amounts of blood came out. The doctors had to transfuse him every few days. From what I could see, the transfusions were all that kept him alive.

He was constantly vomiting. We didn't even know how much fluid he was losing, because he would lean over the side of the bed and vomit into the basin, and the basin would overflow into the wastebasket, and the wastebasket usually had junk in it. Toward the end of his second week back in the hospital, Kelly stopped caring where he vomited. He would just lean over the bed and vomit on the floor. There was no way we could measure what was coming up. But it was in the neighborhood of hundreds of ccs. each time.

As far as I could gather, Kelly's poor condition was the result not of his disease but of the treatment for the disease. He had had so much radiation that tissue inside him was dying from it. From what I could see, none of the support we were giving Kelly was having the effect of allowing the radiation injuries to heal. He just seemed to grow worse.

Yet Rose continued to seem optimistic. That confused me.

One morning I grabbed Rose when he came up on rounds.

"Dr. Rose," I said, "do you really think we're helping Kelly?"

Rose didn't ask what I meant.

"Look," he said. "Cell death is very complicated. Radiation biology is very complicated. I don't know at what point the body starts to recover from the treatments. A lot of radiation people don't know either.

"I'm not even sure that radiation gastritis is the problem at this point. It's possible that Kelly is bleeding because he has an ulcer in the gastrointestinal tract. It's possible—not likely, but possible— that there's cancer inside Kelly that I didn't find when I did the exploratories. It could be just long-term effects of heavy radiation. Most people don't live long enough to suffer long-term effects of heavy radiation.

"That's one reason we can't be sure of what's happening with Kelly. I don't know why he's bleeding. I do know that if the problem is from radiation, sometimes even when the situation seems critical, as it does seem with him, you can't be certain that the patient will not live."

I said, "Do you think he's going to live?"

"I believe he's going to heal. I want him to heal. I want him to turn the corner and go home."

I said nothing. Rose went off on rounds. I sat there wishing that Rose would put himself in the patient's place and let Kelly O'Brien die.

It seemed to me that that's what Kelly wanted. I felt he had given up. He had virtually stopped talking. During his first and second admissions, he and I had had long talks about all kinds of things and had joked around a lot. Even during the third admission, before he had had his five days at home. Kelly had talked a lot.

But this admission was different. After his first week back on Eight, Kelly began blocking everybody out. He wouldn't open his eyes. When we'd ask him a question, there would be no response. None. I'd go in and talk to him or put my hand on his shoulder or say, "Hi, Kelly," just to let him know I was there. Nothing. He was getting Dilaudid, but only enough to keep him pain-free. Not enough to keep him from responding.

"He never talks to me," Mrs. O'Brien said one afternoon, stopping me in the hall. "He never says a word to me. Does he talk to you nurses?"

"No," I said. "He's not talking to us either."

One day one of the new kids, Pam Franklin, was exasperated enough with the situation to confront it.

"Kelly," she said. "I haven't worked with you in a week. If you don't tell me what hurts, I can't know. Does this hurt?"

Kelly didn't open his eyes, but he said, "Yes."

Pam said, "Do you need pain medication?"

"Yes."

That's all he said. But he had heard. He did know what was going on. He just wasn't bothering to talk back.

Taking care of Kelly was very depressing for everybody. He was a heavy load, physically and emotionally. We'd no sooner get him cleaned up than he'd vomit all over the place, and we'd have to change the whole bed again. Or we'd change his dressings, and he'd retch, and the dressings would pull off, so we'd have to straighten those up again. Kelly didn't want to be turned from side to side. Every time we moved him, he was uncomfortable. We felt we couldn't control anything.

Just being in the room was unpleasant, the odor in there was so foul. The heating–cooling unit under the windowsill next to Kelly's bed was covered by a big grill, and often when Kelly vomited, he would spray into the grill. Since it was impossible to clean in there, the whole grillwork was covered with particles of dried vomitus. Once I got in the room, I sort of forgot how it smelled, but each time I walked in, I'd think, "My god. The odor. I can't stand it."

The room always looked dirty. The bedside table and the whole windowsill were full of equipment we were using with Kelly, and the floor was almost always messy. A lot of what Kelly vomited up was Maalox. Maalox is extremely hard to clean up. It just clumps onto everything. No matter what we did, there was always a residue of Maalox on the floor.

Mr. Shorey had a lot of mess on his side too. People were always trying to straighten up the room, but there was so much mess and so much stuff that it was impossible to make a real dent in it. I've never seen anything like it in my life.

I didn't help that Mr. Shorey was getting very bad himself. Since he had CA everywhere, and since none of us really knew him that well, watching him go downhill so fast wasn't as hard on us as seeing what was happening to Kelly. People felt really sad about Kelly.

But having them both on the floor at once was rough. Each man needed so much care that I had to assign two different nurses to that room so one person didn't get them both. People had to be rotated out of that room a lot, because they got depressed. They couldn't take more than two or three days at most.

Mrs. O'Brien was still spending most of each day with Kelly. Though she had shortened her visits to about six hours instead of eight or ten, she didn't look as if she was getting any more rest than she had been. She looked bad physically and seemed really down. Until the time Kelly had gone home, she would sit by his bed and knit. Now she just sat there. Thinking over her question of whether Kelly was talking to the nurses, I decided it was time I had a talk with her.

One afternoon I was just finishing up for the day when I saw her getting her coat on to leave.

"Mrs. O'Brien," I said, "could I speak to you for a few minutes?"

She said, "Yes, of course."

"Come over here." I took her into the little office we sometimes use as a conference room. She sat down on the edge of one of the chairs. I sat down too.

I asked, "What has Dr. Rose said to you about Kelly?"

"He told me he thinks the cancer is burned out, and he wants to give him a chance."

"What do you think?"

She sighed and looked down at her hands. "I don't know. Kelly has been saying to me, 'Don't let them do this to me. Take the feeding tube out. Take the blood out.' "

"I didn't realize he had been asking you to do that."

Mrs. O'Brien looked at me. "Oh, yes," she said. "He has been asking me for a couple of weeks, 'Just pull out the tubes.' "

She took a tissue out of her purse. "It just seems to me as if he's been through so much misery." She blew her nose and said, "I think it's time."

Not so much what Mrs. O'Brien said, but the way she said it made me feel certain that she had accepted that her husband was going to die. Her face looked resigned.

I said, "You seem prepared."

"I guess I'm as prepared as I'm ever going to be."

"What's happening with you?"

"I'm all right. I'm eating dinner with my children. They're taking care of me."

"You're not going to be in the house by yourself, are you?"

"No. I couldn't stand being alone. I've been sleeping over at Pat's on the couch in the living room. She lives just next door, you know."

"Oh, that's good. So you're not alone."

"I'm not alone."

Mrs. O'Brien and I walked out of the office with our arms around each other. When we got back to the nurses' station, I wrote down the Eight Cook telephone number, which is not a public number, and gave it to her.

"You know we'd call you if anything happened," I said to Mrs. O'Brien. "But if you wake up in the middle of the night and start worrying, call. Somebody you know is sure to be here. Anybody will be glad to tell you what's going on."

Mrs. O'Brien's eyes filled up again. "Thank you, Mary," she said. "I'll see you tomorrow."

When I started nursing school, I didn't know what sickness was.

I graduated from nursing school still not knowing.

Only after I had started working did I begin to truly understand what it's like to be sick.

I was shocked.

Doris Russell, a cancer patient who had several admissions on Eight Cook, wrote something for the people close to her on what it means to have cancer. She gave me a copy just before she died. Basically she wrote that cancer patients aren't any worse off than anyone else with a disease that's incurable or hard to cure. Family, friends, and the public in general, she wrote, should not feel especially sorry for CA patients, because many people with other illnesses suffer just as much.

I think what Doris Russell said is true. There are people who are far more debilitated by cardiac disease than some people are with cancer. Stroke patients may lose the use of their bodies. Multiple sclerosis patients may be blind and confined to wheelchairs before they're thirty years old. I'm not saying cancer isn't horrible. But many other diseases are just as bad. Any illness is horrible. What people go through when they're sick is incredible.

They don't go through just the illness. They also go through the cure. Sometimes the remedy seems worse than the disease. To save the life of a diabetic, surgeons might have to amputate the patient's legs, as they did with Emerald Lynch. To stabilize a patient with kidney disease who is on renal dialysis, the doctors may impose fluid restrictions so strict that patients end up begging for an ice cube in the middle of the night.

I know that must be horrible for the patients, because it's an ordeal even for the nurses. I could be walking down the hall in near-dark with a flashlight in my hand and hear, "Nurse. Please. Get some ice." I go in and check the I&O sheet. The patient's intake for the day has been 720 ccs. He's allowed 800 ccs. That means he has less than three ounces left. I know I have to give him a pill at 4:00 A.M. If I give him an ice cube, I won't have enough water to give the pill.

So I refuse the patient's request for one ice cube, and I leave the room feeling like a witch.

It's horrible for any human being to go through treatment for cancer. Chemotherapy and radiation can make you feel worse than the disease did. It's one thing to come in with a big tumor inside your abdomen. You're having pain, you can't eat, you can't swallow properly. While the radiation adds to the discomfort at first, it does shrink the tumor, so that you end up feeling better than you did when you came in.

It's quite another thing for, say, leukemics, who may be basically asymptomatic. They're not uncomfortable. They're not having pain. When they start receiving radiation treatments, they puke their guts out.

Any kind of major surgery is hard on patients. I don't think most people realize how much work is involved. As Stephanie points out, some patients think they're in the Hilton when they come to the hospital. They think they're in to be taken care of, not to get well. They think they're there for recuperation, by which they mean bed rest.

They're not. They're in for a lot of hard work after surgery. We make all patients except the cardiacs do their own A.M. care. Even Kelly O'Brien was doing his until he came back in. This has a therapeutic purpose: the faster the body returns to normal activities, the sooner the person can go home.

That's why surgical patients who have surgery in the morning are usually out of bed in the evening. This helps prevent post-op complications. Most doctors write, "Bed rest till 6:00 P.M., out of bed tonight once, up walking tomorrow." Older men and women need convincing. They'll tell you they used to stay in bed several days after surgery. When you tell them they're going to get up that night, they look at you as if you're crazy.

Getting the body moving is hard work for post-op patients. They're uncomfortable to begin with. Exerting effort makes them even more uncomfortable. To prevent fluid from collecting in a post-op's lungs, a nurse keeps saying to the patient, "Cough. Cough." The patient is coughing, but the nurse is saying, "Cough louder." The patient is trying. Most patients try to do the best they can. But people in the hospital are asked to do more and perform better when they're at their very weakest.

Tests alone are unpleasant for patients. One of the worst is the barium enema. Barium is a thick, chalky substance used in a test called the lower or long GI, which is administered to detect or rule out abnormalities in the lower gastrointestinal tract. I've walked in rooms where they were doing that test. It's uncomfortable and demeaning.

The night before, the patient is given laxatives to clean out the rectum and intestines. Then for the enema he lies on his side on an X-ray table, and an X-ray technician he has never met till that moment hangs up a big bag of barium and releases the barium into the rectum and says, "Okay, honey, we're almost ready to do the films."

The patient has to hold the barium in while the technician is taking X-rays. He feels cramped. Because he's had all the laxatives the night before, his intestines are very irritated. The whole procedure can be done impersonally. I imagine it's very nasty. I half think doctors and nurses should go through all these studies to know what they feel like.

So when Toni Gillette tells me, as she sometimes does, that I baby patients, I have to disagree. I feel very sorry for people in the hospital. It's terrible to be sick. No wonder patients get depressed.

No wonder they get angry. I once had a lung cancer patient who called me in, told me he had gotten the wrong breakfast, then picked up his breakfast tray and threw it against a wall. Before I could react, he stalked out of the room and into the solarium yelling and screaming. The nursing care was terrible, he said, and the doctors didn't give a damn. He was very, very angry.

At first I thought, "Well, if that's the way he wants to act, let him." But something told me to try to talk to him. I went into the solarium and put my hand on his arm.

He pulled away. "Leave me alone. I don't want to talk to you."

"I want to talk to you. There's something wrong. People don't throw breakfast trays because they get the wrong breakfast. What's troubling you?"

At first I didn't think he was going to tell me. But I ended up staying in there for about an hour. The man had suffered enough for twenty people. His wife had died of cancer three years earlier. He had five children ranging in age from five to eighteen. He had lost his job because of his illness. He was a young man—in his forties—but he could not support his family. Sooner or later he was going to die of his disease. He was very, very angry. At everybody. At the world.

Of course I couldn't blame him. He was going through a stage of loss. He had lost his ability to function and thus to control his own life. From what I've read, the stages of loss are similar to the stages of grief. Anger is one stage. The man was grieving for himself.

He calmed down. Eventually he went home, and I don't know what happened to him.

But if he was like most patients, he came to accept his illness and all that went with it.

It's incredible to see what people can accept. People go through hell and complain about nothing. Some people actually experience pain without recognizing it as pain.

I'll walk in a room and say to a patient, "Are you having pain?" The patient says no. Yet I can see that his feet are going, his hands are moving, and he's obviously jittery. I'll say, "Why are you moving your feet?" He'll say, "Oh, I'm uncomfortable." You use the word *pain*, and people think you mean something so terrible that it can't be what they're feeling. Yet they have these horrible sensations.

I'll look at a chart and see that a patient who had abdominal surgery two days earlier has been medicated for pain only once. Occasionally the patient refuses the pain medication out of fear of becoming addicted, something that happens very rarely. Usually the pain medication isn't given because the patient doesn't know he's in pain. The nurses have to stress to the patient, "You have something ordered. Don't lie there and be uncomfortable, for god's sake."

It's incredible to see what the body can take. What the spirit can take. When you consider what patients go through, it seems nothing short of miraculous that so few trays get thrown. I've seen a lot of people with a lot of strength, and I wonder where they get it.

Some seem to get it from religion. I usually don't discuss religion with people, but I guess that the patients who ask to talk to a pastor or rabbi or who read the Bible or use rosary beads are at least somewhat religious. Those who seem to have religion seem to be helped by it. There's a certain calmness about them. The most memorable instances of this were a few older black women, Baptists, who honestly believed that they were in God's hands. They were very calm. It seemed as if they could endure anything.

"Don't worry about me, dear," they would say. "I'm an old lady. My time has come. God is taking care of me."

Maybe these people were strong underneath and would have been calm even if they hadn't been religious. A lot of people who don't seem to have any religion do have strength. Look at what happened to "that repulsive old Al Fortin," as Maureen Shay called him, once he made up his mind to get well. Minus one leg, he picked himself up and started walking again and finally, we heard, went back to work.

Or Sally Morse, a 72-year-old bilateral amputee who was a psychotic. Sally Morse went through a really bad post-op depression on Eight Cook. She was in poor shape. A psychiatrist came in and started giving her anti-depressant medication. You could say that the pills helped her, because when Sally Morse found out what she was getting, she was highly offended. Not only did she start hiding the pills (and she was very slick; we never did catch her at it) but she also decided she had better get better. Last we heard she was making visits to her doctor's office on two artificial legs, using a walker.

That woman was beautiful.

There are lots more like her.

Emerald Lynch. Two and half weeks after her second leg was amputated, Emerald Lynch finally got depressed. Sharon went in to do Lynch's A.M. care one morning, and Lynch hardly said a word the whole time Sharon was in her room. For a week she scarcely spoke to anybody.

I was glad this happened. Some people put up a good front till they get home and then fall apart. I'm sure Lynch would have gotten some support from her boyfriend at home. But in the hospital, she got support from everybody.

As down as she was, for her, Emerald Lynch never came close to falling apart. We were starting to get her out of bed and into the wheelchair, because her stump was healing nicely at last, and Lynch made herself do everything we wanted her to. She was unbelievably cooperative. "Oh, you girls want to make the bed now? Okay, I'll get up." She kept on doing all her own care, except for her back.

One afternoon about a week after her depression began, I was doing something out at the nurses' station when Lynch rolled up in her quote Cadillac and said to me out of the blue, "You know that black and white cat I told you about that my nephew was keeping for me? Well, that cat made the mistake of making a mess on my nephew's bed, and that was that."

Lynch had that old roguish grin on her face.

"So," she said, shrugging, "no more cat."

"So," I said, "one less mouth to feed off your plate."

Lynch threw back her head and laughed. Her whole upper body shook.

From that day till the day she went home, Emerald Lynch was her funny, nutty self.

People are amazing. Absolutely amazing. To think that patients can go through hell and get better, without getting bitter, can go through everything people go through when they are sick and have terrible things happen to them and then still have a life—well, it's really magnificent.

A couple of footnotes about going through hell.

Some people go through it who shouldn't have to. If Al Fortin had taken good care of himself from the time his diabetes was diagnosed, he might not have lost a leg. If Virginia Medlock and Joy Li had gotten treatment when they first began having vaginal discharge, they might still be alive and well.

Yet I can't judge people who ignore warnings or neglect their bodies. I ignore warnings myself. I have cystic breasts. Every so often when I'm examining my breasts, I discover what I take to be a lump. Instead of seeing a doctor immediately, I've waited a couple of weeks, thinking, "Oh, it'll go away." Or I think, "That could never be breast cancer. I'm too young." Of course women my age get breast cancer.

So far the lumps have always gone away. I think if I really had breast cancer, I'd run right to the doctor. But I wonder to myself why I put off finding out.

I've seen articles in nursing journals about other nurses who notice lumps here or a mole changing color there, and these nurses have also waited for a while before seeing a doctor, because they were almost sure what their diagnosis would be. They knew. I mean most people are not dumb. They know what's happening. They're just afraid to face it.

Some people who face the disease can't face the treatment. It may get down to a question of which kind of hell you prefer to go through. Some people refuse to have a leg taken off, even though the doctors have told them that an amputation will prolong their lives.

Some people refuse radiation or chemotherapy. A number of these patients have already had a lot of cancer therapy, are going downhill, have very loving families, and don't want to put their families through any more. Patients who have nobody may not want to put themselves through the treatment. They'll say, "Well, I've got to go home and think about it," and they disappear.

Some patients refuse to have a colostomy done. They honestly think their spouses will hate them if they have the surgery. A woman came in to Eight Cook for tests, and the doctors told her she had cancer and needed a colostomy. She said no. They warned her that if she didn't have it, her life would be shortened.

"That's not a life," the woman said to me. "That's smelly and dirty. I'm not going to let my husband see me with a colostomy. He wouldn't love me any more. I'd rather die with my whole body intact than have him be physically repulsed by me."

The idea of a colostomy seems particularly upsetting to a lot of people. Friends of mine who are nurses have said to me, "I'd die before I'd have a colostomy done. I don't want shit coming out on my stomach." My own views have changed. When we read in a nursing school textbook that people with ulcerative colitis were very happy about having colostomies done, I couldn't believe it. I would think, "Oh, god, who could be happy about having a colostomy?"

Then I met an ulcerative colitis patient. He was a young black guy of about 24 who worked at Central, and shortly after I started on Eight Cook, he was admitted to the floor for an ileostomy. That's a similar operation to a colostomy, an opening from the bowel to the abdomen, but from a lower part of the bowel. I talked to the patient a lot and really got to like him. One day I said, "Can I ask you something? What was your reaction when the doctors first recommended this surgery?"

He grinned. "I was happy!" he said. "I used to sit on the john for hours. I'd be getting ready to go out to work or out on a date, and I'd have an attack of colitis, and I'd have to run to the john and sit. I had no control over my life. I never knew when I was going to be spending a long time on the john. With the ileostomy, I'll have a bag on my stomach, and what comes out goes into that bag. It may not be glamorous, but I have freedom."

What he said made me see colostomies from a different perspective. I've also been enlightened by the perspective of Dean Marco, the stoma therapist. For one thing, Dean gets really upset with nurses who wear gloves to do colostomy care. Gloves, he says, make the patients feel dirty. Dean will walk into a room and say to the nurse, or sometimes to a patient who is irrigating his colostomy with gloves on, "Why are you wearing gloves? You don't wear gloves when you wipe your rear end. It's the same feces. Just because it's coming out of the stomach doesn't make it any less clean. You don't need gloves."

Dean has also pretty well convinced me that if a patient has a good, strong relationship with his or her spouse, that relationship will not suffer as a result of a colostomy. I suppose there are exceptions. But that is Dean's feeling, and that's his experience, and he should know, because he has a colostomy himself. Though I've never asked, I'm guessing that he would agree with my feeling that a colostomy is not the worst thing that can happen to a human being.

The worst thing, from my point of view, is to lose your mind. To be unable to cope with your life. When I did a psych rotation in nursing school, seeing those people coming in and out—totally regressed, chronically unable to deal with their families or their surroundings—bothered me more than anything I have seen in a regular hospital.

Once we had a young woman diabetic on Eight Cook from a nearby psychiatric institute. She had tried to kill herself by jumping out a window. She was not in touch with reality. Seeing her bothered me more than any gaping, pus-filled wound I have ever seen.

Another time we had a 51-year-old black "dump" patient who had colon CA with metastasis to the brain. Mr. Vickers. He was like an animal. He couldn't talk, he couldn't do anything for himself, he seizured and made strange facial movements. One morning we went in and found that he had finger-painted the sheets, the walls, and his whole body, including his face, with his own feces.

He could understand us slightly. When we asked him a question or tried to get a reply to something, there was a certain intelligence that flickered through his eyes. But he couldn't retain anything, and his only means of communication was a growl.

It's terrible to see another human being in that condition. To me what happened to Mr. Vickers was far, far worse than any colostomy.

It's sometimes hard to understand why patients refuse treatment that might make them better. Some doctors become really upset when patients refuse radiation or chemotherapy. Deep down, I guess I feel myself that those patients are making unwise decisions, that if they allowed themselves to go through the treatments, they'd have a longer life. I would prefer to go through the treatment, no matter how uncomfortable it was. To me it would be worth it.

But what if you're a 75-year-old patient who lives alone, has no family, and there's nobody who really cares whether you live or die? Is it worth it to go through all that? Or is it better to say, "Well, I'll take my days as they are and that's it?"

They're awful choices. But I don't agree with doctors and nurses who invariably feel that patients who refuse treatment are being suicidal. Sometimes those patients are being realistic. Everybody's life is precious to the person living it. People have to decide for themselves how they want to spend the days they have left.

The day after I had my talk with Mrs. O'Brien, something really funny happened with Kelly.

It started with a comment Mr. Shorey made early in the morning. Mr. Shorey and Kelly had been too sick to talk to each other much since they had become roommates, but they listened to music or watched television together and sort of watched out for each other, and their families would sit in the room and talk. Mr. Shorey was hard of hearing, so when he did talk, it was in a very loud voice, loud enough that we could often hear him out at the nurses' station.

On this particular day, Kelly looked really bad. Stephanie was taking care of him. She was in there that morning when all of a sudden Mr. Shorey gestured toward Kelly and said to her in a loud voice, "Well, the old man looks pretty bad. I don't think he's going to last much longer."

Stephanie went "SSSSSSHHHHHHHHHH!" She looked over at Kelly, because she was afraid he'd be upset.

Kelly had his eyes closed. Since he had been blocking everybody out for days, Stephanie decided that he probably hadn't heard Mr. Shorey. She went back to whatever she was doing.

In about an hour, when Stephanie had finished Kelly's A.M. care, Kelly suddenly snapped his fingers at her and said, "When am I getting up?"

Stephanie almost fell over. Kelly hadn't been out of bed for two days. He hadn't volunteered a sentence to her for a week.

Well, she got him out of bed and propped him up in his chair. As soon as Kelly had settled himself and all his paraphernalia, he looked over at Mr. Shorey.

"Boy," he said in a loud voice, "the old man looks pretty bad today. Doesn't look like he's going to last much longer."

I've never heard anything like it in my life. We were all talking about it, shift to shift: "Did you hear what happened?" It was just as if Kelly had said, "Hmph. Who the hell does Shorey think he is, saying I'm not going to live much longer? *I'm* going to decide."

All that day Kelly O'Brien really forced himself to do things. Nobody could believe it.

17

ERRORS

Christmas was on a Sunday. I was scheduled to be off on Saturday and Sunday, but I had also asked for two vacation days, so I would be off Monday and Tuesday as well. Four whole days! I was really looking forward to the time, especially to the time after Christmas. As a present to me, Ron had made reservations for us to spend two days at the historic picturesque hotel in the country where we had spent our honeymoon. This would be our first time back to the Green River Inn, our first time away together in nearly a year and a half. I couldn't wait.

Central seemed very quiet when I went in that Friday for my last day of work before the holiday. The patient census was down throughout the hospital. All the patients who could go home had gone. Two sections, the orthopedics floor and the diabetic unit, were closed completely. According to the Eight Cook patient directory next to the front counter in the nurses' station, fourteen out of the thirty-six beds were empty.

"My god," I said jokingly to Mrs. Payne, "Twenty-two patients. Why don't we go out and finish our shopping?"

There were fewer nurses on than usual that morning. Everybody seemed in good spirits. The floor Christmas party had been held the afternoon before, and we gathered for report congratulating Jennie on the beautiful job of organizing she had done. Report revealed no serious problems. While the breakfast trays were being distributed, we got word that three more patients were

271

being discharged, leaving us with a record low census of nineteen. The morning passed uneventfully until noon.

Then two things happened. First, Kelly O'Brien vomited 1,000 ccs. of frank blood—about a quart.

I called Rich Drake, the resident covering Rose's service for December, to let him know.

"How is he?" Drake asked.

"He's rotten," I said. "But if you're asking me whether he's stable, he is."

As soon as he could, Drake came up to check on Mr. O'Brien. Drake looked upset. I felt upset. When he told me he was going to start another unit of blood on Kelly, I said. "For god's sake. Why don't you leave him alone?"

Drake's voice was tight. "Do you think I want to do this?"

"Then why are you doing it?"

"Because you can't legally let a patient bleed to death."

I just looked at Drake. "That's a copout," I said. Doctors do sometimes decide not to transfuse a patient who's hopeless.

Drake returned my look. He sighed. He said, "Because the Big R wants it."

Drake was overweight and slow-moving and, from what I could tell, a good doctor. I liked him almost as much as I liked Jon Benson. I could tell by Drake's face that he was as frustrated as I was. Rose had made up his mind to be aggressive with Kelly O'Brien's care. As long as he felt that way, the residents really had no choice but to go along and take whatever measures Rose wanted them to take. They could object, and I guess they could refuse to give the blood themselves, as Jane and Sharon had refused to give Virginia Medlock her Dilaudid. But a resident rarely goes against a staff doctor. Anyway, for all I knew, the residents shared Rose's belief—or at least respected it—that Kelly could get better, if not well. Rose was, after all, Central's expert on solid-tumor cancers.

But even if Rose was right, it was hard on all of us to see Kelly O'Brien suffer day after day.

After I had had this exchange with Drake, Sharon came up to me looking very troubled.

"Mary," she said, "there's a problem. Mrs. Bishop didn't get her insulin this morning."

Sharon was acting as team leader that day. Like the other new grads, she could supervise a team without much difficulty most of the time. But there was still an occasional slip-up. This was clearly one.

Ordinarily all diabetics receive insulin at 7:30 A.M. However, Mrs. Bishop had been scheduled for a fasting blood sugar test that morning. Dietary had been asked to hold her breakfast tray until after the blood samples were drawn, and the patient's insulin dose was also held. The blood team usually comes up on the floor at about 7:30 or 8:00. After the team had been up that morning, Sharon called Dietary for Mrs. Bishop's breakfast but forgot about giving the insulin.

No irreparable damage was done. We notified the doctor. Mrs. Bishop's blood samples were drawn again, and her next dose of insulin was adjusted according to the sugar levels the doctor found. Sharon wrote a nurses' note saying what had happened. She filled out an incident report, which I signed. There was no emergency.

Still, the insulin should not have been missed.

With another patient, it might not have been. Mrs. Bishop was in her own world. Sometimes on Saturdays and Sundays the blood team doesn't get up to the floor till 10:00, which means the patients waiting for fasting blood sugar tests don't get their breakfast till just about lunchtime. In Mrs. Bishop's mind, getting breakfast so late was just about the worst thing that could happen to her. When I'd go in to give her her insulin, her insulin was the last thing on her mind.

"What's that?" she'd ask distractedly. "My blood thinner?"

"No, Mrs. Bishop. It's your insulin."

"Oh, yeah, I didn't get that this morning, did I?"

Most diabetics are not like that. Most will get their breakfast tray and say, "Where's my insulin?" They get hyper about it. If Mrs. Bishop had been a little more hyper, there might have been no problem. Which is not to excuse the nurses.

I really felt sorry for Sharon. She has fair skin, and as she told me about what had happened, her face got very red. She was almost crying. She knew she had made a mistake, and she took it personally. I would have too, if I had been in her position. You think, "My god. That could have been a serious error. It could have hurt somebody.

Every nurse has made medications errors. I may be wrong, but my feeling is that nurses who say they have not are either liars or they haven't worked long enough.

None of the errors I know of had dire results. Most people probably think of medications errors as overdoses or big doses of the wrong medicine, doses that can cause death or a dramatic change in the patient's condition. From what I know, the system of passing medications involves so many checks on accuracy that it's almost impossible for these errors to occur. In fact most medications errors are, like Sharon's, errors of omission. The nurse forgets to give a pill or a shot. These errors are almost always easily remedied.

I've made two medications errors since I started nursing, or at least two that I'm aware of. The first was while I was a student. One morning I was supposed to pass meds with an instructor. Because I had already had some practice in giving meds, the instructor told me to go ahead and give a patient her 7:30 dose of insulin by myself.

The problem occurred because I was mixed up about the date. It was the 22nd of the month. I thought it was the 23rd. When I looked at the patient's chart, I saw that a dose of insulin had been given and signed off by a nurse on the 22nd. What had happened was that a night nurse had given the insulin only a few minutes earlier, just before she went off duty and I came on.

So I went in and gave the patient what turned out to be her second dose of insulin that morning. The patient was too sick to notice.

When the mistake was discovered, the head nurse hit the roof. I felt horrible. But the doctor just said, "Make sure you check the date before you start giving meds," which seems so obvious that I can't think of it now without smiling.

Actually, the night nurse was at fault too. A nurse going off duty should never give meds after the next shift begins, because—clearly—things could get confusing. In this case as with Sharon and Mrs. Bishop, the next insulin dose was simply adjusted, and there was no problem.

My second meds error occurred shortly after I came to work at Central. I was reading a patient's medication orders which a clerk had transcribed into the medication Kardex. The clerk had missed one of the orders. As I remember, it was for a diuretic, or water pill. I guess my mind wasn't on what I was seeing, because I failed to notice the absence of an order for that medication, something I should have picked up. The patient didn't get the pill that day.

The error was discovered that night by the nurse who was double-checking all the meds orders, which is one of the responsibilities of the night shift. The next morning I notified the doctor and filled out an incident report. There could have been a problem, but there wasn't.

Once in a while there's a mix-up of some sort, and the wrong patient is premedicated for surgery. The error is usually caught when the escort comes up and checks the patient's name band. I've never heard of the wrong patient getting as far as the OR. Even if that happened, so many people check a patient's identity before surgery that I think it would be impossible for a patient to undergo the wrong operation. At least I've never heard of one who did.

Once in a great while we slip up and premedicate a patient who has not signed the hospital consent form. When this happens, we have to let the sedative wear off, get the signature, and start over. We're not allowed to get a signature while the patient is under sedation, and surgery is never supposed to be done without the patient's signature on that form. Of course if a person is badly injured or there is some other emergency, the surgeon will take the responsibility of operating without a signature or the permission of a family member. I'm sure surgery is sometimes done without a signature when there's no emergency. But it's not supposed to happen.

Once I saw a surgeon break the rule against getting a signature from a patient under sedation. This was at Metro. The surgeon was a friend of mine. When I notified him that we had premedicated a patient of his before discovering that the man had not signed the consent form, the surgeon said, "Oh, don't worry, Mary, I'll come right up and straighten the whole thing out."

The surgeon was upstairs in two seconds. I've never seen anybody get anywhere as quickly. He got to the floor so fast that when he arrived, the patient hadn't even started to get groggy.

The surgeon clapped the patient on the shoulder and said, "Oh, by the way, before you go to the OR, I have to have you sign that."

The patient signed.

The surgeon operated.

Today I would say to any doctor who did that, "You're not supposed to have the man sign under those circumstances." Then I was just thankful I didn't get into trouble. Granted, the patient was not out of it. But if anybody had wanted to raise a legal issue, there certainly would have been grounds.

I'm sure medications errors are made that we don't pick up. Though patients don't like to think so, nurses are human beings, just as office workers are or the President of the United States is. That's why it's important for patients to know what they're supposed to get. Many patients don't want to take the trouble to learn. When I pass meds, I explain to patients what they're getting. "This is your Dig for your heart, to make it contract. This is your Lasix to get rid of water so your heart works better. This is your vitamin pill. . . ."

The patients interrupt. "Oh, nurse, don't worry."

I'll say, "I've made mistakes with medications. . . ."

"Oh, nurse, don't worry. I'm not going to die from it."

Which is probably true. But if I go down the line and give pills to eighteen patients, two will look at each pill and pay attention to what I'm saying about it. The rest just throw the pills in their mouths. When a patient takes a handful of pills and gulps them down, I almost die.

From what I've seen, other nursing mistakes, like medication errors, are also usually errors of omission. Treatments and soaks are missed from time to time. I make these kind of mistakes myself, usually because I'm in a hurry and I simply forget to do something. Or I don't follow through as I should.

But I don't think I make life-and-death mistakes. I feel under pressure not to. I think every nurse feels under that kind of pressure. After all, it's more serious than making a mistake with ten dollars in a bank. If a patient's temp goes up to 101° and I forget to call the doctor, the patient could suffer. My forgetting could mean four hours of minor discomfort for that patient, or an extra day in the hospital. Even that's not a life-and-death situation. But I think all of us are aware that the stakes are high even when the situation is not life-threatening and consciously try to avoid mistakes of any kind.

In 1976 I read a survey on quality of care done by a magazine,

Nursing '76. One of the questions asked was, "Did you ever encounter patient deaths accidentally caused by other nurses or doctors?" Forty-two percent of the nurses answering said yes in the case of doctors. Eighteen percent said yes in the case of nurses.

I would have to answer no in both cases. I have heard of a doctor removing a spleen during a cancer operation that did not call for a splenectomy. Apparently, he had cut the spleen by mistake and then took it out. But the patient didn't die. I don't know of any patient who died because of a doctor's error.

However, a patient did die on Jackie Neill's floor recently because of a nurse's error.

The nurse had been hired by the patient's family for private duty. I don't know why the patient was in the hospital, but she was sick enough to be getting blenderized feedings through a nasogastric tube. One day the private duty started giving a feeding without checking to make sure that the NG tube was in far enough to reach the woman's stomach. Apparently the end of the tube was actually somewhere in the esophagus. The patient aspirated some of the fluid and began vomiting and then inhaling the vomitus.

The private duty ran out to the desk and yelled to Jackie, "Stat—page the doctor!"

Jackie did, then ran back into the room with the private duty. The patient was cyanotic from lack of oxygen. Blue.

The two nurses flipped her over the side of the bed and started pounding on her back, trying to get the vomit to come up. Nothing came up.

When the doctor got there, he called for a stat chest X-ray, ordered antibiotics stat, got an IV into the patient stat, got her an electrocardiogram stat, started her on steroids stat, and sent her down to the ICU where they started giving her oxygen stat. None of these measures worked. The patient died.

Jackie was responsible in the sense that any head nurse is responsible for what happens on her floor. But when a nursing registry hires a private-duty nurse, it takes responsibility for her actions. There was no indication prior to this incident that this particular private duty was negligent. The nurse admitted to the doctor exactly what had happened. Still, Jackie felt bad that the patient had died, even though she did not feel personally responsible.

The *Nursing '76* survey also asked nurses whether they themselves had caused the death of a patient. Four percent of the nurses who answered said they had.

I've never done that. But like thirty-eight percent of the nurses who responded to the quality-of-care survey, I have done something that made a patient worse.

Again, this was when I was a staff nurse. I was taking care of a patient named Mrs. Bray, a retired elementary school principal who had CA of the colon with liver metastasis. Her husband was a retired teacher. A really lovely couple. Mrs. Bray had a couple of long admissions at Metro, and I really got close to her.

The doctors were shooting a substance called 5FU chemotherapy up to Mrs. Bray's liver through a catheter that had been threaded from the groin through the vascular system and on into the artery going into the liver. The X-ray Department had had a hard time putting the catheter in. It's not easy to find the right route. The patient has to be anesthetized locally while it's done.

Anyway, the chemotherapy, which was going in under pressure, appeared to me to be having some effect, because the liver was shrinking somewhat. You could feel it.

However, the catheter itself caused Mrs. Bray some discomfort where it emerged from her body. To keep it in place, the doctors had made several loops in the tubing and taped the loops onto a layer of tape against Mrs. Bray's groin. The tape was caught in her pubic hair. The skin was sticky from the tape. Mrs. Bray was having frequent diarrhea and, because of this dressing, could not be adequately cleaned up afterward. The whole area was messy and smelly.

Several times Mrs. Bray mentioned to me that she would like the area cleaned. The problem was that nurses were not allowed to cut or replace the tape around her catheter. Only the doctors were supposed to do that. So I kept telling the doctors, "Mrs. Bray is upset about how dirty and smelly the catheter is. She would really like to have someone clean it up."

The doctors answered, "Oh, we'll get to it." But they didn't get to it. Finally one day Mrs. Bray said to me, "Mary, please fix that catheter. It's so bad I can't stand it."

I said I would.

I was clipping away with the scissors, and I had everything

freed except for one blob of tape, and when I snipped at that, bright purple-red blood started shooting out all over the place. Blood from the artery leading from the liver. I had cut the catheter.

Never in my life have I been so scared. I panicked. I didn't know how to summon anybody, because there was nobody in the room who could run for help. I just stood by the bedside sweating bullets, scared to death that the lady was going to bleed out.

Mrs. Bray knew immediately what I had done. I'm sure she saw the blood spurt out onto the sheets, but she knew just by looking at my face. Even now it almost makes me cry to think of it.

Finally I yelled, "I need a nurse!" Then it occurred to me to fold the catheter and pinch it flat. As soon as I did this, the bleeding stopped.

A nurse walked into the room. I told her quickly what had happened and said, "Get a doctor!"

The nurse left, and in a moment, an intern from another service, a little twerp, walked into the room. I said, "Could you help me? I need some help here."

Well, he took one look at what I had done, and his eyes went up to heaven.

"I've got to go to lunch," he said. "I'll see you later."

He walked out of the room. He was new and, I'm sure, scared to death. He didn't know what to do, so he left.

A couple of nurses came back to help. Holding everything in place, we called the Radiology Department. A couple of radiology people came up and fooled around with the catheter. They couldn't get it reconnected.

"Okay," they said, "we'll take her downstairs."

I looked at Mrs. Bray. I was close to tears. I said, "I'm really sorry."

I'll never forget her reaction as long as I live.

"That's all right," she said. "You didn't mean to do it, did you?"

"No."

She said, "I know one thing. You really like me. Somebody else might have left me here. You stayed with me."

Then, as they were getting Mrs. Bray onto a litter to take her downstairs, she patted me on the head. *She* was comforting *me*.

I stood there with tears in my eyes while they took her down.

Two supervisors came up and started making out an incident report. Everybody wanted to know why I had wanted to clean Mrs. Bray in the first place. I couldn't answer. I just stood there feeling terrible. It seemed unbelievable that I had done what I had done.

The supervisors were saying, "Don't worry about it. You didn't mean to do it. Accidents happen." Interns came up to me and said, "Don't worry about it. I could have done the same thing." Katie came up to me and told me about something she once did that was bad for the patient, but the patient had survived. I still felt terribly guilty.

Later in the afternoon we got word that the people in radiology had not been able to get Mrs. Bray's catheter back in. Her veins were too sclerosed.

I thought to myself, "My god, they can't get the chemotherapy in. If the liver gets big again, it's my fault. If this lady dies, it's all my fault."

That night I went home feeling like a failure.

I came to work the next day feeling as if I had to tell everybody to exonerate myself. The more people I told, I thought, the less guilt-ridden I would feel. A couple of the residents I told also said, "We could have done the same thing." I felt no better.

Finally Black Ollie, who was Mrs. Bray's doctor, came in. I saw him get off the elevator and start walking down the hall. Despite the fact that I was scared to death of the man, I had to try to soothe my conscience by acknowledging to Black Ollie what I had done.

I went after him in the hall and stopped him.

"Dr. Strode," I said. "I have to tell you something."

"Yes?"

I said, "You know that catheter that got cut on Mrs. Bray yesterday?"

"Yes, I heard about that."

"I was the one who did it."

I just stood there.

For a few moments, he looked at me. Then he said, "You're absolved. Don't worry about it. The chemotherapy wasn't working. I was going to stop it anyway."

Whether he was telling the truth or not I don't know. But all of a sudden I felt as if a huge load had been taken off my chest. I remember walking home that day feeling about twenty pounds lighter.

I took care of Mrs. Bray until she died. Neither of us ever mentioned what I had done. Cutting her catheter was the worst mistake I've ever made as a nurse. God, I hope I never do anything like that in my life again.

The day I was least proud of myself as a nurse was the day I hit a patient.

She was a little old lady, not particularly confused, but very combative and nasty. Nobody could get to her. We put jacket restraints on her, but that didn't stop her from smacking or picking at anyone who came near.

Usually when I went in the room, I would grab her hands so she couldn't hit me. But one day, with my mind on something else, I forgot to grab her hands. All I know is that she suddenly started barreling at me with her fists. Before I could stop myself, I smacked her back, once on each hand, saying, "Don't you ever hit me again."

The woman stopped dead in her tracks. She started to cry.

I felt horrible. I couldn't believe what I had done. True, her behavior had made me frustrated and angry. I knew I hadn't hit the patient hard enough to hurt her. But I was upset to think that I would lose my temper enough to smack somebody who was lying in bed and had no defenses.

Whether the woman was totally aware of what had happened, I don't know. I stayed in the room and tried to placate her, and finally she quieted down. She never hit me again. But I was wrong to hit her, and I'll never forgive myself for losing control.

It has been somewhat comforting to me to discover, as I have since that incident, that I'm not the only nurse who's ever lost control on the job. Liz Roberts once slammed her hand down on a bed because she was so fed up with a patient who whined all the time. Maureen Shay once went into an empty room and beat on a bed after a hostile man she had been struggling to feed spit a mouthful of scrambled eggs in her face.

My friend Rebecca once bit a patient. The woman had come in from a nursing home for surgery. She was senile, and after she came out of the anesthesia, she was hitting at people. Rebecca got too close. The woman bit her on the hand and drew blood. So Rebecca bit the patient back, also on the hand, but not hard enough to draw blood, and said, "That's how it feels." I don't think Rebecca felt terrible about what she did, but I'm sure she's not proud of it either.

June Fong has never abused a patient physically, but she once did something that made her feel worse than if she had. A woman came in for open-heart surgery. The patient, Mrs. Crouse, was anxious about the operation and had other problems as well. The Sunday after she was admitted, she got particularly upset because her doctor hadn't gotten up to see her early in the day. June tried to explain that on weekends the doctors often got up on the floor later than usual.

June was having a bad day herself that Sunday. The floor was short-staffed and very busy. June was the only RN on duty. She was going crazy as it was. Then at about noon there was some kind of emergency. To top it off, the lunch trays were late, and all the patients were complaining.

June finally took Mrs. Crouse's lunch tray in to her. The woman was on a restricted diet. Apparently the food on the tray was not the lunch she had ordered. Without warning, Mrs. Crouse picked up the whole tray and threw it at June.

Really angry, in fact thinking "I'll kill her," June marched out of the room with chicken gravy all over her uniform, went straight to a telephone at the nurses' station, and dialed the woman's doctor.

"Your patient, Mrs. Crouse, just threw her entire lunch at me," June said, "and I'm wearing it."

The doctor came up and apologized to June. He talked to the patient. June got cleaned up. That might have been the end of the incident except that when June went in to give Mrs. Crouse her 2:00 heart pills, the patient refused to take them.

June put the pills down on the bedside table. "Well," she said, "I personally don't care if you take them or not." Again June left the room.

"That was really poor," she said when she was telling me the story, "but I really couldn't help it. The whole day had me really frustrated."

When June went into Mrs. Crouse's room on 4:00 rounds, she found the patient crying over what June had said to her earlier about the pills.

June sat down. She tried to talk to Mrs. Crouse, but the patient wouldn't listen. She was too hurt.

Mrs. Crouse died on the operating table.

June felt terrible. She still feels bad about having lost control. So do Liz and Maureen, although hitting a bed is not nearly as bad as hitting a patient. As Maureen says, "These people are sick. They're sick. Sick. You pound that into your head. You're not supposed to lose control."

But some days maintaining control takes all the effort a nurse can muster. And if one time you don't maintain it, you may feel unhappy with yourself for a long time after.

I've never heard of a situation in which loss of control by a nurse has led to a lawsuit. For that matter, it's rare to hear of nursing errors that end up in court. Though medical malpractice suits seem very popular these days, I've been involved in only one situation in five years of nursing that led to a lawsuit being filed.

Technically I wasn't the person responsible. I had just come to Central when the incident occurred and was still on orientation under the nurse who was in charge of Eight Cook at the time.

We had a little old lady who was very, very sick. She was in her eighties and had had surgery done, following which she was very weak and wobbly. She had a concerned husband and very protective children who hired private duties to stay with her around the clock until she began to get stronger.

At the time this woman was a patient, there was an old geriatric chair in the solarium. Nobody used it, because the wheels did not lock. One afternoon this old woman, using an aluminum walker, walked into the solarium with the help of her husband and her private-duty nurse. We were in report when suddenly we heard a loud crash. Apparently the woman had backed up to get into the geriatric chair, and because the chair was not stationary, it rolled backwards. The patient fell on the floor and fractured her hip.

Of course, the supervisor said afterward, the chair should never have been left on the floor. I wasn't even aware that the chair was broken. But I should have been. I felt very guilty about that.

I did not feel guilty about the fact that the patient was walking without one of the floor nurses beside her. She was with her husband and a private duty. Though she was weak, we were getting her ready to go home in a couple of days. Most of our patients walk in the halls with family members. We would caution some of them, like Kelly O'Brien, not to walk by themselves. But we can't be eyes and ears. Nurses can't be in every room every minute to see what's going on.

Some time after the patient's hip healed and she went home, we heard that her children were suing. I haven't heard anything about it since that rumor came through. If I were pulled into court, I don't know what I'd say. I just felt bad that the patient fell and hurt herself.

As soon as the matter of Mrs. Bishop's missed insulin was straightened out, I went into Kelly's room to see how he was doing. Mrs. O'Brien was sitting on the chair at the foot of the bed, her hand over her eyes. She did not look up when I came in. Kelly's radio was playing "Oh Come, All Ye Faithful." Through the window I could see that a heavy sleet had started to fall.

Kelly looked awful. His son was shaving him every day or two, so he didn't have a beard, but his face was very drawn. His wound was still open. He still had the tubes all over his stomach. His legs and arms were all bruised from injections. His skin had taken on a whitish-yellow tinge. His legs, his toes, and his ankles were so swollen that the skin on them looked stretched. The man had not only been through hell but also looked it. I could not imagine why Rose still wanted him to be coded.

I went back out to the nurses' station and unloaded on the first person I saw, who happened to be Dr. Benson.

"I'm not blaming you or the other residents for keeping Kelly going," I said, interrupting Benson's search for a chart in the rack. "I know it isn't your fault. But this is senseless."

Benson nodded. He pulled a chart out and sat down on one of the desks without looking at the chart.

"I know how you feel," he said. "It's hard not to feel that way."

"Then why is Rose doing it?"

"Because he hasn't found any further malignancy. And, as you know, Rose goes gangbusters when he thinks there's a reason to."

"Do *you* think Kelly's going to get better?"

"I can't be certain he isn't. Don't forget that Mr. Shorey has cancer everywhere, and Rose isn't doing anything to keep Shorey going."

That was true. Mr. Shorey was receiving only comfort measures. But I said to Benson, "It doesn't look to me as if Kelly's going to get better."

Benson swung his feet for a moment without talking. Then he said, "Me either."

I couldn't think of anything else to say. It was my turn to clean the utility room. As I started to walk out of the nurses' station, Benson said, stopping me with his voice, "You know, I think Rose is emotionally involved with Kelly. I think Kelly is one of his favorites. Maybe he's having a hard time letting him go."

Reflecting upon this possibility as I scrubbed down the sink and the counters, I thought Benson might be right. For all of Rose's brusqueness, I had seen him take Kelly's hand and hold it while he was talking to one or both of the O'Briens. I had seen this side of Rose before. Yet, thinking back, it seemed to me that I'd seen it more with Kelly than with most of Rose's other patients. Then I remembered one of the supervisors saying that Rose had pets. Well, so did I, and Kelly was one. Maybe he was also a pet of Rose's.

I think patients are sometimes ready to die before other people—nurses, doctors, family members—will let them die. If Rose was having trouble letting Kelly O'Brien die, he wouldn't have been the first doctor who ever tried to keep a patient alive longer than the patient wanted to live. I had seen that happen on Eight Cook once before, with Danny Dawson, an 18-year-old with CA of the naso-pharynx.

Danny was in a lot of pain during his last admission. He had bone metastasis, and he ached all over. His back hurt. His arms hurt. His legs hurt. Also, he became progressively weaker with respiratory problems. The prognosis was clear to everyone, including Danny himself. He knew he was dying. He was ready to die. He had said goodbye to his whole family. He had told his mother the angels were coming to take him away.

But he was still to be coded. The resident taking care of him,

Ramona Garcia, refused to make him a no-code.

Dr. Garcia was very, very close to Danny. Apparently a brother or cousin of hers to whom she had been very close had also died of cancer in his teens. I think Ramona was having a hard time accepting that Danny was going to die too. Danny's respiratory problems could "be taken care of." Dr. Garcia was doing everything she could to take care of them—giving medications and tapping the kid's lungs to keep them free of fluid. She would not let him go.

One morning Danny stopped breathing. Garcia got up to the floor in time to revive him with an Ambu bag, a rubber sac with a flexible, rimmed opening which is placed over a patient's nose and mouth like a mask while the bag itself is manipulated to force air into the lungs. Bagging is sort of a sophisticated version of mouth-to-mouth resuscitation.

After this incident, Danny was fine for a day.

But the next afternoon he stopped breathing again. Ramona happened to be in the room. I was also in there, as was Jennie and Danny's whole family—mother, father, and two younger brothers. Respiratory death is probably one of the most horrible to watch. The person is awake, conscious, and can't get breath. Danny was gasping frantically and turning blue. While Jennie rushed the family out into the hall, Ramona tried to bag Danny again.

Danny wouldn't let her. I've never seen anything like it in my life. Every time she got the mask near his face, he pushed it away.

"No, no, no," he kept saying.

The family heard him and came back in. The mother was hysterical. "Danny, don't!" she kept crying. "Don't! Don't do that!"

Ramona was really upset. Again and again she tried to put the mask over Danny's face, and again and again he put his fingers under the mask so she could not get a tight seal. It never occurred to me to try to hold his hands down out of the way. He had so obviously made a decision that the thought of trying to help the doctor go against it never entered my mind.

Finally Danny's body went limp. Ramona took the mask away. The boy was dead.

I didn't know what was in Dr. Garcia's heart, any more than I know what Rose's philosophy is. But from what I saw, Ramona cared more about Danny and invested more in him than she had done with any other patient. If Rose felt the same way about Kelly, that could be at least part of the reason why he hadn't let the man die weeks earlier.

As I left the utility room, Mrs. O'Brien stopped me in the hall with a hand on my arm. "Mary," she said, "what's keeping him alive?"

I faced her. "The blood."

A pause. "Can I stop it?"

Another pause. "Yes."

Mrs. O'Brien's body sagged. She turned away. With her back to me and tears in her voice, she said, "But I can't."

"It's your choice," I said. "I can't make that choice for you."

I turned away too. I was upset. Disappointed. Deep down I wanted Mrs. O'Brien to be able to take the step that would stop her husband's suffering. Rose hadn't offered her that option. Since the doctor hadn't, I couldn't.

As Mrs. O'Brien and I walked away from each other in the hall, I thought, "God, let me do it for Ron if the time comes. Let me do it for my mother."

A little while later Ken Rose came up on rounds. I told him about my talk with Mrs. O'Brien.

"Can't you give her the option of stopping the blood?" I asked Rose.

He said, "I told the family that I was not going to stop, period, and that if they wanted to stop, they could tell that to Kelly. If there were any malignancy there, I would pull the plug. I like Kelly. He's a good man. I wouldn't support him without reason."

Rose spoke gently. "I didn't find any malignancy," he continued patiently. "I know he's sick. But he doesn't have the cancer any more. There's a chance that we can keep him."

I felt like exploding.

"Keep him?" I said. "For what?"

It wasn't a question, and Rose didn't answer it.

At the end of the afternoon, just before I left on my Christmas holiday, I went in and took Kelly's hand. I told him I was going to be off for a few days and that I hoped he would soon feel more comfortable. Kelly squeezed my hand.

I hugged Mrs. O'Brien. Neither of us said anything.

I walked home slowly. There were Christmas lights on all up and down the streets. It was starting to get dark. The farther I got from the hospital, the better I felt to be free of it. Four days off. Christmas. And Ron would soon be home.

Ron.

18

CHRISTMAS AWAY: A HOLIDAY TO REMEMBER

We had planned to have dinner at my parents' house on Christmas Day. My whole immediate family would be there except my older brother, Jeff. My younger brother, Jerry, was home on leave from the Army, and my sister, Kathy, would also spend the day at my parents' house with her fiancé.

But on Saturday, Christmas Eve morning, I woke up feeling rested and in such good spirits that while I was waiting for the tea to steep, I decided to invite the whole family to our apartment instead.

My mother was surprised at the phone call.

"You realize," she warned me, "that there'll be seven of us altogether."

"I know," I said. "I just want to see if I can do it."

My mother said they'd love to come.

The most I had ever entertained for dinner was four. That's how many our table seats. But Ron had remembered that we kept a card table pushed under our bed, and he offered to stop and borrow some chairs from his aunt on his way home from the hospital that afternoon. That would work fine.

I spent a very nice day. After Ron had left, I sat down with a second cup of tea and balanced my checkbook so I could see how much money I could spend on Christmas food. Then I made out a menu, did the grocery shopping, cleaned the apartment, finished wrapping the last few Christmas presents, put some Christmas records on the stereo, and cooked for the entire afternoon. It was great fun. That evening Ron and I spent with his parents, which I always enjoy, and got to bed early.

In the morning he and I exchanged gifts. I hadn't really expected anything from Ron, since he would be paying for our two days away, but he gave me a beautiful pair of gold earrings. I had bought him two belts and a shirt and tie with Christian Dior labels.

When he opened the shirt, Ron said, "You spent too much. I'd never get something so expensive for myself. I'll never wear it."

"Look," I teased, "You've got to get used to the better things in this life. What about these earrings? They look pretty expensive too."

Ron admitted that he had had to work extra time in the Anesthesia Department in order to buy the earrings. I loved them. He seemed just as pleased with his gifts.

My family came at about noon. While I put the finishing touches on things in the kitchen, we all drank eggnog and opened presents. I got the meal on the table at about one. We sat down to turkey, mashed potatoes, fresh stringbeans, fresh cranberry-orange relish, homemade bread, chocolate cake, and pumpkin pie.

"I thought you were going to start small," Ron said.

Everybody laughed. My mother was very impressed with the meal. I was surprised myself that I had done it. And impressed too, I'll have to admit.

Late on Christmas afternoon, after the dishes had been washed and put away and my family had left for home, Ron and I packed our car and set out for the country.

Snow began to fall before we had gone more than a few blocks. The drive took about an hour and a half. It was well past dark by the time we reached the Green River Inn, just as it was when we first arrived there after our wedding.

We checked in. If there were other guests, we didn't see them. The lobby was deserted. The dining room was open, but neither Ron nor I could even think of eating again.

It was still snowing. We decided to take a walk.

The little town near the Inn is a madhouse of tourists in the summer. The only people we saw that night, however, were natives inside their tree-lit houses, doing Christmas things with their families.

Outside it was so quiet that we could actually hear the snow fall.

For the next two days, Ron and I forgot about medicine, forgot about patients, forgot about work and school. We read, talked, reminisced, planned, and relaxed in front of the hotel's main fireplace. We said again and again how great it was to have some time alone together. We returned home knowing there was nothing wrong with our sex life that being rested didn't cure.

From beginning to end, it was as nice a holiday as I can remember.

19

LAST RESORTS

On Wednesday morning, when I went back to work, Kelly O'Brien was still alive.

He had started going severely downhill on Christmas Day. He was still conscious, but very weak, very depressed, and bleeding—hemorrhaging—everywhere. The fact that Rose had yet to make Kelly a no-code had us sitting in report shaking our heads.

"Several of us talked to Rose about it while you were out," Stephanie said to me. "He did listen, but he told us he wanted to keep trying."

So the nurses on Eight Cook were continuing to be very supportive of Kelly. Ordinarily when we give 10:00 A.M. meds, for example, some patients may not get them till 10:30 or 11:00, because we can't be in every patient's room at precisely 10:00. We give the drugs within a normal range of the specified time. With Kelly, however, because he was bleeding out and getting blood expanders and volume expanders, it was very important that he have his medication exactly on time. The nurses were giving it to him right on time. If a doctor said, "I want this given immediately," someone would run down to the pharmacy or the blood bank and get it.

No one was holding off, in other words. Everybody was doing for Kelly exactly what had been ordered. Deep down I knew that no nurse was doing anything that would have encouraged Kelly to die, even though every nurse on the floor was hoping that he would die.

When Rose came up on the floor that morning, I couldn't help saying to him, "What's with Kelly?"

Rose looked as if he had expected me to ask.

"I know," Rose said. "You're wondering why I'm not giving him the Thorazine–Dilaudid trip out."

"Yes, I am wondering that. He's been through hell. His family is going through hell."

"Don't you think I know that?"

"Yeah, but god, he just needs some peace."

"I want to give him every chance," Rose said.

I didn't know what more I could do. I don't think there was anything else a nurse could have done in that situation. The issue was life or death. When it's a question of something minor, like a soak or sending a patient to physical therapy or even getting a psychiatrist to see a patient, I think a nurse can influence the decision. But with somebody like Rose, when he's decided that he's going to do everything he can, no nurse is going to convince him to let a patient die with dignity.

Actually I wouldn't try to convince a doctor to do that. I'm not God. I don't know what I would have done in Rose's situation. My role, as I saw it, was to raise a question. I did that. Beyond that, I felt I couldn't make a difference, so I didn't try.

The next day I said to Dr. Drake, "If the nurses hadn't done so much for Kelly, he would have been dead by now."

"Why do you think he's on this floor?"

"But he just needs some peace."

"Don't you think this is upsetting me too? We're all upset. Benson, me, the chief resident—we're all as upset as you are. We had four people die of cancer over the weekend. Now Shorey's going bad too. I can't even walk into that room."

I felt sorry for Drake. I had heard about the four patients from Benson who was continuing to follow the oncology patients when Drake was off. Benson was depressed. I tried to console him.

"Everybody has to die sometime," I said.

"Not while they're on my service," Benson replied.

Sometime on Thursday afternoon Ken Rose came up to Eight Cook and wrote in Kelly O'Brien's chart, "Everything short of a code."

20

THE OLD YEAR PASSES

On Friday Kelly was in shock. He started spiking very high temperatures. His blood pressure went down, and he began to have shaking chills. Because his heart wasn't pumping properly, his legs swelled with fluid until his ankles were the size of his thighs. His pulse started going up.

Following Dr. Rose's instructions, the nurses did everything we could for Kelly.

I wasn't in the room that much. But no matter what else I was doing, I found myself thinking about Kelly O'Brien.

It was the day of New Year's Eve. Except for the fact that Kelly and Mr. Shorey were both going bad, the floor was quiet. We had only seventeen patients, even fewer than we had had over Christmas. No new admissions were scheduled.

But at about noon, James called from the Admissions Office to say that Mrs. Petey English would be coming back to Eight Cook that afternoon.

I was upset at the news. So was everybody I told. There wasn't a person on the floor who didn't like Petey English.

Mrs. English had been discharged from Eight Cook just a few weeks earlier. She had come in to have her spleen removed. The splenectomy had been palliative surgery for myelofibrosis, a rare blood cancer. After the surgery, Mrs. English ran into a lot of problems with temp elevations. She was really sick. The cancer had screwed up her immune system, so her body had lost some of its ability to fight infection. The doctors put her on a long course of antibiotics, and she was in the hospital much longer than is normal for a splenectomy.

Petey English was the most un-patient-like patient I had met in quite a while. It's hard to explain, but some people, after they've been sick and in the hospital for a long time, become patients. They act a certain way. They're so knocked down by the disease that they are no longer concerned about the weather, the news, or anything that isn't happening in their immediate environment.

They're interested in their families only from a personal standpoint. They don't ask, "What's happening to my family? What's So-and-so doing?" But, "Does my family love me?" These patients let the hospital, their own condition, become the world.

Petey didn't. She watched TV. She read and told us about what she was reading. When we'd come on duty and go in the room, she would say, "What's it like outside?" Or she'd walk out to the desk and say, "Hi. How are you? What are you doing? What's up with you?" Though she had a serious disease that was going to shorten her life, though she was, I'm sure, afraid deep down, she stayed interested in what was happening in the world outside the hospital.

I had a certain feeling about Petey right from the beginning. Far more quickly than with most patients, I took a real liking to her. She was in her early fifties, not a pretty woman but certainly an attractive personality. An interesting, good person, with a lot of inner strength. She had a job in insurance. Her husband was a quiet person who watched everything but didn't say much. There were no children.

While Petey was recovering from her splenectomy, I spent as much time with her as I could. She talked a lot about the fact that she was getting gradually worse. When she had first been diagnosed two years earlier, the doctors had assured her that it would be a matter of years before the cancer needed any kind of treatment. She would probably need a splenectomy, they said, but maybe not for five years. She would need chemotherapy, but not for five years. Two years after making these predictions, they put her on chemotherapy and told her she needed a splenectomy immediately.

Petey talked to me about all these things with a lot of calm.

"You seem like a very strong person," I said to her one day. "Whom do you get support from? Is your husband supportive?"

"No," she said, "he isn't. I know he loves me, but he can't stand strain. He falls apart."

She then told me that she had been hiding certain facts about her condition from her husband to save him the worry.

I said, "Well, is there anybody you can really talk to when you're upset?"

"I've talked to my sister and my aunt. I can say anything to them."

I felt relieved.

"It's good that you have those two people," I said. "But I want you to know that I'm here. If you ever want to talk to me, just say so, and I'll come in."

"Thank you, Mary," she said. "I won't forget that."

Petey English returned to Eight Cook on New Year's Eve Day with an admitting diagnosis of CVA—cardiovascular accident. According to what James told me over the phone, she had started having weakness and numbness in her right hand. She had gone to her doctor when she began to notice that she couldn't open things. The doctor thought she might have an abscess on the brain.

That's all James could tell me. The whole staff was apprehensive about what we were going to see when Petey English got off the elevator.

"Oh, god, I hope she's not paralyzed," somebody said.

"I hope she can speak," another person said.

But Petey got off the elevator walking, and she was having no trouble with her speech. I came around a corner after doing some errand to see her standing in front of the nurses' station, surrounded by every nurse on duty that day.

"Uh-oh," I said, making myself sound as much like a head nurse as possible. "What's all this? These nurses are supposed to be working. They're not supposed to be standing around talking to you. What are you doing back here, anyway? You just left."

Petey started laughing.

"I asked to come back to this floor," she said. "All my friends are here."

Petey's spirit amazed me. She wasn't dying, but to feel your hand get numb and to know that you're gradually losing control over your body must be terribly frightening, even if you're as realistic and practical a person as Petey.

A little while later I went back to the room to see if Petey had gotten settled. She had a look on her face I had never seen on her before.

"Remember when you told me last time I was here that I was a strong person and didn't look as if I fall apart very easily?"

"Of course I remember."

"I'm ready to fall apart."

She started to cry.

I went to her.

"Oh," she moaned through her sobs, "I'm so embarrassed."

I sat down on the bed and put my arms around her.

"For god's sake," I said. "Don't be embarrassed. I'd be crying right now, too, if I were in your position. Anyone would be."

Her whole body was shaking. She let her head come down on my shoulder. I held her until her sobs began to subside, the tears—my tears—streaming down my face.

And then it was New Year's Eve.

Since Ron and I both had to work the next day, we had decided not to go out. We had done our celebrating a few nights earlier by having dinner with Steve and Susan at one of our favorite Italian restaurants. We would see in the new year by ourselves, in our apartment.

Ron cooked. He had potatoes baking in the oven and a fire burning in the fireplace by the time I got home from the hospital. When the potatoes were done, he broiled two steaks. We got out a bottle of wine and drank some. After we had finished eating, we cleaned the dishes, lit candles, turned off the lights, and sat on the couch together, still sipping our wine.

I started to tell Ron about Petey English. About how terrible I felt for Petey.

The story turned out to be about me. I found myself telling Ron how afraid I had been over the last year that I was holding myself back from patients.

"You know," I said, "I'm almost glad that Petey cried today.

She made me feel the way I used to feel. It makes me glad that I can still act that way. That I can still get involved. That I'm not a cold professional."

Ron put his arm around me. We snuggled close. We kept talking.

I got onto the subject of Kelly O'Brien. Kelly was taking longer to die, I told Ron, than almost any other patient I had known. His dying was one of the hardest I had ever seen. A long string of horrendous days.

Ron wanted to know how I could take it. How I could go in to work day after day and watch human beings going through hell. At such close range.

A few minutes went by. The question called up some of my deepest feelings about nursing. Leaning on Ron, with my cheek against his shoulder, I let them come.

I feel I have a lot to give in that situation, I told Ron finally. Let's face it—when you don't have much time left, you don't want to be just some person lying in a bed. You want somebody to call your name. You want somebody to care about you.

I care about Kelly. I think I have made him feel special. I get satisfaction from knowing I have done the best thing I could have done, which was to help Kelly, and his wife, through what was probably the worst period in their lives—his dying.

That was what they most needed, and that was what I was most prepared to give. Many people—nurses, doctors, family members, friends—can't or don't want to get involved. They don't even use the word death. For some reason I can use it. I can say to a wife and son and daughter, "When he dies. . . ."

When I say those words and the family stands and cries, that's hard for me. But it's necessary for them. Helping a person die, and helping the family, are things I want to do. Doing them makes me feel as though I've done something good. It makes me feel good about myself.

As for watching people in pain, I said to Ron, I get upset about the pain sometimes. I don't like to look at somebody who's very uncomfortable. But if I sat there and cringed, I wouldn't be functioning. I give the person pain medication, and he relaxes.

I still find it upsetting to do something to patients that hurts them. That bothers me a lot. But if I don't do those things, somebody else will. You do them to help the person feel better or get better. When you're doing your best to make a patient comfortable, that's all you can do.

The fire popped. Ron was stroking my hair.

But you don't have to work in a place where people are so sick, he said.

But I enjoy that kind of nursing. I've always worked in areas where people were very sick. Where people died. That's where I feel the most useful. If I worked in a dialysis unit and just put people on and off machines all day, I'd probably be bored stiff.

Or I could become an industrial nurse and go nuts. I'm sure I could do patient teaching, and I'm sure people would come in for aspirin, and I'd do annual check-ups, and I'm sure I'd do resuscitations from time to time. But from what I've heard from my friend Angie, there's really not that much to it. I'm sure Angie would hit me over the head for saying so. She loves that kind of nursing. It's her. It's not me.

I read the want ads every Sunday, I reminded Ron. Once I even sent a resume to a place. But most of the jobs I see in the paper don't seem to offer any more than I already have. I get good money. Central is a good hospital to work at.

Besides, there are fringe benefits. Being in a management position has taught me to stand up for myself. To deal with people more easily. The job has helped form me as an adult woman, an adult person. That pleases me.

Something else, too. I was thinking about this when we were talking about Petey English. Touch.

I used to be very uncomfortable showing physical warmth. My family never did much of that. I had to learn about touch from Katie. She often said how important it was to have that kind of contact with patients. She felt that the patient loses something if touch isn't there, and so does the nurse.

Some people don't need physical contact. Some don't want it, maybe because they've never allowed themselves to learn that that kind of physical warmth is pleasurable. My mother would be one of those people, I said to Ron. I don't think she would want a nurse to put an arm around her. You have to respect that in a person. But some people really appreciate being touched. And you'd be surprised how much easier it is to take care of some people after they realize there's a warmth there.

That lesson has changed me. Because of what I've learned about touch from patients, I've allowed myself to become warmer and more open toward my friends. I've grown to see how important it is to have physical warmth in friendship.

Of course not just in friendship, I teased Ron.

The fire began to get low. After a while we drifted off to sleep.

21

THE NEW YEAR BEGINS

Passing certain houses on the street at 6:40 the next morning, I could hear music, voices, and the tinkling of ice in glasses. The sky was just beginning to get light.

I couldn't help smiling. How strange. People were still having New Year's Eve parties, and here I was, going to work.

Kelly O'Brien looked bad. He had had a very bad night, on and off, with diarrhea almost every hour. He had become disoriented. Then he just sort of slipped out of things. When I arrived, he wasn't acting conscious.

An hour after I got there, Toni Gillette said to me, "I'm having trouble getting a pulse on Kelly."

I went in and felt a pulse, but barely.

Back outside the room, Toni said, "He looks worse than he did on nights." Toni had worked the night shift but had agreed to stay for the day when another nursing assistant had called in sick.

I paged Rich Drake, the resident on call.

"Kelly's pretty bad," I said.

"He's been bad all night," Drake said.

"Well, according to the night nurse, he's worse than he was. Would you please come and take a look at him?"

"Okay. I'll be there in a few minutes."

"Shall I call Mrs. O'Brien?"

"No. Wait till I see the patient."

305

So Drake came and looked at Kelly, and he said, "You'd better call the family."

There was no answer at the O'Brien home. I called the number I had for Pat. Her husband answered.

"I'm not trying to upset you," I said after I had told him who I was. "But your father-in-law's condition has changed. He's a lot weaker. He really doesn't look good. I can't give you a time limit, but I did want to let Mrs. O'Brien know the situation she she could come in now if she wanted to."

Pat and her mother were on the floor within half an hour. Mrs. O'Brien looked as if she had just thrown her coat on and rushed in. Her hair was disheveled. She looked as if she hadn't slept all night. Both she and Pat had bags under their eyes. Mrs. O'Brien was crying. They went in the room and pulled two chairs as close to the bed as they could and sat down to wait. In a little while, Mike came in.

Kelly remained unconscious. We couldn't get a pulse off and on all day. His blood pressure began to drop. To keep it from dropping further, we were giving Kelly a volume expander, a sticky yellow substance that was given intravenously to replace some of the fluid he was losing. We were also giving him fresh frozen plasma so the blood would clot and he would stop bleeding. In addition, he was getting Maalox and a diuretic and a vitamin that was supposed to help in the clotting process.

In other words, per Rose's orders, we were doing everything to give Kelly the chance to live.

Which I thought was senseless. If I had been the doctor, I would have given him none of these things. I would have given him sugar water through an IV. That would have kept him from becoming dehydrated, would have kept his temp from going up, and would have permitted him to die without becoming uncomfortable.

All that day Mr. Shorey was also getting worse. His temp went up to 104°. He was urinating almost every half hour. He was not responsive. He was obviously on the way out.

Between Kelly and Mr. Shorey, nurses were in the room all the time, doing something for one or the other. Mr. Shorey's sister came in. I went in as often as I could during the day to make sure that she and the O'Briens knew I was there if they needed me.

After lunch I was standing at the desk making phone calls when Emerald Lynch came out in her wheelchair on the way to physical therapy. She pressed the elevator button, swung the wheelchair around to face me, and announced, "I suppose you know they're going to spring me next week."

"So I heard. I'm really glad. Except I was sort of hoping you'd move in here. Keep things from getting too dull."

"Hah!"

Lynch was pleased and full of herself. She waited while I made another phone call. Then she said, "I've been in the hospital six months out of the last twelve. Where I want to go now is straight home."

"Can't say I blame you for that."

Again I dialed the phone. Waiting for an answer, I said to Lynch, "Is Larry going to take good care of you?"

She grinned, showing the holes where her back teeth had been. "Yeah," Lynch said slyly, "Larry is going to take real good care of me."

I pretended I didn't understand her double meaning. Hanging up the phone, I said, "Sorry I have to break up this party, but I've got to pick something up in Pharmacy right away."

"Okay, Miss Efficient."

As I passed Lynch on the way to the stairs, she grabbed me by the hand and squeezed. I squeezed back.

"Hurry up, Miss Efficient," Lynch called after me. "Don't be late."

"You're so full of blarney that I can't believe you're not Irish," I called back as I went through the swinging doors.

Lynch broke up. At the bottom of a whole flight of steps, I could still hear her laughing.

Toward midafternoon, while I was in with Kelly, I heard a commotion down the hall. A loud, angry voice I recognized as belonging to the grown daughter of Mrs. Yocum, one of the black patients, was yelling, obviously at somebody on the staff.

I heard "Motherfucker!" and "Yessing Whitey!" and "You people aren't taking care of my mother!" and I got down there fast.

The daughter was obviously drunk. Apparently she had come in with her boyfriend, who was also drunk, and started cursing her mother, Mrs. Yocum. Jeannette, the part-time floor clerk, happened to walk by the room. Seeing trouble coming, she had threatened to call the security guard if the daughter didn't quiet down.

The daughter was furious. As soon as I walked in the room, she turned from Jeannette and started cursing and screaming at me, calling me names and threatening to sue the hospital because her mother wasn't getting good care. She was so loud that I'm sure everybody on the floor heard what was going on. Mrs. Yocum just sat there looking uncomfortable.

"Excuse me," I said to the daughter in a low voice. "If you have a problem, I want you to discuss it with the doctors, but right now I want you to lower your voice."

She answered me quite loudly. "Yes, ma'am. Yes, ma'am. Yes ma'am, Whitey."

I stepped closer to her.

"We have a lot of patients up here who are very sick," I said. "If you don't lower your voice and stop yelling, I'm going to have to ask you to leave. Please. Keep it down."

The daughter was very upset, but she stopped screaming.

When I went back to Kelly's bedside, Pat and Mrs. O'Brien and Mr. Shorey's sister were sitting there talking about the commotion. Ignoring me, they kept on talking about it.

"I don't believe it," Mrs. Shorey's sister said. "What could that woman be thinking of? These nurses take care of the patients so well up here."

"I don't believe it either," Mrs. O'Brien said. "These nurses are so nice. They take such good care of these patients."

They were saying these things, I realized, for my benefit.

When I left for the day, Kelly and Mr. Shorey were both still alive. Because of all the things we had been doing for Kelly, his blood pressure had improved a little.

Something woke me up.

The bedroom was pitch black. Beside me, Ron was sound asleep.

I reached for the clock. It was 4:00 A.M. I sat up, coming to.

I had dreamed that Kelly had died.

It was strange. In the dream, his wife walked out of the room and into the nurses' station and said to me, "I've got to call my children." She put her hands through her hair, pushing it back.

I gave her the phone.

She dialed.

Then I heard the operator's voice say, "I'm sorry. You cannot make a phone call unless it's on hospital business." The voice sounded like a tape.

I grabbed the telephone from Mrs. O'Brien.

"This is hospital business!" I screamed at the operator.

Mrs. O'Brien made her calls.

After she hung up, she said to me, "They're coming in."

Then she said, "You girls have been so good to Kelly. I've got to give a party for you."

Three hours later I got off the elevator on Eight Cook and looked first, as I always did, at the patient directory. Kelly O'Brien's name was not on it.

Sharon was standing at the desk.

"Sharon," I said, "when did Kelly die?"

"Just a little while ago. Stephanie and I went in to turn him over, and we had just gotten our hands under his body when he let out a long sigh and died."

"What time was that?"

"Just about 5:00."

My dream had been a premonition.

One of the residents had called the family. Pat said she would be in in a day or two to pick up Kelly's belongings. The family had refused an autopsy. Kelly had been through enough, they said. So had they.

I felt momentarily sorry for Rose. He would never know

exactly what had caused Kelly's death. But I couldn't blame the O'Briens for their decision.

Not one nurse cried. I don't see how anyone could cry. It was such a blessing.

Every one of us was more than ready. When it happened, every one of us felt relieved and glad.

All day long Mr. Shorey kept calling Kelly's name.

We were astonished. Mr. Shorey had been so out of it because of his high fever that none of the nurses thought he could have known that Kelly had died.

"Kelly!" Mr. Shorey called. "Kelly! Kelly!"

Just before the change of shift, Mr. Shorey stopped breathing and died.

His sister was in the room when it happened. I went in to see her. She was sitting in the chair with her face in her hands. Her body was moving back and forth with sobs.

I put my arms around her.

"It's so much better that he's gone," I said. "He went through hell. Now his suffering is over. That won't take the hurt away from you, because the people who live after go on suffering. But now your brother will have some peace. At least you know that."

The woman kept crying. I didn't try to stop her.

Instead of going right home after work that day, I went in to see Petey English.

She was sitting in bed reading, and she looked like herself. I said so.

"I do feel much better today," she said, "but you don't look so hot. Rough day?"

"You know," I said, "you might think this is really strange when I tell you the reason, but actually I've had a good day. I feel better today than I have felt for a long time."

"Sit down, why don't you?"

I pulled up a chair and sat down. I told Petey a little about Kelly O'Brien.

The Petey told me about a cousin of hers who had also been a policeman.

From there we got onto other subjects. I can't remember what we talked about, but I must have been in there an hour. I remember that we laughed a lot.

Finally I looked at my watch.

"My god," I said. "Mrs. Payne keeps telling me that I'm going to lose my husband if I don't get home earlier. I'm sure she's wrong. But I did promise to make dinner tonight."

"If making dinner is all it takes to keep a man you're obviously crazy about," Petey English said, "get going."

We both laughed.

I got up to leave.

"It's great to see you looking as good as you do," I said to Petey, turning from the doorway.

She grinned. "Come back tomorrow if you think I look good now. I've conned my favorite beautician into coming over in the morning to do my hair. I doubt if she can make me look like Garbo at her peak, but my feeling is that if you go around looking horrible, you make yourself and everyone else feel bad. Who needs that?"

My throat caught. For about three seconds I just stood there.

"You are really something else," I finally said to Petey. "I hope you know I know that."

Petey looked away. "So are you. Now get out of here and get that dinner going."

"You're right." I reached over and gave Petey's nearest foot a squeeze through the blanket. "I'm getting."

I was halfway down the hall when I heard her call, "Hey, Mary?"

I stuck my head back in the room.

"Are you off tomorrow?"

"No," I said. "I'll be here."